DAVID WHITWELL

ESSAYS ON MUSIC OF THE GERMAN BAROQUE: PHILOSOPHY AND PERFORMANCE PRACTICE

WHITWELL BOOKS

Essays on Music of the German Baroque: Philosophy and Performance Practice
Dr. David Whitwell

Copyright © 2015 David Whitwell
All rights reserved.
Published in the United States of America.
These essays were first published between 2000 and 2010.

Cover image: *Statue of Johann Sebastian Bach at the St. Thomas Church in Leipzig* by Zarafa at the English language Wikipedia

ISBN-13 978-1-936512-83-6

Whitwell Publishing
Austin, TX 78701
WWW.WHITWELLPUBLISHING.COM

Contents

1. Thoughts on the Musical Scene in Baroque Germany — 9
2. Leibniz on Music — 25
3. Mattheson on the Nature of Music — 37
4. On Emotion in Music in the German Baroque — 51
5. Mattheson on Emotion in Music — 63
6. On German Baroque Performance Practice — 77
7. Praetorius on Performance Practice — 85
8. Mattheson on Performance Practice — 113
9. Mattheson on the Composition of Good Melody — 129
10. On Court Music in the German Baroque — 139
11. On the Hautboisten — 153
12. On the Golden Age of the Trumpet in Germany — 163
13. On Civic Music of the German Baroque — 169
14. On Church Music in Baroque Germany — 185
15. On Military Music in Baroque Germany — 197
16. On the Influence of Turkish Music — 209

Bibliography	219
About the Author	231
About the Editor	235

I want to express my appreciation for my colleague, Craig Dabelstein of Brisbane, Australia, for his contribution to this volume. His own musicianship, broad education and skill in editing is responsible for thus preserving my essays. Any reader who places value in having these essays in his library is in his debt.

1
Thoughts on the Musical Scene in Baroque Germany

THE SEVENTEENTH CENTURY was a century of crises for the German-speaking nations. Germany itself, hampered by a lack of central authority, was facing increased difficulties in trade both from across the Alps to the South and from the lack of harbors in the North. The growth of the Lutheran populations in the North and the growing of support by England, Spain and France for the Catholic South led almost inevitably to the Thirty Years' War (1618–1648).

The war began when the Emperor Ferdinand II's ambassadors to Bohemia were thrown out of a window in Prague. The fortunes of war caused troops to traverse back and forth across Germany, with Wallenstein first leading the Catholics to victory and then the Protestants under Gustavus Adolphus, King of Sweden, driving them South and defeating Wallenstein at Lützen. Before it all ended with the Peace of Westphalia, France, Spain and the Dutch were all participants. After thirty years of fighting, France and Sweden were stronger and the Dutch and Switzerland became independent. Germany was weaker, with the population in some areas having declined by thirty percent.

The impact of the Thirty Years' War on the arts was, of course, dramatic and far-reaching. With regard to music we have many testimonials to the decline in the fortunes of the musicians. In the writings of Burckhart Grossmann we can see already in the early years of the war wide ramifications in society.

> Noble music is particularly hated today, and that, too, among such as should especially cultivate it and preserve it to the glory of God. Many of these esteem it so little that they derive more pleasure, eloquence, and usefulness from the yelping of dogs, the bellowing of bulls, and the braying of asses than from the most beautiful Orphic strains, or from the well-ordered heavenly choir of our late blessed Michael Praetorius ...
>
> We find Saul's spear at court and especially in the chamber of the exchequer, barring the way to music, singers, and musicians when they approach, or driving them away, so that they must flee as David fled ... One cuts their bread with Saul's spear into such small bits that they almost starve to death, so that of many a one it can be said, as I often heard from the lips of an old singer, "Music benefits well, but nourishes badly."
>
> ......
>
> In some towns and places where music formerly flourished and one praised God on Sundays and festival days with sixteen and more voices in two, three, or more choirs, one can only now engage an old unaccompanied quartet; the cantors and organists, from whom the keys stick and the bellow freeze ...
>
> No peasant familiar with the Thuringian practice ... will believe me that in distinguished universities one is more ashamed of music than of Saul's spear, and that in numerous places it appears as though one wished to weed out music altogether from among its six sisters and no longer wished to acknowledge it as belonging to the liberal arts. This is indeed the actual state of affairs. Formerly honorable and art-loving students in our universities, and among them some from the aristocracy, conducted *collegia musica* at times and places of recreation ... Now they are supplanted by bagpipe players and performers on the shawm, or at best by three fiddlers who play three octaves apart.[1]

In Dresden, by 1633 Heinrich Schütz was so discouraged with conditions imposed by the war that he sought to leave to work in Copenhagen.

---

[1] Burckhart Grossmann, *116th Psalm* (Jena, 1623), quoted in Hans Moser, *Heinrich Schütz* (St. Louis: Concordia, 1936), 15ff.

On account of the war conditions prevailing at present I could readily get away, because the times do not demand or allow music on a large scale, and the more so because the company of instrumentalists and singers has at present considerably diminished. Some are subject to illness and to the infirmities of age; others are occupied with the war, or have taken advantage of other opportunities, wherefore it is now impossible to perform music on a large scale or with many choirs. Furthermore, if God, as is to be hoped, improved the times, and Your Electoral Highness desired my service, a considerable readjustment and improvement of our *Collegium musicum* would have to take place.[2]

[2] Letter of February 9, 1633, quoted in Ibid., 145.

Three years later Schütz pictures a more general decline.

Everyone can see how, as the result of the still continuing, dangerous vicissitudes of war in our dear fatherland of German nationality, the laudable art of music, among the other liberal arts, has not only greatly declined but at some places has even been completely abandoned, succumbing to the general ruination and disorder which unhappy war is wont to bring in its train.[3]

[3] Henrich Schütz, *Kleine geistliche Concerte,* Preface.

In this same year Schütz's pupil, Martin Knabe, wrote of the effects of war in the dedication of his "Lamentation on the Protracted War: When at Last Will My Grief be Ended?"

It is unnecessary to speak at length concerning this long-protracted, wearisome war. Suffice is to say that its destructive fire is still burning at all corners of the Roman Empire. It is enough to observe how daily, yes, hourly, so many countless sighs are emitted with broken words by many thousands of souls: Oh, if there were only peace! Oh, if only the war would come to an end! Not to mention the collapse of studies which bloodthirsty Mars occasions in all the branches of the university and among the other liberal arts, and only to recall with a few words the state of music, how this noble art, even before the other arts, has sunk to the lowest level.[4]

[4] Quoted in Moser, *Heinrich Schütz,* 162.

By 1652, a letter of Schütz to the secretary of the elector of Saxony makes a touching plea on behalf of a court singer.

But now I can no longer conceal from you that the bass singer who some time ago had to pawn his clothes again, and ever since has been living at his house like a wild beast of the woods, has informed me through his wife that he now must and wishes to leave us …

It is a real pity, though, to lose such an exquisite voice in the choir. What does it matter if in other respects he is a good-for-nothing and that he must cleanse his throat daily with a keg of wine? Naturally such a wide throat needs more moistening than a narrow one.[5]

[5] Letter to Christian Reichbrodt, May 28, 1652, quoted in Gertrude Norman and Miriam Shrifte, *Letters of Composers* (New York: Knopf, 1946), 14ff.

Toward the end of the war, the letters of Schütz take on an even more desperate character.

Our music at present practically defunct … I cannot refrain from seeking help for our *corpori musico*, which is in desperate straits, and from petitioning that you intervene as does a *medicus* in a serious illness before that illness becomes altogether fatal.[6]

[6] Heinrich Schütz, letter to the elector of March 7, 1641, quoted in Ibid., 170.

Conditions were such that even a decade after the end of the war Schütz can see no evidence of a restoration of a favorable climate for music. On September 21, 1661, he writes the elector,

In conclusion, so far as I am personally concerned, I must protest that, after promising practically everything but the blood from my veins, actually advancing a part of my means to suffering musicians, it will be altogether impossible for me to continue here in Dresden any longer. With regard to this place I am not merely announcing but stating positively that I would prefer death to living under such harassing conditions.[7]

[7] Quoted in Ibid., 209.

Because of the social disruption of the Thirty Years' War, art music developed somewhat behind that of Italy and France during the seventeenth century. It was natural, therefore, that discussion of the nature of German music was carried out to some degree in the context of reflections on the style found in other countries.

In addition it was a goal of some young men in the Northern countries to travel to Italy to "finish" their education by absorbing the culture there. Thus it should be no surprise to find Heinrich Schütz, in requesting permission for his second trip to Italy in 1628–1629, thinking of a similar trip to improve his spirit. Indeed, years later Schütz would refer to Italy as "the true university of music,"[8]

> ... as from the first I did not come upon this idea prompted by any frivolity, as a mere pleasure jaunt or desire to travel, but through the urge for an improvement in spirit.[9]

After making this trip, Schütz documents his discovery there of a new style of church music:

> When I arrived in Venice, I cast anchor here where as a youth I had passed the novitiate of my art under the great Gabrieli—Gabrieli, immortal gods, how great a man![10]
>
> ......
>
> Staying in Venice with old friends, I found the manner of musical composition [*modulandi rationem*] somewhat changed. They have partially abandoned the old church modes while seeking to charm modern ears with new titillations.[11]

Some years later, in 1647, Schütz provided an interesting reference to the absorption of Italian style in Germany.

> Until now I have been prevented from sending [the *Symphoniae Sacrae*] to press because of the miserable conditions prevailing in our dear fatherland which adversely affect all the arts, music included; and even more importantly, because the modern Italian style of composition and performance (with which, as the sagacious Signor Claudio Monteverdi remarks in the preface to his *Eighth Book of Madrigals*, music is said finally to have reached its perfection) has remained largely unknown in this country.
>
> Experience has proved that the modern Italian manner of composition and its proper tempo, with its many black notes, does not in most cases lend itself to use by Germans who have not been trained for it. Believing one had composed really good works in this style, one has often found them so violated and corrupted in performance that they offered a sensitive ear nothing but boredom and distaste, and called down unjustified opprobrium on the composer and on the German nation, the inference being that we are entirely unskilled in the noble art of music—and certain foreigners have more than once leveled such accusations at us ...
>
> As for others, above all those of us Germans who do not know how properly to perform this modern music,

[8] *Geistliche Chormusik* (1648).

[9] Quoted in Moser, *Heinrich Schütz*, 1936), 126. Bach's son once wrote that his father "did not have the most brilliant good fortune, because he did not do what it requires, namely, roam the world over." [See Hans T. David and Arthur Mendel, *The Bach Reader* (New York: Norton, 1966), 279]

[10] Heinrich Schütz, *Symphoniae sacrae* I, Op. 2, 1629, quoted in Oliver Strunk, *Source Readings in Music History* (New York: Norton, 1950), 433.

[11] Schütz, Ibid., quoted in Moser, *Heinrich Schütz*, 128.

> with its black notes and steady, prolonged bowing on the violin, and who, albeit untrained, still wish to play this way I herewith kindly request them not to be ashamed to seek instruction from experts in this style and not to shirk home practice before they undertake a public performance of any of these pieces. Otherwise they and the author—though he be innocent—may receive unexpected ridicule rather than praise.[12]

At the end of the seventeenth century, after the influence of the court of Louis XIV had begun to make itself felt throughout Europe, one begins to find interesting observations on the French style. An early example of French influence can be seen in Georg Muffat's *Florilegia* (1695), a collection of pieces which he describes as "conforming in the main to the French ballet style."

> In Germany the French style is gradually coming to the fore and becoming the fashion. This same style, which formerly flourished in Paris under the most celebrated Jean Baptiste Lully, I have diligently sought to master, and, returning from France to Alsace, from whence I was driven by the late war, I was perhaps the first to bring this manner, not displeasing to many professional musicians, into Austria and Bohemia and afterwards to Salzburg and Passau. Inasmuch as the ballet compositions of the aforesaid Lully and other things after his manner entirely reject, for the flowing and natural movement, all other artifices—immoderate runs as well as frequent and ill-sounding leaps—they had at first the misfortune, in these countries, to displease many of our violinist, at that time more intent on the variety of unusual conceits and artificialities than on grace; for this reason, when occasionally produced by those ignorant of the French manner or envious of foreign art, they come off badly, robbed of their proper tempo and other ornaments.[13]

If, Muffat suggests, composers would only notice how popular this style was with the aristocrats they might become interested in studying it. He quotes a "discerning prince" who observed that the old-fashioned composers learned more than was necessary for the purpose of "charming the ear."

[12] Heinrich Schütz, *Symphoniae Sacrae*, II (1647), quoted in Sam Morgenstern, *Composers on Music* (New York: Pantheon, 1956), 29.

[13] Quoted in Strunk, *Source Readings in Music History*, 443.

Another interesting discussion on the contemporary assessment of German style is found in Heinichen in 1711.

> Experience teaches that ... paper music receives more credit in one nation than in another. One nation [Germany] is industrious in all endeavors; another laughs over useless school work and tends to believe skeptically that the "Northerners" work like a team of draft horses. One nation [Germany] believes art is only that which is difficult to compose; another nation, however, seeks a lighter style and correctly states that it is difficult to compose light music ... One nation seeks its greatest art in nothing but intricate musical "tiff-taff" and elaborate artificialities of note writing. The other nation applies itself more to good taste, and in this way it takes away the former's universal applause; the paper artists [Germans], on the contrary, with all their witchcraft remain in obscurity and, in addition, are proclaimed barbarians, even though they could imitate the other nations blindfolded if they applied themselves more to good taste and brilliance of music than to fruitless artificialities. An eminent foreign composer once gave his frank opinion ... regarding the differences in music of two nations.
>
> Our nation, he said, ... is more inclined to *dolcezza* in music, so much so that it must take care not to fall into a kind of indolence. Most "Northerners," on the other hand, are almost too inclined to liveliness in music, so that they fall too easily into barbarisms. If they would take pains over adapting our tendresse and would mix it together with their usual vivacite, then a third style would result that could not fail to please the whole world.
>
> I will not repeat the comments I made at that time, but will say only that this discourse first brought to my mind the thought that a felicitous mélange of Italian and French taste would affect the ear most forcefully and must succeed over all other tastes of the world ... Nevertheless, the Germans have the reputation abroad that if they would apply themselves industriously they could usually surpass other nations in learning. From this principle I hope that some day our composers will try in general ... to surpass other nations in matters of musical taste as well as they have succeeded long ago in artful counterpoint and theoretical accuracies.[14]

[14] Johann David Heinichen, *General-Bass Treatise* [1711], quoted in George Buelow, *Thorough-Bass Accompaniment according to Johann David Heinichen* (Ann Arbor: UMI Research Press, 1986), 281ff.

After the beginning of the eighteenth century German self-confidence was rising and occasional comments which were distinctly anti-French in character began to appear. Friedrich Niedt, for example, observed in 1700,

> The final chord must be major regardless of what goes before, except that French composers do the opposite, but everything is not good merely because it comes from France or has a French name.[15]

[15] Friedrich Erhard Niedt, *Musicalische Handleitung* (Hamburg, 1700), quoted in Robert Donnington, *The Interpretation of Early Music* (New York, 1964), 141.

Telemann, in a letter of c. 1751 to Carl Graun, makes a comment which was intended as an unfavorable reference to the theories of Rameau.

> If there is nothing new to be found in melody then we must seek novelty in harmony.[16]

[16] Quoted in Morgenstern, *Composers on Music*, 41.

Of course, the entire discussion of national styles was rapidly focusing on opera. While opera, especially Italian opera, was becoming very popular with the public across Europe, contemporary philosophical discussion of opera lagged somewhat behind, with the exception of France which enjoyed a vigorous philosophical debate. One finds almost no important literature by the Italians. The Germans, lacking the literary heritage of the French and Italians, drew on their greater concern for moral principles. One early reference to opera, in 1624, during the tragic years of the Thirty Years' War, understandably finds its purpose as bringing joy and recollection of the more pleasant things of life to the viewer.

> Lyric poetry, a genre highly suited to music, requires in the first place a free and happy mind; unlike the other genres, it must be adorned with many beautiful maxims and precepts ... Concerning its themes: it is capable of describing anything that can be contained in a brief composition—gallantries, dances, ballets, beautiful women, gardens, vineyards, eulogies of modesty, the vanities of life, etc., but above all exhortation to joy.[17]

[17] Barthold Fend, *Gedanken von der Opera* (1708), quoted in Lorenzo Biaconi, *Music in the Seventeenth Century*, trans. David Bryant (Cambridge: Cambridge University Press, 1989), 225ff.

One of the most valuable German contributions on the subject of opera is by the Hamburg librettist, Barthold Feind (1678–1721). Reflecting the strict Lutheran environment,

Feind disapproves of all attempts to portray religious subjects in opera. Likewise he finds in Hamburg no interest in the ancient Greek subjects.

> In Hamburg, the public is characterized by a notable aversion to the fabulous myths of the pagan deities; I would, indeed, be unable to cite a single example of this kind which had met success—convinced, however, as I am that Hamburg can boast not twenty persons with the ability to pass adequate judgment on the delicacy or virtue of an opera, and that frequently, of these twenty persons, not one can be seen at performances.[18]

[18] Ibid., 312ff.

Feind also believed that any form of low humor, especially clowns, mimes and Harlequins, was inappropriate for the operatic stage. Much to his disgust, however, these were not only popular but demanded by the Hamburg audience.

> Here, whatever seems vulgar and ridiculous to refined tastes now finds maximum approval—as occurred only last year on the occasion of *Le carnaval de Venice,* an opera of such absurdity and so full of nauseating and scornful gestures as to look like buffoonery. Yet this subject met with such applause as can hardly be believed.

With regard to what opera should be, Feind begins by defining opera as "a splendid deception in which poetry and music (both sung and played) combine to the highest perfection." He wishes to stress "deception" for if one takes what occurs on the stage as *real,* then opera makes no sense. This, he finds, is a mistake made by some French philosophers, as for example Saint-Évremond whom he quotes:

> One feature of opera is so contrary to nature as to offend my imagination: that is, that the drama is sung from beginning to end, as though the characters represented therein had for some ridiculous reason agreed to discuss the various questions of their lives—the greatest and most trivial alike—in music.

But opera is *not* real, Feind points out, "one simply tries to *imitate* nature." The value of having everything sung in opera, is because of the power of music to define not only the emotions, but the experiential side of ourselves far beyond speech.

Nor do I believe that anyone can reasonably doubt the assertion that song is capable of imbuing a discourse with ten times more energy than any declamation or simple speech. What, indeed, is song if not a means of sustaining the discourse and voice with maximum energy and force?

In the communication of these emotions to the audience, the first responsibility falls to the poet, the librettist. In acknowledging the endless variety of emotions, Feind touches on the very reason why any "doctrine of the affections," equating specific emotions to specific musical figures, becomes impossible in practice.

> A philosopher, a noble and high-minded person, a man in love, in despair, in frenzy, a suspicious, jealous, faltering or irresolute man, etc.; each must be presented in accordance with his own particular temperament and manner of speech. This, however, requires enormous ability and skill, in so far as hundreds—indeed thousands—of possibilities exist, variable in accordance with epoch, nations and traditions.

Regarding the duties of the poet, he continues,

> The words must interpret the heart of whoever is speaking and allow his temperament to shine through, the temperament of a character must correspond to his "nature" and reflect the influence of the passion by which he is moved. The haughty will be boastful and arrogant, the magnanimous generous, a lover tender and charming, an old hand of the world sober and temperate, the historical tale of a messenger extended, etc. These are the essential elements; two or three scenes are sufficient to form an impression of the spirit and taste of a good poet. And since various characters appear in an opera, each different in passion and nature; since, moreover, each character must express his own will and actions in accordance with his nature and the laws of decorum: this is the principal reason why the opera has come to be seen as the highest yet also the most difficult of all poetic genres.

Beyond this, Feind stresses that the poet must write with the qualities of the specific singers intended in mind, for it will be through them that the emotions are communicated to the audience. The portrayal of an emotion improves in relation to its naturalness in presentation and if effectively done will provoke "wrath, terror, hope, fury or pity in the beholder." He cites, in this regard, English audiences crying bitterly during Shakespeare plays and French ladies crying during the plays of Racine and Corneille.

By the end of the Baroque, reflection on the nature of German music had clearly produced one conclusion: Germany stood pre-eminent in keyboard music. Martin Fuhrmann wrote in 1729,

> When I was at the Easter Fair in Leipzig recently ... I had the good fortune to hear the world-famous Mr. Bach. I thought the Italian Frescobaldi had polished off the art of keyboard playing all by himself, and Carissimi was a most valued and cherished organist. But if one were to put the two Italians with their art on one side of the scales and the German Bach on the other, the latter would far outweigh them, and they would be lifted straight up into the air.[19]

Similarly, Johann Scheibe, writing in his journal, *Der critischer Musicus*, in 1737, observed,

> In some types of clavier pieces there is a clear distinction between the German style and others. In foreigners we find that neither the structure, nor the ornamentation, nor the working out of these pieces, is so perfect as in the Germans. For they know how to exploit this instrument with the greatest strength and according to its true nature better than all the other nations. The two great men among the Germans, Mr. Bach and Mr. Handel, illustrate this most strikingly.[20]

Two years later, in an article on the Italian Concerto, Scheibe adds the comment that in Bach's clavier music "we can certainly defy foreign nations."[21]

Perhaps the most interesting observations on the development of German style are those in which we can see the coming of the *galant* style, if not the Classical Period itself. One prominent characteristic of the new style was the Italian predilection for the dominance of the upper melodic voice. Georg Muffat, who was more inclined to the French style, wrote, in the Foreword to his *Florilegium Secundum* (1698), pleading for a return to balance.

---

[19] Martin Fuhrmann, *Satans-Capelle* (Köln, 1729), quoted in David and Mendel, *The Bach Reader,* 441. Bach himself was more modest. J. F. Kohler relates he once heard Bach suggest that all you have "to do is hit the right notes at the right time, and the instrument plays itself." [Ibid., 291]

[20] Quoted in Ibid., 230.

[21] Quoted in Ibid., 234.

I have sought diligently to soften, by means of the sweetness of agreeable consonances, whatever seemed unusual in the upper voice, namely the violin, and also to lend distinction, by means of the artful setting of the inner voices and the bass, to whatever seemed overly vulgar [meaning, common].[22]

And, again, in the Foreword to his collection of concerti, *Auserlesene Instrumental-Music* (1701), Muffat urges the music director to assign good players as well to the middle voices, for it is no insult to play these parts,

> contrary to the deep-rooted prejudice of certain haughty persons, who faint away on the spot if one does not assign them to the violin or some other prominent part.[23]

One of the clearest harbingers of the new galant style was the appreciation of *Gout*, or taste itself. The most famous Baroque discussion of this among musicians is found in Heinichen, who contends that taste can only be acquired through personal experience.

> If experience is necessary in any art or science, it is certainly necessary in music. In this *Scientia practica*, first of all, we must gain experience ... either at home, provided opportunities are sufficient, or through traveling. But what is it that one believes one must seek in the experience? I will give a single word ... *Gout*. Through diligence, talent, and experience, a composer must achieve above all else an exquisite sense of good taste in music ... The definition of *Gout, Gusto* or *guter Geschmack* is unnecessary for the experienced musician; and it is as difficult to describe in its essentials as the true essence of the soul. One could say that good taste was in itself the soul of music, which so to speak it doubly enlivens and brings pleasure to the senses. The *Proprium 4ti modi* of a composer with good taste is contained solely in the skill with which he makes his music pleasing to and beloved by the general, educated public, or which in the same way pleases our ear by experienced artifices and moves the senses ... In general, this can be brought about through a good well-cultivated, and natural invention or through the beautiful expression of words. In particular, through an ever dominating *cantabile*, through suitable and affecting accompaniments, through a change of harmonies recommended for the sake of the ears, and through other methods gained from experience and

[22] Quoted in Strunk, *Source Readings in Music History,* 446.

[23] Quoted in Ibid., 452. We say today, "No mother raises her child to play *second* violin!"

frequently looking poor on paper, which in our times we only label with the obscure name of "rules of experience..." An exceptional sense of good taste is so to say the musical *Lapis philisophorum* and the principal key to musical mysteries through which human souls are unlocked and moved and by which the senses are won over ... For even the natural gift or talent endowed with most invention resembles only crude gold and silver dross that must be purified first by the fire of experience before it can be shaped into a solid mass—I mean into a finely cultivated and steadfast sense of good taste.[24]

We would like to think that it was this view of the future which Bach had in mind in a note to the Leipzig town council in 1730:

> The present *status musices* is quite different to what it used to be formerly—the art being much advanced and taste marvelously changed, so that the old-fashioned kind of music no longer sounds well in our ears.[25]

And, indeed, an observation by Johann Scheibe in 1737 seems to imply that the Germans now had, in fact, arrived at a sense of taste comparable to their neighbors.

> Indeed, we [Germans] have finally found in music too the true good taste, which Italy never showed us in its full beauty. Hasse and Graun, who are admired also by the Italians, demonstrate by their richly inventive, natural and moving works how fine it is to possess and practice good taste.[26]

But some people, as always, never quite notice what is going on all around them, the foremost example of the German Baroque being, of course, Johann Fux. And we must note a particularly curious comment in 1752 by Friedrich Marpurg which seems to imply a rejection of the new Classical style.

> Thus the manly element which should prevail in music remains quite absent from it; for it may be believed without further testimony that the composer who has made himself particularly acquainted with fugues and counterpoints—however barbaric this last word may sound to the tender ears of our time—will let something of their flavor inform all his other works, however *galant* they are meant to be, and will set himself against the spreading rubbish of womanish song.[27]

[24] Heinichen, *General-Bass Treatise* [1711], quoted in Buelow, *Thorough-Bass Accompaniment according to Johann David Heinichen*, 285ff.

[25] Quoted in Donnington, *The Interpretation of Early Music*, 99.

[26] Johann Scheibe, *Critischer musicus* (1737), trans. Claude Palisca, *Baroque Music* (Englewood Cliffs: Prentice Hall, 1981), 281.

[27] Quoted in David and Mendel, *The Bach Reader*, 268.

Court, civic and church records of payments to musicians and purchases of instruments allow us to set an approximate date of 1550 as the point when professional string players begin to appear, replacing the long tradition of professional wind instrument specialists. During the years when the professional musician was primarily a wind player, string players tend to be wandering beggars often called the "beer fiddler." The Baroque, of course, is when the modern strings of the highest quality were made.

As a salute to the old "beer fiddler," one German book by Grimmelshausen provides one of our most extended and colorful portraits of an old wandering string player called Springinsfeld. Such a musician was still a very frequent figure in the seventeenth century literature in all Western European countries, but almost no details are ever given other than mention of his presence. The colorful descriptions which Grimmelshausen provides are therefore all the more welcome. We first meet this wandering violinist when he enters a tavern.

> There entered the room an old beggar with a pegleg who, like me, had been driven by the cold to the stove in the room. He had hardly warmed himself a bit when he drew forth a small treble violin, tuned it, stepped up to our table, and played a tune. At the same time he so artfully hummed and squeaked with his lips that anyone who only heard him but did not see him would have perforce believed that three different stringed instruments were being played. He was a rather poorly clad for the winter, and to all appearances had not had a good summer either, for his haggard body bore witness that he had been obliged to tighten his belt, and his sparse hair that he also must have suffered through a serious illness.[28]

As we can see from this description, Springinsfeld was primarily an entertainer, not a violinist. Later, in a description of an outdoor performance, we learn more of this fiddler's skills.

> [He] whisked out his fiddle and began to put on a show and at the same time to play the fiddle. He shaped his lips into a triangle, a square, a pentagon, a hexagon, yea, into a

[28] Hans Jacob Christoffel von Grimmelshausen, *The Singular Life Story of Heedless Hopalong* (Detroit: Wayne State University Press, 1981), 6.

heptagon, and while he was playing the fiddle, all the while
he made music with his mouth too, as he had done earlier
in the inn, but since the fiddle, which had been tuned in
the warmth of the room, would not play right in the cold,
he imitated all sorts of bird and animal calls [on it], from
the lovely forest song of the nightingale to, and including,
the frightful howl of the wolf, as a result of which we had
attracted in less than a quarter of an hour an audience of
more than six hundred people, who looked on wide-eyed and
open-mouthed with astonishment, forgetful of the cold.[29]

[29] Ibid., 26.

In another place this fiddler reveals that he did rather well, observing that most of the people who gave him money did not themselves have one-tenth the money he had accumulated.[30] We are also provided with some information on the early education of this wandering entertainer.

[30] Ibid., 102.

> [My father-in-law] raised me till I reached my eleventh year
> and taught me all the principles of his art, such as how to
> blow the trumpet, beat the drum, play the fiddle and the
> pipes (both the shawm and the bagpipes), how to do sleight-
> of-hand tricks, to jump through hoops, and do other strange
> and clownish things.[31]

[31] Ibid., 42.

This fiddler in time married a "hurdy-gurdy girl," in a wedding occurring during a fair and attended by "puppeteers, acrobats, sleight-of-hand artists, ballad singers, pin peddlers, scissors' grinders, tinkers, hurdy-gurdy girls, master beggars, rogues, and other honorable rabble."[32] The reader will notice here the general level of society with which the popular song writer was associated. In another book, Grimmelshausen mentions the "ballads men write in praise of harlots."[33]

[32] Ibid., 86.

[33] Hans Jacob Christoffel von Grimmelshausen, *The Adventurous Simplicissimus,* trans. A. T. Goodrick (Lincoln: University of Nebraska, 1962), I, xxiv.

The hurdy-gurdy girl is also pictured at work for a banquet in the house of a "great gentleman." The sound of this instrument caused the other musicians to flee!

> Now when dessert was on the table and the dancing was
> supposed to begin, unexpectedly the sound of a hurdy-gurdy
> was also heard coming from where the musicians were sitting,
> to the great consternation of all who were in the hall. The first
> to run away were the musicians themselves, who heard the
> rasping sound close by, and yet did not see anyone.[34]

[34] Grimmelshausen, *The Singular Life Story of Heedless Hopalong,* 93.

It is a wonder, the narrator observes, that people were not crushed to death in the doorway.

2
Leibniz on Music

GOTTFRIED WILHELM LEIBNIZ (1646–1716), one of the great figures in early German mathematics and philosophy, was reared in a highly educated family, his father being a professor at Leipzig University. Leibniz also entered Leipzig University, receiving a bachelor's degree in philosophy at age sixteen and two doctorates by age twenty-one. Leibniz was also a brilliant mathematician, having discovered the foundations of differential and integral calculus, which he invented independently of Sir Isaac Newton.

One of the first things one notices in reading German philosophy of the Baroque is the emergence of a new and genuine national self-confidence. Leibniz, for example, freely and without hesitation criticized Descartes, Spinoza, Newton and the entire English School of philosophical writers, not to mention the ancient philosophers including even Aristotle. Inseparable from this self-confidence was also a new sense of nationalism, which is sometimes expressed in interesting characterizations of other nationals. We don't see this yet in Kepler, who, writing at the beginning of the seventeenth century, observed, "Germany is just as famous for corpulence and gluttony as Spain is for genius, discernment, and temperance."[1] By the end of the century, however, Leibniz was feeling a distinct sense of German superiority.

[1] Leibniz, "A New Method for Learning and Teaching Jurisprudence" (1667), I, xxxiv, in Leroy Loemker, *Philosophical Papers and Letters* (Dordrecht: Reidel, 1956), 89.

One need not worry about the Italians, who are ready to receive the yoke, and who have degenerated from the virtue of their ancestors.[2]

The Frenchman, in Leibniz's view,

> allows himself no repose, and leaves none to others; the grave and the serious pass for ridiculous, and measure or reason for pedantic; caprice, for something gallant, and inconstancy in one's interactions with other people, for cleverness: everyone meddles with others' affairs in private houses, and pursues people to their very homes, and picks shameful fights. Youth above all glories in its folly and in its disorders.[3]

From the background of his somewhat old-fashioned Scholastic background, it did seem obvious to Leibniz that speech itself must be an important key to the function of the thought process. For this reason he speculated rather broadly on the origin of speech and on the chronological development of the parts of language. He wondered, for example, which came first, proper or generic names.[4] And he wondered about the possibility of a language based on musical tones, a subject of many future philosophers and most successfully attempted by François Sudre. After noting that monkeys have the physical components for speech, but do not speak, Leibniz adds,

> We must also consider that we could *speak,* i.e., make ourselves understood by the sounds of the mouth without forming articulate sounds, if we availed ourselves of musical *tones* for this effect; but more art would be necessary to invent a *language of tones,* whilst that of words may have been formed and perfectly gradually by persons who found themselves in a state of natural simplicity. There are, however, people like the Chinese, who by means of tones and accents vary their words,[5] of which they have only a small number.[6]

Although extensively trained in Scholastic perspective, and its foundation of 1,000 years of arguments on behalf of Reason, Leibniz had difficulty explaining the experiential, non-rational side of man. In the following passage he makes a point obvious to us today, but most confusing to earlier

---

[2] Leibniz, "Mars Christianissimus" (1683), in *The Political Writings of Leibniz,* trans. Patrick Riley (Cambridge: Cambridge University Press, 1972), 133.

[3] Leibniz, "Manifesto for the Defense of the Rights of Charles III" (1703), in Loemker, *Philosophical Papers and Letters,* 157.

[4] Curiously, among his various speculations, the one obvious factor which apparently did not occur to Leibniz at all was the fact that all languages use the same five vowel sounds. This has immense implications regarding the relationships of vocal sounds and emotions in early man. In his discussion of a few vowel sounds he does refer to Johann Becan (1518–1572), a Belgian scholar who believed that Adam spoke German!

[5] I have wondered if the unique singing/speech of Chinese opera might be our last glimpse of the art of the ancient Rhapsodist.

[6] Leibniz, *New Essays Concerning Human Understanding* (1704), trans. Alfred Langley (La Salle: The Open Court Publishing Company, 1949), III, i, 1. Leibniz himself was inclined to believe that mathematics was the universal language and in a treatise, "The Art of Discovery" (1685), he suggests that a way might be found for mathematics to express basic grammar, etc.

centuries, that we can have an occasion where we understand something on the experiential level and yet fail to be able to explain it on a rational level.

> In order better to understand the nature of ideas, we must to some extent touch upon the various kinds of knowledge. When I can recognize one thing among others but cannot say in which its differences or properties consist, my knowledge is *confused*. In this way we sometimes know *clearly*, and without having a doubt of any kind, if a poem or a picture is well done or badly, because it has a certain "something, I know not what" which either satisfies or repels us.[7]

This Truth is proved everyday all over the world, of course, by people who listen to, and love, music, but "know nothing" about it. He finally comes to the correct explanation, even if he knows nothing about the true arrangement and function of the brain.

> There remain two ways of knowing contingent truths. The one is experience; the other, reason. We know by experience when we perceive a thing distinctly enough by our senses; by reason, however, when we use the general principle that nothing happens without a reason.[8]

When Leibniz began to reflect on the nature and definition of music he first seemed to reflect only the old medieval Church definition of music as a branch of mathematics.

> Music is subordinate to Arithmetic and when we know a few fundamental experiments with harmonies and dissonances, all the remaining general precepts depend on numbers; I recall once drawing a harmonic line divided in such a fashion that one could determine with the compass the different compositions and properties of all musical intervals. Besides, we can show a man who does not know anything about music, the way to compose without mistakes.[9]

But, it is one thing to know *how* to write and something different to know *what* to write and Leibniz apparently realized this was too narrow and calculated. This definition also omits the artistic aspect entirely and fails to account for the artist who appears to write without regard to "the

[7] Leibniz, "Discourse on Metaphysics" (1686), xxiv, in Loemker, *Philosophical Papers and Letters*, 318.

[8] Leibniz, "On Freedom" (c. 1679), in Ibid., 265.

[9] Leibniz, untitled manuscript, known as "Precepts for Advancing the Sciences and Arts" (1680), in *Leibniz Selections*, ed. Philip Wiener (New York: Scribner's, 1951), 42ff.

rules" as well as the performer, who requires practice and not just knowledge of the rules of the art. Therefore he expands his scope considerably, beginning with the aspects of the beautiful and the eloquent. With regard to music he seems to suggest that it is better to learn from listening, from listening to good music by successful composers. The "rules of music" are employed only later, to correct mistakes.

> ... so in music what a man needs in order to compose successfully are practice as well as a genius and vivid imagination in things of the ear. And as the making of beautiful verses requires a prior reading of good poets, noticing turns and expressions which gradually tinge one's own style, "as they who walk in the sun take on another tint," in the same way a Musician, after noticing in the compositions of talented men a thousand and one beautiful cadences and, so to speak, phrases of Music, will be able to give flight to his own imagination furnished with these fine materials. There are even those who are naturally musicians and who compose beautiful melodies just as there are natural poets who with a little aid and reading perform wonders, for there are things, especially those dependent on the senses, in which we do better by letting ourselves go automatically by imitation and practice than by sticking to dry precepts. And as playing the clavichord requires a habit which the fingers themselves have to acquire, so imagining a beautiful melody, making a good poem, promptly sketching architectural ornaments or the plan of a creative painting require that our imagination itself acquire a habit after which it can be given the freedom to go its own way without consulting reason, in the manner of an inspired Enthusiasm ... But reason must afterwards examine and correct and polish the work of imagination; that is where the precepts of art are needed to produce something finished and excellent.

But, when Leibniz turns his attention to the amateur, he retreats back to the safety of Scholasticism and the importance of rules. Here he says that one must know the basic rules.

> As the common man is eternally befogged by a badly understood distinction between practice and theory, it is still appropriate to explain in a few words what is solid in that distinction and how it should be understood. I have already explained that there are things which depend rather on the

play of imagination and on spontaneous impressions than on reason and that in such things we need to form a habit, as in bodily exercises and even in some mental exercises. That is where we need practice in order to succeed.

There are other matters in which we can succeed through reason alone, aided by a few experiments or observations. We can even learn these at some other person's expense. We see excellent geniuses succeeding in their first attempt within the profession they apply themselves to, and by virtue of their natural judgment put old practitioners to shame. But that is not a usual occurrence, and this is how we must regard it.

In all matters where it is possible for judgment aided by a few precepts to avoid application and experiment, we can always reduce all of a science with its subordinate parts to a few fundamentals or principles of discovery sufficient to determine all the questions which can arise in the circumstances by combining with the principles the exact method of the true Logic or art of discovery.

But to succeed actually with this precept in practice we must distinguish among the things encountered; we must know whether decisions must be made immediately or if we have the leisure time to reflect with exactness. In the first case, the precepts combined with the method will not suffice, at least in the present state of the art of discovery, for I believe that if it were perfected as it should, and as it could be, that we might penetrate with ease a vein of thought which now takes too much time and explanation. Therefore, in order to obtain good decisions quickly in an embarrassing situation we have to have an extraordinary power of genius or long enough practice to make us think automatically and habitually what otherwise would require investigation by reason. But when we have the leisure time to reflect, I find that theory can forestall practice in all matters capable of precepts and reasons even if the latter are based on the foundation of experience provided that after the foundation is laid we can give a rational account of everything done. But this holds only if we know how to reflect methodically in order not to let anything escape of the circumstances to be accounted for.

And even theory without practice will incomparably be superior to blind practice without theory, when the practitioner is obliged to face some situation quite different from those he has practiced, because not knowing the reasons for what he is doing, he will be stopped short, whereas he who possesses the reasons discovers the exceptions and the remedies.

An important element of the definition of music is that it is a form of truth, a direct form of truth between composer and listener. Indeed, it should be noted that the experiential aspect of music, whose fundamental characteristic is the communication of feelings, is located in the right hemisphere of the brain, and it is one of the realities of the right hemisphere that it cannot lie. It is truth personified, and Leibniz seemed to be aware of this. However, it is a different kind of truth, an experiential truth, not a rational truth. Again, Leibniz's Scholastic and mathematical background made it difficult for him to fully grasp this, as well as the apparent problem that men do not seem to agree on artistic truths.

> Wit and imagination is better received than truth wholly dry. It goes well in discourse where you only seek to please; but at bottom, order and clearness excepted, all the art of rhetoric, all these artificial and figurative applications of words, serve only to insinuate false ideas, to excite the passions and seduce the judgment, so that they are nothing but pure frauds. Nevertheless this fallacious art is given the first rank and rewards. It is evident that men care but little for truth and much prefer to deceive and to be deceived. This is so true that I doubt not that what I have just said against this art is regarded as the result of an extreme audacity. For eloquence, like the fair sex, has charms too powerful to allow itself to be opposed.[10]

[10] Leibniz, *New Essays Concerning Human Understanding*, III, x, 34.

Later in this discussion, Leibniz makes a passing reference to this aspect of truth in painting and in music. Painting, he says, makes the truth vividly clear. Music makes it believable.

> It is as in painting and music, which are [also] abused, one of which often represents grotesque and even hurtful imaginations, and the other softens the heart, and the two amuse in vain; but they can be usefully employed, the one to render the truth clear, the other [music] to make it effective, and this last result must be also that of poetry which contains rhetoric and music.

The aspect of the perception of music which Leibniz seemed most comfortable in explaining was its expression of pleasure and pain by means of consonance and dissonance.

He first mentioned this in 1671, in a letter to Magnus Wedderkopf. Leibniz several times uses the word "harmony" in the Platonic idiom meaning God's perfect organization of the world. Then, in suggesting that some evil must always accompany good, he observes that dissonance was a necessary part of pleasing music.

> Sins are good, that is, harmonious, taken along with their punishment or expiation. For there is no harmony except through contraries.[11]

In a record of a conversation with Baron Dobrzensky, in 1695, Leibniz mentions this again, actually calling dissonance an "imperfection."

> I believe that God did create things in ultimate perfection, though it does not seem so to us considering the parts of the universe. It's a bit like what happens in music and painting, for shadows and dissonances truly enhance the other parts, and the wise author of such works derives such a great benefit for the total perfection of the work from these particular imperfections that it is much better to make a place for them than to attempt to do without them.[12]

But Leibniz was wrong about this. Dissonance is not a contrast with consonance, but rather simply another tool for expressing emotion.

In the following, Leibniz's first analogy would seem to us to suggest that one cannot judge the whole by a single part. When he continues with the subject of music, the analogy is not the same, but rather an analogy of the mixing of pleasure and pain in life.

> If we look at a very beautiful picture but cover up all of it but a tiny spot, what more will appear in it, no matter how closely we study it, indeed, all the more, the more closely we examine it, than a confused mixture of colors without beauty and without art. Yet when the covering is removed and the whole painting is viewed from a position that suits it, we come to understand that what seemed to be a thoughtless smear on the canvas has really been done with the highest artistry by the creator of the work. And what the eyes experience in painting is experienced by the ears in music.

[11] Leibniz, Letter to Magnus Wedderkopf (May, 1671), in Loemker, *Philosophical Papers and Letters*, 147.

[12] Quoted in *Philosophical Essays* [of Leibniz], trans. Roger Ariew and Daniel Garber (Indianapolis: Hackett, 1989), 115.

Great composers very often mix dissonances with harmonious chords to stimulate the hearer and to sting him, as it were, so that he becomes concerned about the outcome and is all the more pleased when everything is restored to order. Similarly we may enjoy trivial dangers or the experience of evils from the very sense they give us of our own power or our own happiness or our fondness for display ... By the same principle it is insipid always to eat sweets; sharp, sour, and even bitter things should be mixed with them to excite the taste. He who has not tasted the bitter does not deserve the sweet; indeed, he will not appreciate it. This is the very law of enjoyment, that pleasure does not run an even course, for this produces aversion and makes us dull, not joyful.[13]

[13] Leibniz, "On the Ultimate Origination of Things" (1697), in Loemker, *Philosophical Papers and Letters,* 489ff.

Finally, one comment of 1704 is quite different. Here he seems to credit the production of pleasure and pain in music [*sound*] not to the composer and his materials, but to God.

> [When] the body produces pleasure or pain or the idea of a color or sound, we seem compelled to abandon our reason, to go beyond our own ideas, and to attribute this production solely to the *good pleasure* of our Creator.[14]

[14] Leibniz, *New Essays Concerning Human Understanding,* IV, iii, 7.

Leibniz's most extensive writings on the general subject of genetic knowledge is found in his *New Essays on Human Understanding* (1704) which was written in refutation of John Locke's *Essay Concerning Human Understanding* (1690). In his preface, Leibniz associates Locke with those who believe man is born a "blank slate," whereas he finds a passage in the New Testament to prove this is not true.

> Our differences are upon subjects of some importance. The question is to know whether the soul in itself is entirely empty as the tablets upon which as yet nothing has been written (tabula rasa) according to Aristotle, and the author of the Essay [Locke], and whether all that is traced thereon comes solely from the senses and from experience; or whether the soul contains originally the principles of many ideas and doctrines which external objects merely call up on occasion, as I believe with Plato, and even with the schoolmen, and with all those who interpret in this way the passage of St. Paul where he states that the law of God is written in the heart.[15]

[15] Leibniz, *New Essays Concerning Human Understanding,* Preface. The St. Paul reference is found in Romans 2:15:

> They show that what the law requires is written on their hearts, while their conscience also bears witness and their conflicting thoughts accuse or perhaps excuse them on that day when, according to my gospel, God judges the secrets of men by Christ Jesus.

A very important aspect of the perception of music is the genetic musical information which is carried into birth, a fact which modern clinical research has convincingly demonstrated. Since Leibniz was a great believer of genetic knowledge in general, we notice two passages which seem to suggest that perhaps he was thinking of this with respect to music as well. In the first passage he speaks of the unconscious memory of music, in the context of a discussion of genetic knowledge.

> It seems that our clever author claims that there is nothing *virtual* in us, and indeed nothing of which we are not always actually conscious; but he cannot take this rigorously, otherwise his opinion would be too paradoxical; since, moreover, acquired habits and the stores of our memory are not always perceived and do not even always come to our aid at need, although we often easily recall them to the mind upon some slight occasion which makes us remember them, just as we need only the beginning of a song to remember it.[16]

[16] Leibniz, Ibid., preface.

Some philosophers have suggested that genetic information contributes to our dreams.[17] We were thinking of this when we read a passage in Leibniz, who believed that the average man often dreamed of music, although if he were awake he would find it difficult to recreate this music.

[17] As for example, Carl Sagen who believed that the monsters which occur in the dreams of children, who have never seen monsters, represent genetic memory of the dinosaur period.

> Noteworthy, too, is what Colomesius tells in his lesser works about a song which Gaulminus dreamed about the immortality of the soul. I do not believe that there is a mortal man who would not confess to me that there have often occurred to him while he dreamed, spontaneously and as if made in a moment, elegant visions and skillfully fashioned songs, verses, books, melodies, houses, gardens, depending upon his interests—visions which he could not have formed without effort while awake. Even such unnatural things as flying men and innumerable other monstrosities can be pictured more skillfully than a waking person can do, except with much thought. They are sought by the waker; they offer themselves to the sleeper.[18]

[18] Leibniz, "A Fragment on Dreams" (c. 1666–1676), in Loemker, *Philosophical Papers and Letters*, 115.

For Leibniz the primary purpose of music was simply to provide pleasure. We can see a hint of this in a passage where he is expressing the thought that a physician should not just concentrate on our pain, but should also study the source of our pleasures. "To this end he should make use of such aids as characteristics, optics, *music*, perfumes, cooking."[19]

In a treatise of c. 1695, our mathematician–philosopher finds pleasure in music in the rules of harmony. He must have regarded it as a paradox, that when one follows *these* rules too consistently the result may not be so good.

> The pleasures of sense which most closely approach pleasures of the mind, and are the most pure and the most certain, are that of music and that of symmetry, the former [being pleasure] of the ears, the latter of the eyes; for it is easy to understand the principles [*raisons*] of harmony, this perfection which gives us pleasure. The sole thing to be feared in this respect is to use it too often.[20]

The problem of a philosophy based on finding pleasure in music from the prospective of identifying the rules is that we can also find pleasure in a composition which seems to break, or ignore, the rules. From his background of mathematics, Leibniz could not adequately explain this obstacle to otherwise finding his pleasure in music in "the numbers."

> Even the pleasures of sense are reducible to intellectual pleasures, known confusedly. Music charms us, although its beauty consists only in the agreement of numbers and in the counting, which we do not perceive but which the soul nevertheless continues to carry out, of the beats or vibrations of sounding bodies which coincide at certain intervals. The pleasures which the eye finds in proportions are of the same nature, and those caused by other senses amount to something similar, although we may not be able to explain them so distinctly.[21]

Finally, there is only one place where Leibniz touches on the most important purpose of music, to move the feelings of the listener. In addition to his observation that music "moves the mind," perhaps we might regard it as another of his suggestions of genetic understanding of music, when Leibniz says the performance "creates a sympathetic echo in us." His comments on the relationship of rhythm and the emotions here are also interesting. This passage follows a discussion of happiness, joy, and pleasure which begins, "Wisdom is

[19] Leibniz, "Elements of Natural Law" (1670–1671), in Ibid., 132.

[20] Leibniz, "On Felicity" (c. 1694–1698), in *The Political Writings of Leibnniz*, trans. Riley, 83.

[21] Leibniz, "The Principles of Nature and of Grace, Based on Reason" (1714), in Loemker, *Philosophical Papers and Letters*, 641.

merely the science of happiness or that science which teaches us to achieve happiness."

> We do not always observe wherein the perfection of pleasing things consists, or what kind of perfection within ourselves they serve, yet our feelings [*Gemuth*] perceive it, even though our understanding does not. We commonly say, "There is something, I know not what, that pleases me in the matter." This we call "sympathy." But those who seek the causes of things will usually find a ground for this and understand that there is something at the bottom of the matter which, though unnoticed, really appeals to us.
>
> Music is a beautiful example of this. Everything that emits a sound contains a vibration or a transverse motion such as we see in strings; thus everything that emits sounds gives off invisible impulses. When these are not confused, but proceed together in order but with a certain variation, they are pleasing; in the same way, we also notice certain changes from long to short syllables, and a coincidence of rhymes in poetry, which contain a silent music, as it were, and when correctly constructed are pleasant even without being sung. Drum beats, the beat and cadence of the dance, and other motions of this kind in measure and rule derive their pleasure from their order, for all order is an aid to the emotions. And a regular though invisible order is found also in the artfully created beats and motions of vibrating strings, pipes, bells, and indeed, even of the air itself, which these bring into uniform motion. Through our hearing, this creates a sympathetic echo in us, to which our animal spirits respond. This is why music is so well adapted to move our minds, even though this main purpose is not usually sufficiently noticed or sought after.[22]

Finally, we should bring to the reader's attention a treatise of 1675, called "An Odd Thought Concerning a New Sort of Exhibition."[23] Here Leibniz outlines an interesting proposal for a world's fair. Although nothing on this scale would actually be held until the nineteenth century, it is interesting to read his long list of curiosities which he recommends be exhibited. In addition to Magic Lanterns, artificial meteors, unusual and rare animals, races between artificial horses and "the man from England who eats fire, if he is still alive," he lists "Rare instruments of Music" and "Instruments that play by themselves." In addition he recommends there be

[22] Leibniz, "On Wisdom" (c. 1690–1698), in Ibid., 425ff.

[23] This treatise can be found in *Leibniz Selections*, in *Leibniz Selections*, ed. Wiener, 585ff.

concerts, galleries of paintings, conferences and lectures for the public, with the entire exposition concluding with an opera. As for the public who would attend, Leibniz observes,

> All respectable people would want to see these curiosities in order to be able to talk about them; and even ladies of fashion would want to be taken there, and more than once.

Finally, he makes an appeal for the private support which would be necessary to make this great exhibition a reality.

> Perhaps some curious Princes and distinguished persons would contribute some of their wealth for the public satisfaction and the growth of the sciences. In short, everybody would be aroused and, so to speak, awakened; and the enterprise might have consequences as fine and as important as could be imagined, which would someday perhaps be admired by posterity.

3
Mattheson on the Nature of Music

JOHANN MATTHESON (1681–1764) was the most prolific German Baroque writer on a wide variety of musical subjects, but also an experienced singer, performer on organ and harpsichord and respected composer. Although educated in law, he became an opera singer while young and it was this experience, no doubt, which most shaped his views on music, particularly his strong belief in the fundamental importance in music of emotions and melody. His exhaustive defense of these ideas made him an important advocate for Humanism in music in Germany.

In Mainwaring's biography of Handel, Mattheson came across a reference to himself in which he is described as a good composer, but "no great singer, for which reason he sang only occasionally." In his translation of this book, Mattheson added the following note which seems to us to confirm how his philosophy developed from his activity as an artist:

> To say that he sang only occasionally is simply ridiculous, when the statement is made of a man who remained on the stage for fifteen years, who nearly always played the chief role and whose natural manner of singing, whose gestures and whose action—all of which are most essential in every opera—aroused in the audience feelings of fear and terror, pity and lament, joy and pleasure.[1]

---

[1] Quoted in Beekman Cannon, *Johann Mattheson, Spectator in Music* (Archon Books, 1968), 27.

He was also fundamentally a religious man and concluded, after considering theories advanced earlier, that music had its origin with the angels, before the creation of the earth.[2] While vocal music must be older than instrumental music with man, he finds no reason to doubt that the angels played instruments. While man might have once heard such music in Paradise, after the Fall and the expulsion from the Garden of Eden, this knowledge was lost.

The great hallmark of Renaissance and Baroque music is the rediscovery of the importance of emotions in music, a subject which the Church tried to hide for one thousand years by inventing a bizarre theory that music was a branch of mathematics. As with other humanists, this was a topic of great concern with Mattheson and in his philosophical writings one can see a careful, lengthy and constant effort to explain why mathematics cannot be the basis for music.

In his *Neu-Eröffnete Orchestre* Mattheson attacks the old notion of mathematics-based theory in music by going directly to the elements upon which the older theorists had based their reasoning, in particular the nature of the intervals. In his discussion of whether the interval of the fourth should be regarded as a consonance or dissonance, Mattheson concludes it is not a matter of mathematics, but rather a matter of the ear, that is how the fourth is used. The reader should particularly notice, as a hallmark of the Baroque's movement away from music based on intellectual concepts to music based on feeling, that Mattheson specifies here that music communicates with "the inner soul."

[2] Johann Mattheson, *Der vollkommene Capellmeister* (1739), trans. Ernest Harriss (Ann Arbor: UMI Research Press, 1981), Foreword III. He apparently finds his evidence for this in Job 38:7,

> when the morning stars sang together,
> and all the sons of God shouted for joy.

In his book, *Behauptung der Himmlischen Musik...* (1747), Mattheson elaborates on his belief in the existence of music in Heaven and the origin of music in angels worshiping God.

> Numbers in music do not govern but merely instruct. The Hearing is the only channel through which their force is communicated to the inner soul of the attentive listener ... The true aim of music is not its appeal to the eye, nor yet altogether to the so-called "Reason," but only to the Hearing, which communicates pleasure, as it is experienced, to the Soul and the "Reason." Hence, if the testimony of the ear is followed, it will be discovered that in its relation to the surrounding sounds and harmony, the fourth will be either consonant or dissonant.[3]

[3] Johann Mattheson, *Das Neu-Eröffnete Orchestre* (Hamburg, 1713), 126ff. Mattheson also writes at length in opposition to the old dogma that mathematics is the basis of music in his book, *Das Forschende Orchestre* of 1721.

Such views, which would seem obvious to most modern readers, were nevertheless a direct attack on the old mathematics-based theories of music and resulted in letters and books attacking Mattheson for his views. Johann Buttstedt, an organist in Erfurt, attacked Mattheson in a book, *Ut, Mi, Sol, Re, Fa, La, Tota Musica et harmonia Aeterna ... entgegen gesetzt Dem neu-eröffneten Orchestre,* in which he contends that since German music is now practiced only by craftsmen [*Spielmanns-Wesen*] the current musicians are not even educated in the older rules.

> How many musicians will one find today who have real knowledge? Most of them do not even know how many styles and modes there are and what music is suitable for ecclesiastical or motet styles. The knowledge of such styles is almost entirely lost ... Why? [It is] is hard to understand and not well paid for. And so, instead of correct knowledge mere *Galanterie* suffices, just as the finery of ladies once consisted of pearls and golden chains but now of mere ribbons and laces.[4]

[4] Quoted in Cannon, *Johann Mattheson*, 135ff.

To defend himself, Mattheson published a new book, *Das Beschützte Orchestre,* in which he appealed to a number of distinguished German musicians to join in the debate over mathematics versus feelings. One who responded was one of the most old-fashioned and dogmatic Church representatives yet composing, Johann Fux (1660–1741), the author of the monument to the former style, *Gradus ad Parnassum.* He was particularly angered by an attack, in this latest book by Mattheson, on the medieval theorist, Guido d'Arezzo (991–1033 AD), to whom Fux believed all subsequent music was indebted.

> I am not at all a blind worshiper of superstitious antiquity; but until something better has been invented, I shall venerate in every way what through so many centuries the noblest masters have held to be good and proper.[5]

[5] Ibid., 140.

Some distinguished musicians, however, came to the defense of Mattheson. Handel wrote Mattheson at this time, taking a very practical approach to the debate.

> The question seems to me to reduce itself to this: whether one should prefer an easy & most perfect Method to another

that is accompanied by great difficulties capable not only of disgusting pupils with Music, but also making them waste much precious time that could better be employed in plunging deeper into this art & in the cultivation of one's genius?[6]

Johann Heinichen, in language much stronger than Mattheson's, ridiculed the old-fashioned theorists as having wasted their entire life in pursuit of *rudera antiquitatis.*

> All will be sheer Greek to those steeped in prejudices when nowadays they hear that a moving music composed for the ears requires even more subtle and skillful rules—to say nothing of lengthy practice—than the heavily oppressive music composed for the eyes which the cantors of even the tiniest towns maltreat on innocent paper according to all the venerable rules of counterpoint … And we Germans alone are such fools as to jog on in the old groove and, absurdly and ridiculously, to make the appearance of the composition on paper, rather than the hearing of it, the aim of music.[7]

Johann Kuhnau also was strong in his support of Mattheson.

> As regards the great controversy that the gentleman of Erfurt has brought upon you, I do not believe that, save for him, anyone will disapprove of your *Orchestre.* This is especially true of your point of view in matters of the solmisation and the old ecclesiastical modes; for you wrote your *Orchestre* for a *galant-homme* who, being no professional musician, has not the least interest in amusing himself with innumerable old freaks which are usually outmoded at best and worth—virtually nothing.[8]

In his *Der vollkommene Capellmeister* of 1739 Mattheson returns to this question.[9] Here he begins with the basic point that mathematics is an aid to music, as it is to most disciplines. However, "they are wrong who believe or want to teach others that mathematics is the heart and soul of music" or that it is responsible for changes in emotion in the music. He begins his argument with the concept of proportions in general, which he finds in natural, moral, rhetorical and mathematical relationships. For the first three of these, natural, moral and rhetorical relationships, Mattheson maintains

[6] George Friedrich Handel, letter to Johann Mattheson, February 24, 1719, quoted in Piero Weiss, *Letters of Composers Through Six Centuries* (Philadelphia: Chilton, 1967), 63.

[7] Quoted in Cannon, *Johann Mattheson,* 141ff.

[8] Quoted in Ibid., 142.

[9] *Der vollkommene Capellmeister,* Foreword, VI.

no precise mathematical measure is possible. One cannot, for example measure the distance from the earth to the sun precisely because the flames leaping out from the sun render no fixed edge. His comment regarding precision in language is quite perceptive. Everyone would agree, he supposes, that "life" is a positive, happy word. But if one says, "life is denied," the meaning is changed. Thus, "the heart's emotion no longer has its basis in mere sounds and words."

Turning to music, he proposes two rhetorical questions:

1. If someone wants to be a sound musician, must he not attain this through mathematics?

2. Cannot one become an admirable composer and musician without thorough knowledge of the arts of measuring?

> Now if someone says yes to the first question, and no to the second, then he contradicts ancient and modern experience, indeed, his own eyes, ears, hands, the combined senses of all mankind, and shuts the only door through which his intelligence gives him what he has. Whereas if he answers no to the first question and yes to the second, then mathematics cannot possibly be the heart and soul of music.

From this he concludes mathematics can measure, but not determine the essence of a thing. "Everything that goes on in music is based on mathematical relationships of intervals just about as much as seamanship is based on anchors and cables."

> However one defines the mathematical relationships of sounds and their quantities, no real connection with the passions of the soul can ever be drawn from this alone.

Mathematics is only the "science, theory and scholarship" of music. To introduce what exists beyond this he quotes Andreas Papius.

> The mere *cognition of the ratio* of a step, a half step, a comma, the consonances, etc., will bring the name virtuoso or artistic prince to no one, but rather the minute examination *according to the laws of nature* of the various works which are produced by great artists: from this we can understand the composer's

soul, in regard to how and to what extent, in his particular work, one thing more than another masters the *human mind and emotions,* which is the *highest pinnacle of the discipline of music.*

Again, his point here is that mathematics can measure the elements of music, but not how these elements are used. It is the latter, not the former, which concern feelings in music.

> A perfect understanding of the human emotions, which certainly are not to be measured by the mathematical yardstick, is of much greater importance to melody and its composition than the understanding of tones ... This is certain: it is not so much good *proportion,* but rather the apt *usage* of the intervals and keys, which establishes the beautiful, moving and natural quality in melody and harmony. Sounds, in themselves, are neither good nor bad; but they become good and bad according to the way in which they are used. No measuring or calculating art teaches this.

How then does one describe the role mathematics plays in music, together with its other elements? Mattheson offers the following metaphor:

> The human mind is the paper. Mathematics is the pen. Sounds are the ink; but Nature must be the writer. Why have a silver trumpet if a competent trumpeter is not available?

Mattheson points out that sculptors know and can measure the proportions of the human body, but "heart and soul ... and beauty is not on this account to be found in such mathematical measuring; but only in that force which God put in Nature." Similarly, in painting, when "mathematics ceases entirely, true beauty really first begins." And so with music,

> A composer can succeed quite well without special mathematical skills. Many who virtually climbed to the pinnacle of music can hardly name or interpret all parts of mathematics; not to mention anything more ... However, the best mathematician, as such, if he were to want to compose something, could not possibly achieve this with mere logic.
>
> Let it be said once in fact for all: Good mathematical proportions cannot constitute everything: this is an old, stubborn misconception.

The point, he says, is this: "music draws its water from the spring of Nature; and not from the puddles of arithmetic." The composer expresses something understood from Nature. Only then can this be mathematically expressed, but not the other way around. Mattheson, in other words, equates music with Nature and God and as something above intellectual skill.

> Mathematics is a human skill; nature, however, is a divine force ... Now the goal of music is to praise God in the highest, with word and deed, through singing and playing. All other arts besides theology and its daughter, music, are only mute priests. They do not move hearts and minds nearly so strongly, nor in so many ways ...
> Music is *above,* not in *opposition* to mathematics.

In conclusion, Mattheson cannot resist taking a shot at those remaining exponents of the old mathematics-based polyphony, but admits the possibility that history may again in the future see such foolish endeavor.

> I have occupied myself with music, practical as well as theoretical, with great earnestness and ardor for over half a century already: I have also met many very learned *Mathematici* in this not insubstantial time who thought they made new musical wonders out of their old, logical writings; but they have, God knows! always failed miserably. On the other hand, I have quite certainly and very often experienced that not a single famous actor, musician, nor composer, not only in my time but as far as I can remember having read or heard about, has been able to construct even a simple melody which was of any value on the feeble foundations of mathematics or geometry ... What will happen in the future is yet to be seen.

In another place, Mattheson makes this point again.

> The entire art of harmonic calculating and measuring, even if we also were to include algebra, cannot alone produce a single skilled Capellmeister; whereas our very best composers have scarcely ever taken a ruler in hand for the sake of their beautiful work.[10]

[10] Ibid., I, vii, 11.

It is also with respect to the older polyphonic style that Mattheson contends it is wrong to say that melody derives from harmony, as was the case in that style. Rather, harmony derives from melody.[11] It is a point made confusing by comments by Rameau and is still misunderstood by some today.

[11] Ibid., Foreword, VII.

A question which had been debated throughout the early Christian era by philosophers was the relationship between Reason and the emotions. Under the influence of the church, these early philosophers assigned little value to the emotions in general. It is only with Humanism that the emotions began to be understood as an important part of man. Today we understand Reason and the emotions to be separate but equal, represented by their respective hemispheres of the brain. Mattheson was one of a number of early writers who attempted to begin to balance the scales.

> Science differs from Art in this, that the former comprehends and comprises a matter from its principles through reasoning only; whereas the latter requires practical application, and as an inseparable component.[12]

[12] Ibid., I, i, 5.

In his discussion of the classifications of music, Mattheson reaches back to the familiar distinction made by the medieval universities: *speculative*, or *theoretical*, "which deals only with inner consideration and deliberation," and *practical* music, which is performance.[13] Contrary to the medieval tradition, and that of some universities today, which labored to keep these disciplines separate, Mattheson makes a determined effort to connect the two.

[13] Ibid., I, ii, 24ff.

> That type of contemplation or theory is however to be preferred to all others which does not delve so deeply into shallow, mental considerations that action is forgotten; but turns its main aim toward actual practice and usage ... Whoever wants to make good use of both aspects must never separate them, but keep them fast together, like body and soul.

He observes that while it is an intelligent thing to ponder, contemplate and reflect on a piece of music before performing it, it sometimes works the other way around. That is, the study seems to be a "corroboration of that which one finds to be true in practice."

Matheson's understanding of the nature of music, like that of the ancient philosophers, included movement. No doubt due to his experience on the stage, he has left a discussion under the title, "On the Art of Gesticulation," which, he says, is a study of emotions as expressed by gesture.[14] The proper term he gives for this art is *Hypocritica,* which Matheson says Cassiodorus defined as "silent music." Quintillian defined it as "the science of hand gesticulation," but used the term *chironomy.*

[14] Ibid., I, vi.

But the word Hypocritica, for Matheson, means more than chironomy, for *Hypo* (under) and *Crisis* (criticism) suggests the submission of one's thoughts for judgment. This should be thought of in a positive sense, as a form of stimulation, and not in the ill-meant "hypocrisy." The origin, and source of power, for gesture is found in its universality. First, Matheson points out that language itself only developed as a shadow of action.[15] Second, he touches on a very important point.

[15] Ibid., I, vi, 5.

> Words do not move a person who does not understand the language; discriminating words are good only for discriminating minds; but everyone understands the well-used facial expression, even young children with whom neither words nor beatings have as much effect as a glance.[16]

[16] Ibid. I, vi, 6.

This observation is more important than Matheson realized, with respect to universality, for modern research has shown that both facial expressions and the basic emotions are universal and the latter are formed before birth and are thus not learned, but genetic.

Matheson classifies this subject under *oratorical,* which directs the movement of the body; the *histrionic,* which belongs to plays and requires much stronger gesturing than the first; and the *saltatorial,* which deals with all kinds of steps and leaps.

The oratorical is closely related to music, for, he says, music is "an oratory in tones" and the ancient orators "gleaned their best rules from music." It is here, of course, that Matheson becomes most critical. Regarding the singers in church he writes,

> It would be desirable that if no proper gestures take place out of bad habit, at least nothing of a quite inappropriate, indecent, or cold and indifferent mien would occur: of which unfortunately! we are so little lacking that often the most serious and sacred pieces are sung and played in such a shameless manner, chattering, smirking, trifling, so that devout listeners are very annoyed.
>
> I have attended many, many a Passion and Requiem which to my great chagrin evoked audible joking and laughter.[17]

[17] Ibid., I, vi, 11ff.

Secular concert music is criticized for similar reasons.

> If we go from the church to the concert room, one likewise encounters quite marvelous and diverse unseemly poses at Concerts which sometimes do not have anything in common with what is going on … [Most players] seem to me like people who care only about filling their stomach and not about elegant taste.
>
> Can the attentive listener be moved to pleasure if he is constantly disturbed by the noise of someone beating time, be it with his feet or hands? If he sees a dozen violinists who contort their bodies as if they are ill? If the clavier player writhes his jaw, wrinkles his brow, and contorts his face to such an extent that it could frighten children? If many of the wind instrumentalists contort or inflate their facial features so that they can bring them back to their proper shape and color in half an hour only with difficulty?[18]

[18] Ibid., I, vi, 15ff.

The true goal for both church and concert performance, Mattheson summarizes, is "that gesture, words and music form a three-part braid, and should perfectly harmonize with each other toward the goal that the feeling of the listener be stirred."

Turning to the theater, here, he says, is "the real college for all sorts of gesticulations."[19] *Hypocritica*, communication through gesture, is what an actor does. It is in pretending what he is not, notes Mattheson, that we get the origin of "hypocrite." Here also one finds the dance, in which *Hypocritica* "is as indispensable as the feet themselves." So closely related are the dancer's gestures and the music, that he finds most dancing masters prefer to write their own melodies. If the composer is to compose the dance music, then he must understand dance and in this regard Mattheson points to

[19] Ibid., I, vi, 23ff.

Lully who "personally instructed all his actors, actresses, and male and female dancers in this art of gesticulation."[20]

In conclusion, Mattheson points to the importance of gesture in all the arts of ancient Greece and Rome, including mime and pantomime which he says often moved the spectators to tears. The system of notation of gesture, of which he regrets precise knowledge is now lost, was called *Orchesin* in Greek and *Saltationem* in Latin. As a summary of the importance of these relationships in the ancient world, he quotes a contemporary, Charles Rollin, *Histoire ancienne* (Paris, 1730–1738).

> The art of gesticulation also belongs to music, it illustrates and teaches the steps and postures of dance as well as of the common walk, together with the postures which one uses in a public oration. In short, music comprehends all the art of composing and writing public utterances that have nothing to do with singing, through which annotations the sound of the voice is speech as well as the tempo and movement of the gestures would be ordered: which was a very useful art to the ancients but is completely unknown to us.[21]

As part of his contemplation on the nature of music, Mattheson also gave some thought to music and society in a broader sense. In fact, he began his first important book, *Das Neu-Eröffnete Orchestre* with the startling chapter title, "The Fall of Music and its Cause." By this he meant, in 1713, that "through misuse and ignorance the noble art of music, contrary to its very purpose, causes, alas!, more ill-humor than pleasure among many."[22] The first reason Mattheson gives for this decline must be seen in context with his belief expressed in his later writings, that the true essence of music was something very close to Nature. But, if we may paraphrase him in modern terms, left-brained man, the product of traditional education (then as now), is compelled to think that the Truth of a thing can be evident only if it can be expressed in rational thought. The academic world therefore tends to turn music, which is by nature associated with the non-verbal right hemisphere of the brain, into a series of concepts understandable by only the left hemisphere. The student, and unfortunately especially the

[20] Ibid., I, vi, 26.

[21] Ibid., I, vi, 35. Mattheson concludes this part of his discussion with an account of the Imperial composer in Vienna in 1730, Francesso Conti, who, having "used his art of gesticulation in a most wicked manner," was placed on bread and water, beaten by a priest and forced to stand before the doors of St. Stefan Cathedral in a long hairy coat holding a black candle for an hour!

[22] *Das Neu-Eröffnete Orchestre*, 1. We cite the original page numbers, but the English translation is by Cannon.

layman, is therefore led to believe that he knows nothing of music unless he knows the conceptual form of it. Mattheson expressed it in this way:

> For they are persuaded that this beautiful and perfect creation, which a beneficent God has given us men for our pleasure, and likewise as a model of the eternal, harmonious Splendor, depends solely upon deep learning and laborious knowledge. To prove this, they dispense their philosophical rules and scholarly vagaries, not only with great authority, but likewise with such obscurity that one has a rightful aversion for the stuff, and would rather remain in permanent ignorance than to go through such *horrenda*.[23]

But Mattheson, having been a performer, knew that rational concepts cannot well describe the experience of music. Thus he advises the pursuit of performance, after the necessary foundation, as a means of finding a "healthy idea of music, purified of all unnecessary school-dust."

Mattheson himself could not entirely escape the Germanic need to conceptualize music, as can be seen in his attempt to explain melody through the rules of rhetoric. And so another reason he gives for the decline of music, not quite the reverse of the first one, was that there are too many composers who just write lots of notes without knowing what they are doing. His third cause for the decline of music is also education oriented: the ancient guild system, through which music was learned as a trade rather than as an art.

Two additional negative circumstances, Mattheson finds, the artist must simply accept as being the way things are. These are the ignorance and poor taste of the general public and the fact that good musicians are not well paid.

In the Foreword to his *Der vollkommene Capellmeister*,[24] Mattheson continues his somewhat pessimistic view of the relationship of music and society. He finds many noble and educated persons who know nothing about music, either because they lack the time to study it or fail to understand the "dignity and great benefit" which derives from music. On the other hand, most of those who practice music are rarely scholarly. They merely take pleasure from music, turning it into,

[23] Ibid., 2ff.

[24] *Der vollkommene Capellmeister*, Foreword, II.

a menial trade, an item to market, a means to obtain food, indeed even into a society of flagellants, and nothing more.

At the same time, he finds some who merely collect beautiful musical instruments (and are called "true connoisseurs") and others who think music exists merely to please and to pass the time. All of the above, he says, are on the wrong path.

In a chapter called, "On the Use of Music in the General Public,"[25] Mattheson focuses primarily on the need for civic and church officials to be musically educated in order to oversee the use of music under their supervision. His most extensive complaint regards a custom ushered in Germany with the Reformation under which no music could be performed for an entire year as part of the observation of the required period of mourning following the death of a noble.[26]

In his *Das Neu-Eröffnete Orchestre,* Mattheson makes a few interesting observations on current national styles.[27] He finds in the compositions of the Italians the most beauty, due in part to "their polished and *insinuante* artistic ideas." There is no question, he concludes, that all nations who desire to be distinguished in music "have borrowed nearly everything from the Italians, and have imitated them completely in all things."

The fame of the French lies not so much in their composition as in their execution, especially in dance music where they are the masters. The English style he characterizes as a "flat-footed imitation of the Italian style." And as for the music of his own country,

> Among the educated Germans the esteem for music has never been really small or thoroughly prosperous either. In fact, this noble art ... has come to be treated somewhat sleepily and indifferently; hence the great revolution in musical affairs has not come to my countrymen as it has to those in other lands ... Our German virtuosi, who are—to speak dispassionately—altogether worthy to bear such a title with honor, are much more deserving of esteem than whole bands of foreigners ... But a contemptible custom affecting these matters has come to pass; we prefer anything that is foreign,

[25] Ibid., I, v.

[26] Ibid., I, v, 30.

[27] *Das Neu-Eröffnete Orchestre,* 200ff.

not necessarily because of its beauty and value, but merely because it is foreign to our own people, and things which are not bad or simple in themselves suffer the odium of being merely native.

He would not find much has changed in our society today.

4
On Emotion in Music in the German Baroque

> All musical expression has an emotion for its foundation.[1]
> F. W. Marpurg, 1749

[1] F. W. Marpurg, *Der critische Musicus an der Spree* (Berlin), September 2, 1749.

IN THE RENAISSANCE the most frequently given purpose for music was to "soothe" the listener's feelings. During the Baroque, as we approach the modern concept of a concert, this purpose is transformed into something with a more Aristotelian ring to it, more like the description of a catharsis, "to refresh the spirit." Georg Muffat, in the Foreword to his *Auserlesene Instrumental-Music* (1701) explains that in his previous collections he has sought to draw "liveliness and grace" from the "Lullian well." But, in the present collection he now presents "certain profound and unusual affects of the Italian manner, various capricious and artful conceits, and alternations of many sorts, interspersed with special diligence between the [ripieno] and [concertino]." The purpose of this music, as he makes very clear, is to listen to, it is concert music. It is also important to notice the variety of situations which he equates with "concert music," considering how limited a definition we acknowledge today (concert hall, lights off, white tie, programs, etc.).

> These concerti, suited neither to the church (because of the ballet airs and airs of other sorts which they include) nor for dancing (because of other interwoven conceits, now slow and serious, now gay and nimble, and composed only for

the express refreshment of the ear), may be performed most appropriately in connection with entertainments given by great princes and lords, for receptions of distinguished guests, and at state banquets, serenades, and assemblies of musical amateurs and virtuosi.[2]

In the title pages of Bach's *Clavier Übung*, Part III, and the "Goldberg Variations," he gives the purpose to "refresh the spirits." Similarly, when he was looking at a position in Halle, he was sent a contract which specified that the church music should have the result that "the members of the Congregation shall be the more inspired and refreshed in worship."[3]

The most important purpose of music is to communicate feelings, a purpose to which Johann Scheibe paid tribute in 1739.

> Music which does not penetrate the heart nor the soul
> Does indeed consist of tones yet only is compelling to the ears,
> Which nature and art have not given sound, grace, strength,
> Is quite dead, and lacks spirit and vitality.[4]

A more typical expression of this purpose during the Baroque is given by Georg Muffat, in his *Florilegia* (1695). He writes that he has given each suite the name of "some state of the affections which I have experienced," namely, Piety, The Joys of the Hopeful, Gratitude, Impatience, Solicitude, Flatteries, and Constancy.

To understand what Muffat means by this, we must pause to consider the influence on Baroque composers of what Bukofzer names "the principle of the doctrine of affections and figures."[5] Nearly every writer on Baroque music mentions this "doctrine," but we believe it is incorrect to suggest this was something composers thought about before or while composing. The "doctrine" was really the creation of theorists, not composers, and the epitome of it lies in the difficulty we all experience in trying to talk about emotions, or to employ the left hemisphere of the brain to describe something it knows nothing about. And it is this central irony, using intellectual concepts to explain feeling, which

[2] Quoted in Oliver Strunk, *Source Readings in Music History* (New York: Norton, 1950), 449.

[3] Quoted in Hans T. David and Arthur Mendel, *The Bach Reader* (New York: Norton, 1966), 65. J. F. Reichardt reports an occasion when Bach needed to refresh his own spirits. He had entered a room where a harpsichordist was performing. Upon seeing Bach, the performer suddenly stopped, leaving a dissonant chord hanging in the air.

> Bach, who heard it, was so offended by this musical unpleasantness that he passed right by his host ... rushed to the harpsichord, resolved the dissonant chord, and made an appropriate cadence. Only then did he approach his host and make him his bow of greeting. [Ibid., 291]

[4] Poem in honor of the publication of Johann Mattheson, *Der vollkommene Capellmeister* (1739), trans. Ernest Harriss (Ann Arbor: UMI Research Press, 1981), 74.

[5] Manfred Bukofzer, *Music in the Baroque Era* (New York: Norton, 1947), 5.

makes this "doctrine" impossible, then or now, as a practical technique of composition.

Baroque theorists, who had essentially the same experiences as we, although they knew nothing of modern brain research, inherited a frame of reference which included a scholastic tradition thousands of years old beginning with the ancient writer's endless theoretical contemplation about the emotions of the soul and continuing in the medieval Scholastic concentration on "speculative music." Thus, after composers began to re-establish the primary purpose of the expression of feelings in their music, by the late Baroque some theorists felt compelled to explain, in the context of this long history of philosophy, and emboldened by the spirit of the oncoming Enlightenment, what they were hearing and to attempt to conceptualize it.

The theorists who began to write treatises on this subject were mostly German and mostly very minor figures. Paul Henry Lang finds "Manuals containing musical 'figures' which corresponded to certain affections began to appear with Mauritius Vogt's *Conclave Thesauri Magnae Artis Musicae* (Prague, 1711)."[6] Bukofzer provides a more extensive list,[7] but some of the treatises he cites, such as Praetorius, only discuss feelings in music but do not construct a "doctrine," and others, such as Heinichen, are more than skeptical of the idea to begin with. For the most part, these attempts to create a "doctrine" are attempts to correlate musical composition, in particular melodies, with the academic terms used in the teaching of rhetoric and oratory. In the material by Mattheson the reader will find an adequate sampling of a typical effort to do this. The musical examples which Mattheson provides, however, are really nothing more than what we would call "text-painting" today, and this was certainly not a new idea to the seventeenth or eighteenth century. Neither, of course, was the expression of emotions a new idea. Indeed, Emilio de' Cavalieri had already written in 1600 that the purpose of his *Rappresentazione di Anima, et di Corpo* was to "move the listener to different emotions, as pity, joy, tears, and laughter, and other similar emotions." Since late Re-

[6] Paul Henry Lang, "Musical Thought of the Baroque: The Doctrine of Temperaments and Affections," in *Twentieth-Century Views of Music History*, ed. William Hays (New York: Scribner's, 1972), 201.

[7] Manfred Bukofzer, "Allegory in Baroque Music," in *Journal of the Warburg and Courtauld Institutes*, 1939–1940 (Vaduz: Kraus Reprint, 1965), III, 5, cites S. Calvisius, *Exercitationes duae*, 1600; J. Nucius, *Musices poeticae*, 1613; M. Praetorius, *Syntagma musicum* III, 1619; J. Cruger, *Synopsis musica*, 1624; Volupius Decorus, *Architectonice musices universalis*, 1631; Chr. Bernard, *Tractatus compositionis augmentatus*, c. 1650; J. C. Printz, *Phrynidis Mytilinaei*, I, 1696; Chr. Caldenbach, *Dissertatio musica*, 1664; D. Speer, *Grundrichtiger . . . musikaliches Kleeblatt*, 1697; J. Heinichen, *Anweisung zum Generalbass*, 1711; M. Vogt, *Conclave thesauris magnae artis musicae*, 1719; J. Mattheson, *Critica Musica*, 1725; J. Mattheson, *Der vollkommene Capellmeister*, 1739 and J. Scheibe, *Critischer Musicus*, 1743.

naissance music clearly had both emotion and text-painting, do we really have much left to dignify with the name, "doctrine?" Can we really imagine that the composers of the Baroque followed the instructions of the theorists? And in the theater, where this idea was supposed to be centered, one not only had extra-musical considerations, but as Heinichen observes the composer might compose emotions not intended by the poet at all.

> I would never suggest to anyone to fill up the theatrical style with too many serious inventions ... For pathetic, melancholic, and phlegmatic music (in so far as it is based on tenderness and good taste) is effective in the church and chamber styles; but it is not well suited to the theatrical style, and one uses serious pieces simply for judicious [variety]. And if their lordships, the poets, overload us with pathetic and sorrowful arias, we [the composers] must try to sweeten these either with mixed inventions or effective accompaniments; or in those arias containing a double affection, one turns the invention more gradually to the lively element rather than the serious one. Thus, for example, with the melancholy of love, one should rather express the pleasantness of love and not the blackness of melancholy ... In summary, the theatrical style for the most part requires something moving or adroit, though I should not call it simply merry. For merry music in itself can easily degenerate into barbarism and is unpleasant to sensitive ears.[8]

[8] Johann David Heinichen, *General-Bass Treatise* [1711], quoted in George Buelow, *Thorough-Bass Accompaniment according to Johann David Heinichen* (Ann Arbor: UMI Research Press, 1986), 282.

Heinichen also questions whether there can be any meaningful association between emotions and tonality. This relationship, one of the most fundamental questions in early philosophy, had long been assumed to be the key to how emotions affect the listener. The long history of this idea in literature left Heinichen somewhat ambivalent. He appears to want to believe that keys have certain emotional qualities, but he immediately casts doubt on the general idea by pointing out that the real emotional meaning is found in the actual music the composer writes.

> The aria begins in Eb; for this reason, however, the invention need not be sad, serious, or plaintive, for brilliant concerti as well as joyous arias in certain cases can be composed with the greatest effect in this beautiful key. Furthermore, the

previous examples ... clearly show that one can express the same words and affections in various and, according to the old theory, opposing keys. For that reason, what previous theorists have written and rewritten about the properties of the modes are nothing but trifles, as if one mode could be merry, another sad, a third pious, heroic, war-like, etc.

He continues by noting that even if this were true, it would be rendered void by the conflicting tuning systems and lack of agreement on a standardized pitch. Following this, he concludes,

> In my opinion, the ancient theorists erred in their research of modal characteristics, in the same way as we continue to err today in judging a musical work. If we, for example, find for this or that key ... one or more beautifully tender, plaintive, or serious arias, we prefer to attribute the fine impression of the aria to the key itself and not to the excellent ideas of the composer; and we immediately establish a *proprietas modi,* as if contrary words and affections could not be expressed in this key. This, however, is worse than wrong, as can be proved to the contrary by a thousand beautiful examples. In general, one can say that one key is more suitable than another for expressing affections. Thus in the practice today using well-tempered scales, the keys indicated with two and three sharps or flats are particularly beautiful and expressive in the theatrical style ... Yet, to specify this or that key especially for the affection of love, sadness, joy, etc., is not good. Should someone object at this point and say that D, A, Bb major are much more suited to raging music than the calmer scales of A minor, E minor, and similar ones, then this actually does not prove the *proprietas modorum* even if it were so, but it depends on the inclination of the composer. For we have heard famous composers write the saddest and tenderest music in D, A, and Bb major, etc., whereas in A minor, E minor, C minor; and in similar scales we have heard the most powerful and brilliant music.[9]

[9] Ibid., 283.

All things considered, we think there is a danger in making more out of "the doctrine of affections" than was ever recognized by the actual composers, that is, more meets the eye than ever met the ear of the Baroque listener. Certainly we recognize that it is the glory of the Baroque that the true purpose of music, expressing feeling, had conquered the old

Scholastic understanding of music as a branch of mathematics. Therefore we may suppose people were talking more about emotions in music than ever before. But just because people were discussing emotions, it does not necessarily follow that there was a universally understood "doctrine." Therefore, we believe that some sixteenth century composers would be surprised to be excluded, if we say, as does Palisca,

> If we want to ascertain whether we have crossed the boundary into the baroque or out of it, there is no better test than to ask whether the expression of the affections is the dominant goal in fashioning a piece of music.[10]

Bukofzer's discussion on "Allegory in Baroque Music" is again primarily a discussion of text-painting. However, he clearly maintains a different purpose for the Baroque composer, almost as if his emotions were not as sincere as those of the composer of the Classical Period. We can only suppose he were thinking primarily of Baroque church music in arriving at such a conclusion. Further, his conception of the "rigidity of baroque music, especially from the rhythmic point of view," an idea which surely no one today believes any longer, is a conclusion which can only be reached if one only looks at the Baroque music as it appears to the eye and overlooks the entire aspect of improvisation which was so fundamental to it.

> The counterblast to baroque music took precisely the form of the discovery how to express feelings *without the intervention of the intellect*. Music no longer *meant* this or that emotion; it was itself the immediate expression of that emotion. This transition from the notion "it means" to that of "it is" marks the transition from the baroque style to its successor, the classical-romantic style ...
>
> Baroque music is not, like modern music, a language of feeling, which expresses its objects directly, but a sort of indirect iconology of sound. For this reason it lacks all psychology in the modern sense. The rigidity of baroque music, especially from the rhythmic point of view, has long since been remarked upon. But this is not a weakness of such music; on the contrary, it is its very strength. The humanization of music by means of a dynamic emotional conception of its nature appears only during the first half of the eighteenth century.[11]

[10] Claude Palisca, *Baroque Music* (Englewood Cliffs: Prentice Hall, 1981), 5.

[11] Manfred Bukofzer, "Allegory in Baroque Music," III, 20ff.

Surely no one today would so describe Baroque music. If "baroque music is not ... a language of feeling," then what was Corelli doing in performance when he,

> suffered his passions to hurry him away so much ..., whose eyes will sometimes turn as red as fire; his countenance will be distorted, his eyeballs roll as in an agony, and he gives in so much to what he is doing that he doth not look like the same man.[12]

Bukofzer was closer to the truth in his later book when he concluded,

> Since [the doctrine of figures] did not "express" but merely "presented" or "signified" the affections, musically identical figures lent themselves to numerous and often highly divergent meanings. It is therefore misleading to isolate certain figures and classify them in a system of absolute meanings as joy, steps, beatitude, and so forth.[13]

We believe the conclusion by Hans T. David and Arthur Mendel more accurately describes not only Bach, but all serious Baroque composers.

> Attempts have been made to describe [the doctrine of the affections] as a kind of formula technique: a set of symbolic patterns to which Bach would recur whenever the textual situation required. But to ascribe to Bach a predominantly intellectual routine of this sort is to overestimate the importance of certain elements apparent in his music. He was neither so poorly endowed with imagination that he had to establish for himself a whole reservoir of ready-made patterns, to draw on whenever inspiration failed, nor so theoretically minded that he would heed the pedantic attempts of his contemporaries to establish music as a branch of rhetoric.[14]

The most accurate testimonial of the view of the Baroque composer may be the one inadvertently expressed in 1711 by Heinichen. He means to complain that no theorist has really written the definitive work on the "doctrine of affections." But he was describing musicians at large, including composers, when he admits that no one is interested in this topic. For this is how it has nearly always been: composers compose and the theorists come along later, and not before.

---

[12] Oliver Strunk, "François Raguenet, Comparison between the French and Italian Music (1702)," *The Musical Quarterly* 32, no. 3 (1946), 419fn.

[13] Bukofzer, *Music in the Baroque Era*, 389.

[14] David and Mendel, *The Bach Reader*, 34.

What a bottomless ocean we still have before us merely in the expression of words and the affections in music. And how delighted is the ear, if we perceive in a refined church composition or other music how a skilled virtuoso has attempted here and there to move the feelings of an audience through his *galanterie* and other devices that express the text, and in this way to find successfully the true purpose of music. Nevertheless, no one wants to search deeper into this beautiful musical *Rhetorica* and to invent good rules. What could one not write about musical taste, invention, accompaniment, and their nature, differences, and effects? But no one wants to investigate the matters aiming at this lofty practice or to give even the slightest introduction to it.[15]

In the end, no matter what emotions the composer was feeling and attempting to notate, a great responsibility remains to the performer if these emotions are to be perceived by the listener. A student of Bach relates that the latter had this foremost in mind even in the performance of the most simple music.

> As concerns the playing of chorales, I was instructed by my teacher Kapellmeister Bach, who is still living, not to play the songs merely offhand but according to the feeling [*Affect*] of the words.[16]

Heinichen concurs that the notes are not sufficient for this purpose.

> It is impossible to find the tenderness of the soul of music with mere numeric changes of dead notes.[17]

The German writer, Christoph Bernhard (1627–1692), in a treatise on singing, expresses his concern that gesture correspond with feeling.

> The question may here be raised, whether a singer's face and bearing should reflect the affects found in the text. Thus let it be known that a singer should sing modestly, without special facial expressions; for nothing is more upsetting than certain singers who are better heard than seen, who arouse the expectations of a listener with a good voice and style of singing, but who ruin everything with ugly faces and gestures.[18]

[15] Heinichen, *General-Bass Treatise*, 326. In a footnote, Heinichen observes that some attempts at expressing emotions in music sound mannered and make people laugh. Thus, he says, "a mighty chasm stretches between knowledge and ability."

[16] Johann Ziegler (1746), quoted in David and Mendel, *The Bach Reader*, 237.

[17] Heinichen, *General-Bass Treatise*, 330.

[18] Quoted in Ellen Harris, "Voices," in *Performance Practice: Music after 1600* (New York: Norton, 1989), 100.

On the other hand, Bernhard's description, in 1649, of the singer's range of emotion in the Florentine style is rather remarkable.

> In the recitative style, one should take care that the voice is raised in moments of anger, and to the contrary dropped in moments of grief. Pain makes it pause; impatience hastens it. Happiness enlivens it. Desire emboldens it. Love renders it alert. Bashfulness holds it back. Hope strengthens it. Despair diminishes it. Fear keeps it down. Danger is fled with screams. If, however, a person faces up to danger, then his voice must reflect his daring and bravery.[19]

[19] Quoted in Ibid., 110.

Marpurg confirms a wide variety of emotions in performance and provides an interesting discussion of the integrity of the performer.

> All musical expression has an affect or emotion for its foundation. A philosopher when expounding or demonstrating will try to enlighten our understanding, to bring it lucidity and order. The orator, the poet, the musician attempt rather to inflame than to enlighten. The philosopher deals in combustible matter capable of glowing or yielding a temperate and moderate warmth. But in music there is only the distilled essence of this matter, the most refined part of it, which throws out thousands of the most beautiful flames, always with rapidity, sometimes with violence. The musician has therefore a thousand parts to play, a thousand characters to assume at the composer's bidding. To what extraordinary undertakings our passions carry us! He who has the good fortune at all to experience the inspiration which lends greatness to poets, orators, artists, will be aware how vehemently and diversely our soul responds when it is given over to the emotions. Thus to interpret rightly every composition which is put in front of him a musician needs the utmost sensibility and the most felicitous powers of intuition.[20]

[20] F. W. Marpurg, *Der critische Musicus an der Spree* (Berlin), September 2, 1749.

Finally, from Forkel we have the interesting insight that even the instrument was a consideration for Bach in this regard.

> Bach preferred the Clavichord to the Harpsichord, which, though susceptible of great variety of tone, seemed to him lacking in soul.[21]

[21] Quoted in Robert Donnington, *The Interpretation of Early Music* (New York, 1964), 576. Bach apparently also gave active consideration to the acoustics of the room as well as in the plan for seating his musicians. See David and Mendel, *The Bach Reader*, 276, 278.

The most dramatic concept of the expression of emotions through music is what is generally known as "ethos," the ability of music to change the character of the listener. The sixteenth century nobles, especially in Italy, felt that after a dinner party, during which there was much debating and arguing, it was important to conclude the evening by singing in order to bring everyone into "harmony." We find it somewhat charming, therefore, that Johann Kuhnau makes a similar argument when discussing the virtues of the collegium musicum.

> The musicians in cities commonly hold a collegium musicum every week or two. That is indeed a laudable undertaking, in part because it provides them with the opportunity to refine further their excellent art, and in part, too, because they learn from the pleasing harmonies how to speak together concordantly, even though these same people mostly disagree with one another at other times.[22]

Finally, may we remind the reader of the chronology of this topic. First, the Church opposed emotion in general in the life of the Christian for one thousand years. Then, Humanism, especially in the field of music, begins to reintroduce the true definition of music, that it is a vehicle for communicating emotions. By the Baroque Period this has become the center of attention for musicians, representative views of which in Germany have been presented above. Given this history, it is interesting, even ironic, that one also finds in Germany during the Baroque even some religious poetry which has now adopted the focus of Humanism. C. Eltester has written an extraordinary religious poem describing a young lady singing a song to the accompaniment of a theorbo, which is almost sensual in its imagery.

> When, fairest maid, there stirs your mouth all filled with sense,
> And then there through your lips a tone inspired does sing,
> Which by sweet song does bear the Lord His offering,
> The heavens are themselves seduced to reverence.

[22] Johann Kuhnau, *Der musicalische Quack-Salber* (Dresden, 1700), Chapter I. Kuhnau (1660–1722), like Bach, was the music director of St. Thomas in Leipzig. Although known today as a composer, he was educated in law and mathematics and was capable in Hebrew, Greek and Latin.

A something which comes near to bearing us from hence,
A hidden current shows—our heart enamoring,
And even through secret force the spirits capturing—
That paradise within your voice has residence.

It seems the angels are descended from the sky
And make themselves through you our choir's ally,
For what men everywhere do round them hear and heed,
And what your lovely mouth in heaven's wise has sung,
That is a masterpiece poured from the angels' tongue,
Which does the very soul from out its being lead.[23]

A poem by Daniel Omeis was intended to help fill the listener with religious ecstasy. It was a rare religious poem before the Baroque Period which used such language.

If here sweet notes can bring me near to ecstasy,
How blissful I shall hear the angels' melody,
My God, when they for You Your thrice blest praises sing,
And through eternity Your grace and glory ring.

My soul turns full of soul, when it a sweet sound hears.
The sweetest song of all, oh God, from You appears.
Oh, in Your awfulness let key and tune resound,
That, where I pleasure find, Your pleasure too be found.[24]

[23] C. Eltester (d. c. 1732), "Als sie ein Lied in die darzu gespielte Theorbe sangl," in George Schoolfield, *The German Lyric of the Baroque* (New York: AMS Press, 1966), 93.

[24] Magnus Daniel Omeis (1646–1708), "Wenn du etwas Liebliches horest," in Ibid., 239. Omeis studied law at the Universities of Altdorf and Strassburg and eventually became a professor of poetry at the former.

5
Mattheson on Emotion in Music

THERE IS NO DOUBT that Johann Mattheson (1681–1764) believed the central purpose of music, after praising God, was the communication of emotion. The whole question of the "passions," Mattheson suggests, is perhaps more the province of the philosopher than the Kapellmeister, but on a practical level it is fundamental to composer and performer if they are to communicate with the listener.[1]

In reflecting on the emotions in general, he observes that "most are not the best, and certainly must be curtailed or kept in check." Love is an emotion frequently represented by music and in these cases the composer should "consult his own experience." Sadness is second only to love in its use by composers, no doubt, he observes, "because almost everybody is unhappy." It is for this reason that sacred music employs this emotion so effectively, because it represents the "penance and remorse, sorrow, contrition, lamentation and the recognition of our misery."

Regarding the expression of emotions through music, Mattheson first gives several obvious illustrations which we might recognize today as simple text-painting: Joy, being an expansion of our soul, represented by large and expanded intervals; Sadness, being a "contraction of these subtle parts of our body," represented by small intervals and Hope and Depression through obvious melodic direction.

---

[1] Johann Mattheson, *Der vollkommene Capellmeister* (1739), trans. Ernest Harriss (Ann Arbor: UMI Research Press, 1981), I, iii, 52ff.

Mattheson then turns to more specific prescriptions for representing emotions through music.² Pride, Haughtiness and Arrogance are represented by a "bold, pompous style ... majestic musical figures which require a special seriousness and grandiloquent motion." For these, the melodic line must invariably ascend. The opposite emotions of Humility, Patience, etc., are represented by humble music with descending melody.

Stubbornness "deserves a special place among the affects that are appropriate to musical rhetoric," and is represented by "so-called capricci ... namely when one writes such peculiar passages in one or another voice which one is resolved not to change, cost what it may." For Anger, Ardor, Vengeance, Rage, Fury and other such "violent affections" it is not enough,

> that one rumbles along strongly, makes a lot of noise and boldly rages: notes with many tails will simply not suffice, as many things; but each of these violent qualities requires its own particular characteristics, and, despite forceful expression, must still have a becoming singing quality.

Hope, "is a pleasant and soothing thing, consisting of a joyful longing which fills the spirit with a certain courage." This, therefore, "demands the loveliest use of the voice and the sweetest combination of sounds in the world."

Mattheson assigns dissonance to the expression of the unpleasant, disagreeable, frightening and horrible, although interestingly enough "the spirit even occasionally derives some peculiar sort of comfort from these." Despair should be represented by "unusual passages and strange, mad, disordered sequences of notes." In contrast, Composure is best represented by a "soft unison."

In summary, Mattheson, in acknowledging the difficulty of his subject, makes some comments which reflect on the characteristics of the left and right hemispheres of the brain. First he observes that although the emotions are like a bottomless sea, one can write very little about them. And, he says, where nature and morals are shortchanged, "reason and wisdom cannot be diverted and naked wit takes the lead."³

² Ibid., I, iii, 72ff.

³ Ibid., I, iii, 83, 88.

Finally, he suspects most composers who fail to effectively express emotions in music do so because they do not know their own desires or what they actually wanted to achieve. But failure in this has significant implications for the listener. He says here, in effect, that whatever is written which represents only the "theory" of music communicates nothing to the listener. It is a fundamental lesson which is rarely taught in music schools.

> Is it then astonishing that with pieces thus formed, where true natural theory of sound together with the pertaining science of human affections are completely absent, merely the ears of the poor, simple, and self-righteous listeners are tickled, but their hearts and minds are not aroused in proper measure.[4]

[4] Ibid., I, iii, 89.

Mattheson did not attribute as much influence on the emotions to tonality as one might have expected. In his review of tonality[5] he does refer to the association of the Greek modes with the peoples for whom they were named.

[5] Ibid., I, ix.

> It is probably that the Dorians had a coarser, more manly, and deeper speaking voice than the Phrygians; and that on the other hand the Lydians sang finer and more effeminately than the others. For the Dorians were a modest, virtuous and peaceful people; the Phrygians however used more noise than foresight; whereas the Lydians, forefathers of the Tuscans, were everywhere described as sensual people.

He also observes that noticeable differences can still be found in the singing of the various areas of Italy during his time, not to mention in other countries. The Mixolydian mode he claims was invented by the lyric poetess, Sappho, to accommodate the fact that she could not sing low enough for the Lydian mode. The voice, Mattheson assures us,

> stemmed from quite natural causes in a young voluptuous widow, since the heat of passion in the long run dries out and contracts certain tubes so that they, especially in the throat, from a lack of sufficient humors cannot stretch adequately enough and cannot produce a low-pitched sound.[6]

[6] Ibid., I, ix, 16ff.

Turning to the Middle Ages in his survey of tonality, Mattheson calls this long period "the worst and most confused theory on modes that one at any time could have invented." And he was right, it was a long struggle to try to explain the laws of tonality in mathematical terms, without reference to the listener.[7]

Mattheson devotes little space to the theories of tonality of his own era, the late Baroque. He principally points out that music was now based on the triad and states, without elaboration here, that,

> the nature and character of each key, namely whether it is happy, sad, lovely, devout, etc., are actually matters of the science of melody.[8]

He is absolutely correct, of course, and it would be very interesting to know how he himself arrived at this truth.[9]

In his *Neu-Eröffnete Orchestre,* Mattheson discusses in more detail the natural affections of specific scales, yielding some interesting conclusions.[10] The key of F-sharp minor, for example, he finds,

> is a key characterized by sadness, but a sadness more pensive and lovelorn than tragic and gloomy; it is a key that has about it a certain loneliness, an individuality, a misanthropy.

Mattheson's discussion of style in music is also closely tied to the general topic of the emotions. He begins with the classification of music into church, theater and chamber,[11] but this too was synonymous with style, for the church style, for example, exists apart from whether the music is performed in a church building. Beyond this, Mattheson considers it more important to think of the distinctions "high, middle and low" styles, or "noble, moderate or trifling." These classifications are also considered apart from those of church, theater and chamber, or location of performance. Thus, one can speak of "high" as meaning something different in different mediums, as for example, "what is *elevated* in the theater is very different from what is elevated in dinner music." Or, one can speak of high, medium and low within a single medium. In the case of church music, for example, Mattheson suggests that,

> "Divine majesty, heavenly splendor, rapture and magnificence" are naturally required for the *elevated* style; "Devotion, contemplation, etc.," belong to the *middle* style; while "Repentance,

[7] Ibid., I, ix, 23ff.

[8] Ibid., I, ix, 47.

[9] For those readers who wish to explore this further, we highly recommend the book, *The Language of Music,* by Cooke.

[10] Johann Mattheson, *Das Neu-Eröffnete Orchestre* (Hamburg, 1713), 231ff.

[11] *Der vollkommene Capellmeister,* I, x. Mattheson attributes this classification to Marco Scacchi, an Italian Kapellmeister for the kings of Poland and to his manuscript book in "the public library of St. John in Hamburg."

supplient entreaties, etc.," stand under the banner of the *low* style.[12]

[12] Ibid., I, x, 10.

Mattheson adds here some additional aesthetic qualities, beginning with "expressiveness." Expressiveness, he finds, must exist in all music, apart from any regard to other classifications. "Naturalness," he regards as somewhat different. Naturalness is required if an elevated style is to sound magnificent. A low style with artistic elaborations, on the other hand, would be unnatural.

Now Mattheson attempts to address the emotions with the purpose of establishing some correlation with style.[13] His discussion is so interesting, from the perspective of illuminating late Baroque thought on the "affections," we will quote it at length.

[13] Ibid., I, x, 22ff.

> Among those affections which one commonly attributes to the high style are many which do not deserve to be called high at all, in the good sense. For, what can be lower than anger, fear, vengeance, despair, etc. Beating, boasting, snoring is indeed not true nobility. Arrogance is itself only an inflating of the soul, and actually requires more bombast than nobility for expression: now the most haughty are again unfailingly the most angry, in their feelings one debility after another takes the helm. For, though anger will have the *appearance* of being action of a great spirit, still it springs in *fact* from an effeminate heart: one would have to consider it then a special, holy, and just bureaucratic wrath, which nevertheless should punish and discipline, without any indignation.
>
> Great and valiant spirits are forbearing; but small and timid souls can endure nothing. Frivolous people are easily provoked and are as quickly moved to anger, as is the turning around of weather-cocks or weather vanes on the roofs. In short, anger is a ridiculous affection. It sounds quite base and does not entail an elevated presentation.
>
> Fear and fright are indeed probably the most foolish emotions in the world, and really deserve nothing so little as something of the elevated in their expression. Alas! One finds these unfortunate impulses in all creatures, even in those which seem to have no other emotion and are scorned. Nothing can however be lower than miserable human vengeance, which has so little noble in it that it finds a place only in the most depraved hearts.

If we come to despair, then that is the extreme to which fear can lead: hence one would have to set it on the highest peak of sadness if it really is to have something of nobility. The Italians therefore rightly call all malicious and dangerous people, whose spirit is dejected and lost, *Huomini tristi*.

I will meanwhile not deny that something of strength, turbulence, passion and ecstasy is required if one desires to express properly these and similar passions in music; just as the affections of impetuosity, vengeance, etc., are so constituted that they, according to the difference in station, have the appearance of a high proud quality, although they deny its strength. Here one must also admit that this presumptuous arrogance occasionally requires something of the stately in oratory and music (yet greatly different from the true type); but which is not at all of the mighty, majestic, etc.

Shrieking and grumbling is suitable in anger and quarreling; an uneven, broken, shocking, trembling style in fright; something of daring with vengeance; something frantic with despair; something turgid with arrogance; as long as it did not come out too naturally and arouse disgust: but all of this has nothing to do with the elevated style.

But whoever would want to relegate devotion, patience, diligence, desire, etc., to the middle style might be considered only as moderately devout, moral, patient, diligent and desirous. Indeed, desire corresponds in very many ways with the highest and most emphatic affection in and outside of the world, namely love, how then can it be relegated to the middle of the road? It is true that desire is according to the nature of the desired object also small or large, high or low, and so on; yet it is the same with almost all emotions.

On the one hand diligence can have much of nobleness, on the other it can have something trifling as the goal. In the last case it would be a work in the dark so to speak (*obscura diligentia*) and would not even deserve to stand in the middle, but rather at the low end. There is nothing at all high-flown about patience, though always something noble: and everyone knows that devotion serves to lift the spirit.

Finally, common dance songs either all, or at least most of them, would indeed have to embody something of the beggarly, slavish, cowardly, disconsolate, base, boorish, stupid, and clumsy, if these qualities of the low style were to be found in them. Low and base are again very different, and if we indeed should exclude from this the most nonsensical peasant dances, though not the clever *Land-Tanze, Country*

Dances, then for all of that there probably would be no one who would expect beggars in a spirited minuet, slaves in a happy rigaudon, cowards in an heroic entree, despair in a lusty gavotte, or base spirits in a magnificent chaconne.

Drinking songs and lullabies, amorous little pieces, etc., must not always be indiscriminately called trifling: if they are done quite naturally they are often more pleasing and have greater impact than high and mighty concerti and stately overtures. The former no less require their master in their own way than the latter. Yet, what am I to say? Our composers are all kings; or of royal descent ... They do not fret over trivialities.

Mattheson also finds specific associations between forms and emotions.[14] He begins his discussion with vocal music and in particular *chant* which he considers the epitome of "noble simplicity." Mattheson does not speak much of contemporary church vocal forms here, but does make a remarkably negative reference in passing to the motet style of the sixteenth century.

[14] Ibid., II, xiii ff.

> [In the motet] there were no passions or affections to be seen for miles; no breaks to be found in the musical rhetoric, indeed rather caesuras in the middle of a word with an adjacent pause; no true melody; no true charm, indeed no meaning: all based on a few words which often meant little or nothing, such as *Salve, Regina Misericordiae,* and the like.[15]

[15] Ibid., II, xiii, 72.

Mattheson adds, in case anyone should think he has been too severe, that he can show contemporary examples of famous composers who are still writing works "with all the above defects." How, he wonders, can intelligent composers issue such works and call them good?

The nature of the *aria* is to express a "great affection,"[16] whereas the *cavatina* (madrigals, sonnets and poems) aim rather for a "penetrating observation." Mattheson's discussion of the *recitative* reflects his concern that it must have as much emotion, with as clearly defined accents, as the principal song. He recognizes its greater rhythmic freedom, noting "the recitative has a beat; but it does not use it."[17] He means there is a beat on paper, but live performance can be, and should be, very different.

[16] Ibid., II, xiii, 56, adds that the principal emotion in opera is "intense love."

> However, it invariably excites a large amount of disquiet and emotionalism with jealousy, sadness, hope, plea, vengeance, rage, fury, etc. I really would seek the most important character of an opera in *disquiet* itself, if that would not make me suspect.

[17] Ibid., II, xiii, 22.

Turning to vocal music of a lighter nature, Mattheson gives one of the most detailed discussions of the *serenade* to be found in early literature.[18] First of all, of course, he associates the form with outdoor music, and in particular evening music.

[18] Ibid., II, xiii, 40ff.

> Nowhere can a serenade better be heard than on the water in calm weather: for then one can use *in their full strength* all sorts of instruments, such as trumpets, drums and Waldhorns, which in a chamber would sound too intense and deafening.

Mattheson then makes a number of very interesting remarks about how the emotions of this kind of music contrast with other vocal forms.

> The principal characteristic of serenades must always be tenderness, *la tendresse*. I say the principal characteristic: for there are very many secondary qualities with this form. The cantatas, each for itself, employ all sorts of affections and passions; though only one at a time, and they use these in a historical manner, narratively. Serenades on the other hand tend to deal mainly with nothing other than with tender and strong love, without pretense, and moreover the composer as well as the poet must certainly construct everything accordingly with these, if he wants to bring out their true nature. There is not a melody so small and not a piece so large that it can forego having a certain principal characteristic prominent before others and over others, and distinguishing it clearly from the others: otherwise it signifies little or nothing.
>
> Consequently it runs against the true nature of the serenade if one makes use of it so to speak outside of its element (I mean the emotion) with felicitations, public pageants, commencements at universities, etc. Political and military affairs are foreign to it; for the night is devoted to nothing with such intimate acquaintance as love and sleep. These other affairs are served by oratorios and aubades or morning-songs of all kinds,[19] and are particularly characterized by a grandiose, pompous, rousing quality, in secular matters, which harmonizes badly with the tenderness and secret emotions of the heart. Hence oratorios need more voices; whereas a solo or only a couple of singers can be used for serenades; which is another good mark of distinction.

[19] The *aubade* had its origin as a morning song in the medieval tradition of the watch tower musician playing special music just before dawn to warn illicit lovers that it was time to hurry back to their own beds!

For two other lighter vocal forms, Mattheson identifies the principal affections for the *balletto* as "pleasure and amusement" and for the *pastorale* as "a certain purity and kindheartedness."

Among Mattheson's discussion of the major instrumental forms,[20] his comments on the Sonata are most enlightening. The Sonata, he says, is a form,

[20] *Der vollkommene Capellmeister*, II, xiii, 137ff.

> whose aim is principally towards complaisance or kindness, since a certain Complaisance must predominate in sonatas, which is accommodating to everyone, and which serves each listener. A melancholy person will find something pitiful and compassionate, a sensuous person something pretty, an angry person something violent, and so on, in different varieties of sonatas ...
>
> For some years rudimentary sonatas for the clavier have been composed with good success ... [but] they aim more toward movement of the fingers than the heart. Yet amazement over uncommon dexterity is also a type of affection, which often gives rise to envy; although it is said, its true mother is ignorance.

He does not find as much variety in emotions in the *Concerto grosso*, but rather curiously a tendency toward "sensuous pleasure." To this he adds a fascinating reference to the concerto *style* of the late sixteenth century definition.

> Most [concerti] depend upon the full elaboration, indeed, one even overdoes it, so that it resembles a rich table which is set not for hunger but for show. Once can easily guess that in such a contest, from which all concerti get their name, there is no lack of jealousy and vengeance, or envy and hate, as well as other such passions.[21]

[21] Ibid., II, xiii, 139.

Mattheson also mentions a large number of other instrumental forms, each of which is identified with specific emotional qualities.[22] Among these are,

[22] Ibid., II, xiii, 81ff.

Minuet	moderate cheerfulness
Govotta	true jubilation
Bourree	contentment and pleasantness, not so degenerate as the gavotte
Rigaudon	somewhat trifling joking
La Marche	somewhat heroic and fearless, yet not wild and running

Entree	noble and majestic
Gigue[23]	ardent and fleeting zeal
Polonaise	frank and free
Angloise	stubbornness
Hornpipe	frivolity
Sarabanda	to express ambition
Courante	sweet hopefulness
Allemanda	a content or satisfied spirit
Chaccone	more satiating than tasteful
Intrada	to arouse longing

[23] Mattheson associates with the Gigue the French *Loure*, which he identifies with "a proud, arrogant nature"; the Spanish *Canarie*, "eagerness, swiftness and simplicity"; and the Italian *Gige*, used for "fiddling, ... extreme speed and volatility."

For all of Mattheson's pleas that the purpose of music was to move the listener, he appears to have been reluctant to go beyond this to an ancient Greek concept of ethos. He appears to want to believe that music can change character, and appears to accept the basic logic, but nevertheless he hesitates.

> Plato thought men's habits change with music, namely when [the mode] is changed; Cicero maintained however if habits were to change, then music would change. Both can serve our purpose, and neither is wrong. Music and customs should be altered together, so that the former does not damage the latter, nor the latter the former. It is the same with the political ...
>
> Besides it is quite regrettable that none of us now knows what constitutes *Musica moralis*. If ethical, or moral philosophy, which concerns the inner man, were only well cultivated; then morals, or ethics which concern the extrinsic, would function better.[24]

[24] Ibid., I, v, 33ff.

Mattheson also quotes the author Lohenstein, in this regard, observing that this is "a statement which can arouse to deeper insight."[25]

[25] Ibid., I, iii, 26. The source for Lohenstein he gives as *Arminio*, II, 90.

> The eyesight, the sense of smell, the sense of taste and the sense of touch serve the body; but only the sense of hearing is reserved for the soul and our morals.

On the other hand, Mattheson seemed comfortable with the concept of music therapy and not only reviews many of the anecdotes of the healing powers of music found in ancient literature, but he also provides some contemporary examples.[26] He says he received a letter from the Queen of Spain in 1737 in which she testifies that her husband was completely cured of "black melancholy" by her having organized a concert every evening before dinner. So impressed was the King, that he began to study music himself.[27] He mentions a professor at Göttingen who attributed the alleviation of pain in limbs with the effect music has on muscles. A particularly interesting report is that seventeenth century native Americans,

> use no other means than their somewhat coarse method of playing, by means of which they occasionally suppress and alleviate difficult infirmities and pains if not heal them.[28]

In chapter seven of his famous book on everything a Kapellmeister should know, Mattheson discusses emotion with respect to the difference between mensuration and movement. Mensuration, for Mattheson, is meter, but his descriptions have to be read in the context of their era for he says some things are impossible, metrically, which are common today. It is in connection with mensuration that he places *arsis* and *thesis*.

First, the reader needs to understand that the use of the word "movement" here refers to the moving of the emotions in the listener. It is in this sense that earlier musicians spoke of the 1st movement, or 2nd movement, in a sonata or sinfonia as meaning different emotions. The "second movement" meant a second emotion, etc. We use the word "movement" today, in regard to form, without reference to the emotions. Returning to Mattheson, movement is, he says, "what the Italians commonly indicate only with some adjectives such as *affettuoso, con discrezione, con spirito*."[29] While he does not list in that sentence, *allegro, adagio* and *vivace*, etc., his choice reminds us that all these terms originally carried some character association and not just speed. We can also see this in the chapter of a contemporary book he cites here, "*Les mouvements differents sont le pur espirit de la Musique.*"[30] Mattheson himself says movement is a "spiritual thing," not a physical thing (meter), and depends not on "precepts and prohibitions," but "feeling and emotion."

[26] Ibid., I, iii, 43. Here he cites three publications: the *Quintessence des Novelles*, 1727, Nr. 18, which contains a Rondo which can be used as a cure for the bite of the tarantula; the *Observations de Medecine sur la maladie, appellee convulsions par un Medecine de la Faculte de Paris*, a Paris, 1732, xii, 32, which contains "examples of music helping sick people to health"; and the *Leipziger Zeitungen von gelehrten Sachen*, 1733, 626, which discusses the author's father being cured of melancholy by music, all other remedies having been in vain.

[27] Ibid., I, iii, 45.

[28] Ibid., I, iii, 47 . He quotes François La Mothe le Vayer, *Oeuvres de François de la Mothe le Vayer* (Paris, 1656), I, 521.

[29] Mattheson, *Der vollkommene Capellmeister*, II, vii, 7.

[30] Jean Rousseau, *Methode claire, certaine et facile pour apprendre a chanter la musique* (Paris, 1678).

To find the correct movement, the performer must "probe and feel his own soul" as well as "feel the various impulses which the piece is supposed to express."[31] The ability to correctly find the movement, Mattheson observes, is a knowledge which "transcends all words" and "is the highest perfection of music, and it can be attained only through considerable experience and great gifts."

Since the previous chapters had their focus on the expression of the feelings of the text through melody, Mattheson now addresses the question of the expression of emotions in instrumental music in a chapter called "On the Difference between Vocal and Instrumental Melodies."[32] Before getting to the most important topic, Mattheson offers a few interesting observations such as "instrumental melody will always have more fire and freedom than vocal melodies"[33] and that vocal music is never concerned with key, whereas this question is a significant one in instrumental music.

Mattheson finds "instrumental music can indeed do without the words themselves, but not the emotions."[34] That instrumental music can indeed express emotions is obvious in practice, he observes, but "never in theory." By this he means it is a subject difficult to write about, although he himself makes an admirable summary.

[31] *Der vollkommene Capellmeister*, II, vii, 18ff.

[32] Ibid., II, xii.

[33] Ibid., II, xii, 21, says the French can't give up their dotted instrumental rhythms because they would be "like chefs without salt." He finds these to be used much less in vocal music.

[34] Ibid., II, xii, 30ff.

> The proper goal of all music [melody] can be nothing other than the sort of diversion of the hearing through which the passions of the soul are stirred: thus no one at all will obtain this goal who is not aiming at it, who feels no affection, indeed who scarcely thinks at all of a passion; unless it is one which is involuntarily felt deeply. But if he is stirred in a more noble way and wants to move others with harmony, then he must know how without the words to express sincerely all the emotions of the heart through selected sounds and their skillful combination in such a way that the listener might fully grasp and clearly understand therefrom, as if it were actual speech, the impetus, the sense, the meaning, and the expression, as well as all the pertaining divisions and caesuras. It is then a joy! Much more art and a better imagination is required if one wants to achieve this without, rather than with words.[35]

[35] Ibid., II, xii, 31.

With the absence of text, the performer must take even more careful note of the Italian expressions at the beginning of the composition for clues to the emotions. Here the reader may be surprised by Mattheson's understanding of the characters and emotions associated with the familiar "tempo" terms.

> An *Adagio* indicates distress; a *Lamento* lamentation; a *Lento* relief; an *Andante* hope; an *Affetuoso* love; an *Allegro* comfort; a *Presto* eagerness ...[36]

[36] Ibid., II, xii, 34ff.

These qualities, Mattheson finds, can appear in a composer's music, "out of his genius," even if he is unaware of it.[37] He also finds emotional content in larger formal designs.

[37] Which raises the possibility that our right-hemisphere of the brain may be contributing something of its own.

> If I hear the first part of a good overture, then I feel a special elevation of soul; the second expands the spirits with all joy; and if a serious ending follows, then everything is brought together to a normal restful conclusion.

And finally a wonderful observation on the listener.

> Whoever pays attention can see in the features of an attentive listener what he perceives in his heart.

6
On German Baroque Performance Practice

> He gave it life when it had none.
> *Johann Daube, on J. S. Bach's improvisation*
> *in place of the notated music.*

THERE ARE SOME INTERESTING COMMENTS in seventeenth century German literature which suggest that the dynamics which appear on paper as contrasting were in fact blended together through crescendo and diminuendo. Benedict Lechler, writing c. 1640, says such markings "stand, not for a series of abrupt steps, but for gradual diminuendos or crescendos." W. M. Mylius, in 1686, makes a crescendo and diminuendo where only piano is given.

> Yet with both piano and forte it is to be noted that one does not go so suddenly from piano to forte, but one should gradually strengthen the voice and again let it decrease so that at the beginning piano is heard, forte at the middle, and once again piano as one comes to the close.[1]

On the other hand, we have quite a different, and even more subjective, concept of dynamics by Georg Muffat, in the Foreword to his collection of concerti, *Auserlesene Instrumental-Music* (1701).

> At the direction *piano* or *p* all are ordinarily to play at once so softly and tenderly that one barely hears them, at the direction *forte* or *f* with so full a tone, from the first note so

[1] Both are quoted in Robert Donnington, *The Interpretation of Early Music* (New York, 1964), 484.

marked, that the listeners are left, as it were, astounded at such vehemence.[2]

"Astounded" seems a strong expectation of the listener, but Muffat mentions this again with respect to tempo.

> In directing the measure or beat, one should for the most part follow the Italians, who are accustomed to proceed much more slowly than we do[3] at the directions *Adagio, Grave, Largo*, etc., so slowly sometime that one can scarcely wait for them, but, at the directions *Allegro, Vivace, Presto, Piu presto*, and *Prestissimo* much more rapidly and in a more lively manner. For by exactly observing this opposition or rivalry of the slow and the fast, the loud and the soft, the fullness of the [ripieno] and the delicacy of the [concertino], the ear is ravished by a singular astonishment, as is the eye by the opposition of light and shade.

Later he implies this sense of tempo continues to the very end.

> It is earnestly requested that the listeners be maintained in continuous attention from beginning to end, until, at a given moment, all end the concerto together, forcibly and, as it were, unexpectedly.[4]

Some scholars have taken comments such as this to suggest that there were no cadential *ritards* before the Classical Period. I disagree.

Perhaps the least familiar aspect to most readers, with regard to Baroque performance practice, is improvisation. But it seems very clear that performers were expected to finish the composition through improvisation (called *ornamentation* by modern theorists) or by the addition of ornaments (not the same thing as ornamentation!) as can be documented throughout the Baroque. Early in the seventeenth century, for example, Heinrich Schütz, in the preface to his *Resurrection History* (1623), recommends that the long sustained chords in the organ part should be performed with "decorative and appropriate runs or passages."[5] Again, in his *Cantiones sacrae*, Op. 4, of 1625, he writes,

---

[2] Quoted in Oliver Strunk, *Source Readings in Music History* (New York: Norton, 1950), 451.

[3] Yet Quantz in his Flute Treatise gives the tempo for Adagio as quarter-note = 16.

[4] Quoted in Ibid., 452. The philosophy expressed by Praetorius and Arbeau is the opposite.

[5] Hans Moser, *Heinrich Schütz* (St. Louis: Concordia, 1936), 367.

You organists, however, who wish to satisfy more sensitive ears I request not to spare the pains to fill in all [!] the voices. If in customary manner you accompany only according to the *basso continuo*, I would consider this wrong and unmusical [*vanum et inconcinnum*].[6]

By "wrong and unmusical" Schütz really meant that the composition had been left in such a manner that the details must be added by the performer.[7] This is surely what Heinichen meant as well, when he wrote of an aria,

In this aria there is no embellishing of notes [on paper], but in a complete performance [*elaboration*] it may be so embellished with good taste, brilliance, and accompaniment that it necessarily will encounter complete success in public.[8]

It is our opinion, in this regard, that all instances where "Alberti bass" figures are found invite improvisation.

Regarding a different kind of improvisation, Georg Muffat mentions the adding of ornaments in 1696, in writing of performance in the French ballet style of Lully.

One must use with discernment certain ornaments making the pieces much more beautiful and agreeable, lighting them up, as it were, with sparkling precious stones.[9]

We also have testimonials to the public improvisation of a number of Baroque musicians. Bach, in particular, is frequently mentioned in this regard. Marpurg, writing in 1752, recalls,

In the minds of all those who had the good fortune to hear him, there still hovers the memory of his astonishing facility in invention and improvisation.[10]

Contemporaries recalled many fascinating demonstrations of Bach's ability to improvise, such as when a famous French organist suddenly left town rather than compete in public with Bach in improvisation.

Marchand, who had hitherto defied all organists, had to acknowledge the undoubted superiority of his antagonist on this occasion. For when Bach made bold to invite him to

---

[6] Ibid., 402. See Ibid., 294 for references to other contemporaries who disliked thorough bass technique—one called it "cabbage chopping." Schütz discussses the "basso continuo" at length in the preface to his *Geistliche Chormusik* (1648) where his principal concern is that this practice not substitute for the ability to understand and write out a full score, knowledge of counterpoint, etc. Praetorius is of a similar mind in his *Syntagma Musicum*, Book III.

[7] An extraordinary example of music as Handel left it on paper, together with how he played it can be seen in Manfred Bukofzer, *Music in the Baroque Era* (New York: Norton, 1947), 376.

[8] Johann David Heinichen, *General-Bass Treatise* [1711], quoted in George Buelow, *Thorough-Bass Accompaniment according to Johann David Heinichen* (Ann Arbor: UMI Research Press, 1986), 372.

[9] Quoted in Strunk, *Source Readings*, 447ff.

[10] Marpurg's preface to the 1752 edition of the *Art of the Fugue*, quoted in Hans T. David and Arthur Mendel, *The Bach Reader* (New York: Norton, 1966), 267.

engage in friendly competition with him on the organ, and for this purpose gave him a theme which he jotted down with pencil on a scrap of paper, to be made the subject of improvisations, asking Marchand for a theme in return, Marchand, so far from putting in his appearance at the scene of battle, thought it better to leave Dresden by special coach.[11]

[11] Marpurg, *Legende einiger Musikheiligen* (Köln, 1786). See also David and Mendel, *The Bach Reader*, 445, 453.

And of course another famous occasion was Bach's improvisation before Frederick the Great, which resulted in the composition we know as "The Musical Offering."[12]

[12] See Ibid., 176, 179, and 260.

Contemporary musicians seemed most impressed in hearing Bach's improvisation while realizing a thorough bass. His son, K. P. E. Bach, recalled,

> He accompanied trios on more than one occasion on the spur of the moment and, being in a good humor and knowing that the composer would not take it amiss, and on the basis of a sparsely figured continuo part just set before him, converted them into complete quartets, astounding the composer of the trios.[13]

[13] Quoted in Ibid., 277.

A similar description of Bach's improvisation was recorded by Johann Daube.

> By his exceedingly adroit accompaniment he gave it life when it had none. He knew how to imitate it so cleverly, with either the right hand or the left, and how to introduce an unexpected counter-theme against it, so that the listener would have sworn that everything had been conscientiously written out. At the same time, the regular accompaniment was very little curtailed. In general his accompanying was always like a *concertante* part most conscientiously worked out and added as a companion to the upper voice so that at the appropriate time the upper voice would shine. This right was even given at times to the bass, without slighting the upper voice. Suffice it to say that anyone who missed hearing him missed a great deal.[14]

[14] Ibid., 256.

And while Bach was still alive, Lorenz Mizler wrote,

> Whoever wishes truly to observe what delicacy in thorough bass and very good accompanying mean need only take the trouble to hear our Kapellmeister Bach here, who accompanies every thorough bass to a solo so that one thinks it is a

piece of concerted music and as if the melody he plays in the right hand were written beforehand. I can give a living testimony of this since I have heard it myself.[15]

[15] Ibid., 231.

While it appears that most listeners were most appreciative of Bach's musicianship, on at least one occasion, his superiors in the church resolved to reprove him,

for having hitherto made many curious *variationes* in the chorale, and mingled many strange tones in it, and for the fact that the Congregation has been confused by it.[16]

[16] Ibid., 52.

In an atmosphere where literally all performers improvised on the basis of the music before them, one must imagine that such distinguished composers as Bach would have become discouraged at hearing lesser musicians transforming their music. Bach, in particular, towards the end of his life began to write out "all the notes." This was the beginning of the end of the tradition of the player contributing to the text of the composition, although it would take until the middle of the nineteenth century for this kind of improvisation to finally die out.[17]

This new practice brought the complaint from players that the composer was doing *their* job, that the music had become so cluttered that one could no longer see the important notes of the melody, etc. In 1737, Johann Scheibe anonymously wrote a "Letter from an able Musikant Abroad" which attacked the new practice.

[17] Thus the touching scene of Berlioz pleading with an oboist in Frankfurt to just play what he wrote. Even today we do not aspire to play exactly what is written.

Every ornament, every little grace, and everything that one thinks of as belonging to the method of playing, he expresses completely in notes; and this not only takes away from his pieces the beauty of harmony but completely covers the melody throughout. All the voices must work with each other and be of equal difficulty, and none of them can be recognized as the principal voice. In short, he is in music what Mr. von Lohenstein was in poetry. Turgidity has led them both from the natural to the artificial, and from the lofty to the somber; and in both one admires the onerous labor and uncommon effort—which, however, are vainly employed, since they conflict with Nature.[18]

[18] Quoted in David and Mendel, *The Bach Reader,* 238.

Since this was obviously directed at Bach, a lengthy series of publications began debating this point. The first to come to the defense of Bach was written by Johann Birnbaum the following year, who reminds the reader that not all performers were as gifted at improvisation as Bach.

> The Honorable Court Composer is neither the first nor the only man to write thus. From among a mass of composers whom I could cite in this respect, I will mention only Grigny and Du Mage, who in their *Livres d'orgue* have used this very method. If the latter, I can find no reason why it should deserve the name of fault. On the contrary, I consider it, for reasons which cannot be disregarded, as a necessary measure of prudence on the part of the composer. To begin with, it is certain that what is called the "manner" of singing or playing is almost everywhere valued and considered desirable. It is also indisputable that this manner can please the ear only if it is applied in the right places but must on the contrary uncommonly offend the ear and spoil the principal melody if the performer employs it at the wrong spot. Now experience teaches further that usually its application is left to the free whim of singers and instrumentalists. If all such men were sufficiently instructed in that which is truly beautiful in the manner; if they always knew how to employ it where it might serve as a true ornament and particular emphasis of the main melody; in that case it would be superfluous for the composer to write down in notes once more what they already knew. But only the fewest have a sufficient knowledge, and the rest, by an inappropriate application of the manner, spoil the principal melody and indeed often introduce such passages as might easily be attributed, by those who do not know the true state of affairs, to an error of the composer. Therefore every composer, including the Hon. Court Composer, is entitled to set the wanderers back on the right path by prescribing a correct method according to his intentions, and thus to watch over the preservation of his own honor.[19]

[19] Ibid., 236.

We must not omit one contemporary, Johann Gesner, who has left a description of Bach conducting in 1738. In this, which must have been a rehearsal, he appears to have been as florid as his counterpoint.

> If you could see him ... singing with one voice and playing his own parts, but watching over everything and bringing

back to the rhythm and the beat, out of thirty or even forty musicians, the one with a nod, another by tapping with his foot, the third with a warning finger, giving the right note to one from the top of his voice, to another from the bottom, and to a third from the middle of it—all alone, in the midst of the greatest din made by all the participants, and, although he is executing the most difficult parts himself, noticing at once whenever and wherever a mistake occurs, holding everyone together, taking precautions everywhere, and repairing any unsteadiness, full of rhythm in every part of his body ...[20]

There is a comment about the public which is worthy of quotation. Gesualdo once complained that a noble to whom he had given some madrigals kept them closely guarded for himself, preventing any opportunity for a wider public to get to know them. Samuel Scheidt (1587–1654) curiously makes the opposite point in a letter to Duke August of Brunswick.

> Since I do not desire to have these symphonies appear in print, whereby they would become common, I have made bold to dedicate them, together with some spiritual madrigals, to Your Lordship for your ducal chapel.[21]

We have seen above the appreciation of Bach's improvisation with a thorough bass. One who held a different view was Heinichen, who reminds the keyboard accompanist that his job is "to second the voice and not to stifle or disfigure it." He finds there are accompanists who add so much improvisation in showing their "clever vanity" that they hurt the performance.

We mention this here because of a subsequent comment which offers an enlightening view of the developing attitudes toward real concerts. He suggests that the art is more important than the individual.

> Whoever plays in a concert must play for the honor and perfection of the performance and not for his own particular honor. It is no longer a concert when each plays only for himself.[22]

Finally, with the developing seventeenth century official civic music, and the growing middle-class participation in

[20] Ibid., 231. His son reported that Bach conducted an orchestra with a violin as he played. See Ibid., 277.

[21] Letter to Duke August of Brunswick, June 19, 1642, quoted in Gertrude Norman and Miriam Shrifte, *Letters of Composers* (New York: Knopf, 1946), 16.

[22] Johann David Heinichen, *Thorough-Bass Accompaniment*, 215.

music, music was clearly leaving the protected environments of court and Church. We imagine some serious composers must have worried about the future of the art. We think perhaps this is reflected in a poem about a civic music guild that Johann Scheibe wrote in 1739 when apparently worrying that music was changing from art to entertainment.

> Your absurd guild which loves only laziness,
> Which denominates as masters those who are yet unskilled,
> Which in fact wants much written; yet never thinks,
> Which dispatches musical foolishness into the world day and night,
> Which so frightfully tortures and torments the sensitive ear,
> Which almost rejects music's cause out of tastelessness,
> Must throw down pen and paper, reflect,
> and examine yourself.[23]

[23] Poem in honor of the publication of Johann Mattheson, *Der vollkommene Capellmeister* (1739), trans. Ernest Harriss (Ann Arbor: UMI Research Press, 1981), 73.

7
Praetorius on Performance Practice

> Music has reached such a high level that
> any further advance would seem inconceivable.
> *Michael Praetorius, 1619*

IN 1975 WE HEARD A MUSIC PROFESSOR at the University of California, Berkeley, declare in public, "The study of the clarinet is to music, as the study of the typewriter is to English literature." This statement reflected an ancient view among music historians, that the actual performance of music is not of particular interest. It is this long held view which has, for example, for so long delayed serious publication in the field of performance practice. And it is this view, we presume, which can only explain why the third volume of Praetorius' *Syntagma Musicum*, the single greatest contemporary discussion of early performance practice, has never been published in entirety in any modern language to this very day in so far as we know.[1] Music historians have long been interested in, and have translated and published in modern editions, the first two volumes, which deal basically with theory and physical descriptions of instruments, but not the third volume, which deals with how music functioned in society.[2]

Although not published until 1619, the third volume is a description of both late Renaissance and Baroque style as practiced in Italy and Germany until about 1675. It is partic-

---

[1] A facsimile of the original German publication has been printed by Bärenreiter Kassel, 1958. The page numbers we cite, therefore, are from the original print.

[2] Praetorius speaks of a fourth volume, which apparently he never actually wrote. Praetorius (1571–1621), whose real name was Schultheiss, studied in the Latin school at Torgau and worked in the court of the Duke of Brunswick and later as Kapellmeister in Wolfenbüttel.

ularly valuable as Praetorius gives us a first-hand look at a critical moment in performance history, just when the use of Italian words for tempi were being introduced, when the slur designation was first introduced, when written dynamic markings were first being used, when thorough-bass was being introduced and, most importantly, an eyewitness account of the new form, the church concerto form, known to most musicians today in the music of Gabrieli.

Starting with the category of works with text, he begins with the concerto,[3] which he seems to have understood both as a style and a form. Here he presents the meaning of the term as a style, whereas below we shall see his extensive remarks on the practical application of this style. Before presenting Praetorius' comments on the concerto style, we should remind the reader that between the late Renaissance and the late Baroque, this term went through three distinct transformations in meaning. The term first meant the name of a group, as we might use the term "ensemble" today, such as "Concerto di Milano." Then it became a style word and only later a form.

To Praetorius, "concerto" as a style, was "a dialog in which different voices or instruments are combined."[4] In an apparent reference to Church polychoral form, he adds that the pleasure comes not from the craft involved, but from the variety.

He associates the style of a concerto with a multi-voice composition in which separate choirs alternate. This follows from the term itself, which he says derives from *concertare*, "to compete with one another."

> Let us imagine several of the best and most competent musicians singing or playing on various instruments—such as cornetts, trombones, recorders or transverse flutes, cromornes, bassoons or dulcians, racketts, viols, large and small violins, lutes, harpsichords, regals, positives, or organs—alternating in the manner of choirs and striving, as it were, to outdo one another.[5]

When he adds, "more properly a composition is called a concerto if a high and a low choir are heard in alternation

[3] In this essay we focus on Praetorius' discussion of church music.

[4] Ibid., 4. For "concerto" he gives *concertatio* in Latin and *ein Concert* in German. He also adds that *Cantio*, *concentus* and *symphonia* all mean at this time, "a composition for several voices."

[5] Ibid., 5.

and together," we can see the roots of what we understand today as *concertato* style.

Curiously, when Praetorius speaks of the English practice, he reverts to an older use of this term, meaning simply a group of players.

> The English call this a Consort, from *consortium*, as when several people with various instruments such as harpsichord, large lyra, double harp, lute, theorbo, pandora, *penorcon*, cither, viol, small violin, transverse flute or recorder, sometimes also a soft trombone or rackett, play together quietly and softly, forming a pleasant and harmonious relationship with one another.[6]

[6] Ibid.

In the case of the motet Praetorius provides a description of the style of the motet, in particular "elegance" and a work which "moves one most profoundly by its seriousness and artfulness."

Praetorius also points out that this form is sometimes confused with concerto, but he recognizes a distinction in style.

> The concerti should be set for several choirs and composed quite plainly, without particular elaboration and imitative passages; the motet, however, should be written with greater artfulness and care and for not more than eight voices.[7]

[7] Ibid., 8ff. He adds that Gabrieli has composed works for up to sixteen-voices which are "motets" in style, but organized into choirs as concerti.

Other church forms which Praetorius mentions include dialogues and canzoni. The Dialogue he does not define, because "everyone knows what dialogues are." It is interesting that he includes echo songs in this category.[8] The canzoni he understands first as "rather worldly" songs with varying orders of verses. He is also familiar with the Italian instrumental form and he recognizes that many beautiful canzoni are being composed there, particularly by Gabrieli.[9] Shorter songs carry the diminutive, canzonette, and usually have secular texts. It is interesting that he identifies this form with the German *Mestergesange*.

[8] Ibid., 16.

[9] Ibid., 17.

Praetorius' second large division of forms, those without text (or instrumental music), also include some forms associated with the church. Praetorius was under the impression that ricercar was merely the Italian name for fugue. He devotes little space to these forms, although he notes that the composer who can write them suited to particular modes and construct them correctly will be held in the highest esteem.[10]

Sinfonia means, to the Italians, he says, an instrumental work in four or more voices in the manner of a toccata, pavan, galliard or similar "Harmony." His most interesting observation is that while the sinfonia may be used at the beginning, it is often used inserted in the middle of a polychoral concerto![11] This apparently corresponds to the practice of having instrumental canzoni or other works performed between movements of the Mass.

Praetorius' brief discussion of the sonata is quite interesting. He finds the word itself is derived from *sonare* [Latin, "to sound"], which he says simply refers to the fact that it is an instrumental work. He seems, moreover, to have associated the word with *style*, for he adds that beautiful examples of sonatas can be found *in* the canzoni and sinfonias of Gabrieli and other composers. He elaborates on the style association as follows:

> In my opinion there is this difference: the sonatas are composed in a stately and splendid manner like motets, but the canzoni have many black notes and move along crisply, gaily and fast.[12]

As an after thought, Praetorius adds that the word "sonata" is often used in reference to the music performed by trumpet corps for banquets and dances.

Book Two, of his third volume, is devoted to "Necessary Precepts" of music. Much of this is theoretical in nature, dealing with the modes, harmony and notation and we shall mention only a few very interesting passages which offer insight to performance.

We find it quite striking that he begins by suggesting that complex ligatures should be replaced with the slur indication.[13] Ligatures are usually presented in early notation literature as a kind of shorthand and we know of no place

[10] Ibid., 21ff. In the original publication, page numbers 22 and 23 were mistakenly omitted.

[11] Ibid., 24.

[12] Ibid.

[13] Ibid., 29.

where there is a suggestion that there was a phrase association, such as would be indicated by a slur. The slur mark itself, of course, was new to notation at this time.

In discussing the necessity of *musica ficta*, the necessary alterations when changing modes, or to avoid the tritone, Praetorius advises the composer that this should *not* be left to the performers.

> Composers would do well, as an excellent precaution, to indicate clearly the two chromatic signs, the *cancellatum* [sharp sign] and *rotundum* [flat sign] whenever they are to be employed, in order to prevent hesitation or doubt. This is useful, convenient, and also most necessary to keep singers from becoming confused, as well as for the benefit of ignorant town musicians and organists who cannot read music, let alone sing correctly.[14]

Some of Praetorius' recommendations are of a very practical nature, such as advising that everyone should start expressing in *numbers* the number of rests in the various parts. He observes that he has learned from experience, "not without some embarrassment," that this is necessary as musicians are inclined not to pay strict attention or are sometimes caught up in listening to the music.[15]

He also offers a system he devised for numbering the separate parts of large concerti, to avoid confusion, since in a polychoral work there will be several parts named "tenor," etc. He also mentions that he made it a habit to count the number of breves in a composition and notate it at the end of his score. Then, when planning the music for a service, by glancing at a chart he had worked out, he could immediately determine how long it would take to perform the composition.[16] This, he observes, is important so as not to delay the remaining church ceremonies. Similarly, he describes a system of marking cuts,[17] in case the latter does not work, which enables the musicians to stop in a hurry,

> in case the conductor finds the composition before or after the sermon threatens to last too long—since a musician is likely to overdo things.

[14] Ibid., 31.

[15] Ibid., 33ff.

[16] Ibid., 88. He had found, for example, that a composition of 640 breves required one hour to perform.
[17] Ibid., 35.

Another instance of practical advice, which Praetorius has learned from his own experience, has to do with his recommended seating plan for singers.

> I have always put the sopranos together with the tenors and the altos with the bass ... The reason is that I have not only seen most other composers do the same, but that it is because of the harmony and the intervals. If the singers stand close to each other and have to read and sing from one part, sopranos and tenors will produce pleasant sixths and the alto and basses fifths and octaves. Otherwise a singer would fill the other's ears with unpleasant fourths, the usual progressions between soprano and alto, or tenor and alto, spoiling the music and making singing distasteful, particularly if the performers carrying the other two parts are not placed near enough to complete and round out the harmony.
>
> Nevertheless I do not want to dictate to anyone in this or other matters, but merely to give my own modest ideas and to tell what I have found to be good from my own experience; for everyone will have his own ideas and will act accordingly.[18]

[18] Ibid., 90.

When discussing various signatures at the beginning of compositions, Praetorius finds a general lack of agreement. He suggests that the slower common time signature is used in madrigals and the faster alla breve sign is used in motets.[19] However, he has noticed that in *all* the compositions of Gabrieli, he uses only the alla breve sign. In the works of Viadana, he finds the alla breve sign in compositions with text and the common time sign in instrumental works. His own opinion, agreeing with what he has found in the works of Lassus and Marenzio, was that, the common time sign should be used,

[19] Ibid., 48ff.

> for those motets and other sacred compositions which have many black notes, in order to show that the beat is to be taken more slowly ... Anyone, however, may reflect upon such matters himself and decide, on the basis of text and music, where the beat has to be slow and where fast.

In concerti, where madrigal and motet *styles* are found, it is necessary to change tempo. Here, instead of using the common time and alla breve signs, Praetorius suggests it might be better to employ the new practice of using Italian words, such as *adagio, presto*, etc.[20]

Praetorius also treats proportional signs and their meaning here, as a topic which he obviously related to the speed of a given beat. Here he feared the conductor might end up beating so fast that,

> we make the spectators laugh and offend the listeners with incessant hand and arm movements and give the crowd an opportunity for raillery and mockery.[21]

That tempo in the sixteenth century was a decision made by the performer, and not the composer, may surprise some readers. Praetorius clearly recommends[22] a level of rubato rarely mentioned in other treatises. First he makes two general rules, that a performance must not be hurried and that all note values must be observed. Then he adds,

> But to use, by turns, now a slower, now a faster beat, in accordance with the text, lends dignity and grace to a performance and makes it admirable ... Some do not want such mixture of [tempi] in any one composition. But I cannot accept their opinion, especially since it makes motets and concerti particularly delightful, when after some slow and expressive measures at the beginning several quick phrases follow, succeeded in turn by slow and stately ones, which again change off with faster ones.

The purpose of this he says is to avoid monotony and he adds the same advice relative to dynamics.

> Besides, it adds much charm to harmony and melody, if the dynamic level in the vocal and instrumental parts is varied now and then.[23]

Later Praetorius returns to dynamics, mentioning that the Italians are beginning to use *forte, piano*, etc., to mark changes within a concerto. It is interesting that, in this case at least, he seems to suggest the two, dynamics and tempo, go together.

> I rather like this practice. There are some who believe that this is not very appropriate, especially in churches. I feel, however, that such variety [in dynamics] and change [in

[20] Ibid., 51.

[21] Ibid., 74.

[22] Ibid., 79ff.

[23] Later he mentions, with regard to concerti, that a softer dynamic level can also be achieved by simply not having as many instruments doubling in a particular choir. [Ibid., 128 (108)].

tempo] are not only agreeable and proper, if applied with moderation and designed to express the feelings of the music, and affect the ear and the spirit of the listener much more and give the concerto a unique quality and grace. Often the composition itself, as well as the text and the meaning of the words, requires that one [change] at times—but not too frequently or excessively—beating now fast, now slowly, also that one lets the choir by turns sing quietly and softly, and loudly and briskly. To be sure, in churches there will be more need of restraint in such changes than at banquets.[24]

[24] Ibid., 132 (112).

It is particularly interesting here, that Praetorius gives one Latin term, *lento gradu*, which he says was understood to mean that the voice became both softer and slower.

Now Praetorius makes two quite extraordinary suggestions regarding performance, and both have to do with the performance of cadences.[25] Moreover, he switches his text from German into Latin for this discussion, making us wonder if this were exclusive information allowed only to those who were formally educated. In any case, the importance of these two observations cannot be stressed enough, in our view.

[25] Ibid., 80.

Some modern scholars believe that a modern *ritard.* is usually inappropriate for Renaissance music, especially as the composer so often accomplishes this effect through a gradual lengthening of note values at the final cadence. But we have never read elsewhere of making a fermata on the next-to-last harmony, which he suggests was common practice by fine musicians!

> It is not very commendable and pleasant when singers, organists, and other instrumentalists from habit hasten directly from the penultimate note of a composition into the last note without any hesitation. Therefore I believe I should here admonish those who have hitherto not observed this as it is done at princely courts and by other well-constituted musical organizations, to linger somewhat on the penultimate note, whatever its time value—whether they have [already] held it for four, five, or six *tactus*—and only then proceed to the last note.

His second "secret" regarding the performance of cadences is based on a principle which can be found in earlier literature, having to do with acoustics. Most musicians know that music sounds better if balanced in such a way that the lower tones are performed louder than higher tones. What is surprising here is the extent to which Praetorius carries this.

> As a piece is brought to a close, all the remaining voices should stop simultaneously at the sign of the conductor or choir master. The tenors should not prolong their tone, a fifth above the bass or lowest voice ... after the bass has stopped. But if the bass continues to sound a little longer, for another two or four *tactus*, it lends charm and beauty to the music [*Cantilenae*], which no one can deny.

One of the chapters in this volume Praetorius calls, "The Method of Teaching Choir Boys who Love and Enjoy Singing, According to the new Italian Style."[26] Praetorius begins this discussion by presenting his primary aesthetic purpose in music. As the orator must, through his style of speaking, arouse the emotions of the listeners, it follows that,

> A musician must not only sing, but he must sing artfully and expressively in order to move the hearts of the listeners, to arouse their emotions and to allow the music to accomplish its ultimate purpose.

In order to accomplish this, Praetorius says the singer must have a naturally fine voice, a good mind and a thorough knowledge of music. But he must also understand what makes good taste in music, in particular the art of improvisation.

> He must know ... where to introduce runs or coloraturas (called *passaggi* by the Italians), that is, not anywhere in a composition, but appropriately, at the right time and in a certain way, in order that the listener may not only be aware of the loveliness of the voice, but also be able to enjoy the art of singing.

The singer who has been gifted with a fine voice, but does not know how to do these things correctly will "provide little joy for the listeners, particularly those who have some

[26] Ibid., 229ff.

knowledge of the art; on the contrary, it makes them sullen and sleepy."

Learning the art of beautiful singing, says Praetorius, as in all the other arts, is a matter of Nature, Doctrine and Practice. Regarding Nature, Praetorius says again that the singer must have a beautiful, pleasantly vibrating voice ("not, however, in the manner to which some singers in schools are accustomed, but with moderation"), a smooth round throat (which apparently was thought to aid improvisation), be able to sustain a long tone and find some range in which he can produce a full sound without falsetto. The undesirable qualities in a voice are taking too many breaths, singing through one's nose and keeping the voice in the throat and singing with the teeth closed.

Praetorius mentions two specific sixteenth century vocal techniques which are quite interesting. The first, *Intonatio*,

> refers to the manner in which a vocal piece is started. Opinions vary about this, some wanting to start the tone on the proper written pitch, some a second below, but in a way that the pitch is gradually raised. Some prefer to begin on the third, some on the fourth, some with a delicate and soft voice. All these methods, for the most part, are designated by the term *accentus*.

The second vocal technique, *Exclamatio*,

> is the proper means of moving the emotions and must be achieved by increasing the voice. It can be employed with all dotted minims and semiminims in descending motion. Especially the following note which moves somewhat fast, arouses the emotions more than the semibreve, which is more frequently used and more effective with a raising and lowering of the voice, and without *exclamatio*.

By Doctrine, Praetorius seems to mean the proper art of embellishment and improvisation. He provides considerable discussion, including musical examples, but we shall only quote his basic definitions. He begins with diminution.

> One speaks of diminution when a longer note is broken up into many other faster and smaller notes. There are different kinds of them [including] accent, tremulo, groppi and tirata.

His examples of "accent" appear to be single and multiple passing tones, in a variety of rhythmic configurations.

Tremulo "is nothing but a quiver of the voice over one note; organists call it a mordent."

Gruppi "are used in cadences and have to be executed more sharply than the tremuli." His examples appear as main-note trills.

Tirate "are long, fast, diatonic runs up or down the keyboard." The examples, in each case, fill an octave diatonically.

Trills, although he provides numerous configurations in which a trill may be found, he finds more difficult to explain.

> These can only be learned through live demonstration and the efforts of a teacher. Then one may learn from the other just as one bird learns by watching another.

Passaggi "are fast runs which are employed over longer notes, both diatonically and in skips of any size, ascending as well as descending." In other words, a form of improvisation.

Regarding the third essential, Practice, Praetorius says it would take too long to discuss—better to just study everything he has provided in this volume!

An idea new to the sixteenth century, but one which would of course become a fixture of the Baroque, was the thorough-bass. The discussion of this new idea by Praetorius[27] is interesting not only because it permits us to observe an early contemporary reaction, but for how he discusses its use in actual practice. It is clear that the chief value, in so far as Praetorius was concerned, was that the organ part of a larger work, often called "General Bass," was in effect transformed into a kind of miniature score. Previously organists would attempt to fill in harmonies above this single-line general bass part, without, of course, having any real idea what the composer wrote. As a working organist himself, Praetorius is quick to accept this new idea for its help in preventing the organist from being embarrassed in public.

> To be sure, the thorough-bass was not invented for the benefit of negligent or unwilling organists who dislike preparing their scores ...

[27] Ibid., 144 (124) ff.

> In my humble opinion the greatest advantage of the thorough-bass lies in the fact that it furnishes a fine summary for the benefit of a Kapellmeister or other music director. When several copies are made of such a thorough-bass, especially in concerti for several choirs, these can then be distributed among the organists and lutenists of each choir ... marking in red ink the passages they are to play. The conductor should keep one copy for himself, in order to have the entire composition before him, not only because of changes in the *tactus*, to *tripla* and other kinds of time, but also in order to be able to cue the individual choirs.

Before continuing his discussion of thorough-bass, Praetorius digresses to discuss the player who will most use this new form of notation, the organist.[28] The organist, he says, must have three qualifications:

[28] Ibid., 145 (125) ff.

1. He must know counterpoint or at least be able to sing reliably, recognize proportions and the tactus or mensuration correctly, know how to resolve dissonances into consonances on any degree ...
2. He has to have a good grasp of the score and be well practiced in handling the keys, keyboards, or stops on the neck of his instrument, be it organ, regal, lute, theorbo or a similar fundamental instrument, so that he does not have to grope for the intervals ... For he knows that the eye has to be turned toward the score, and the motet, concerto, madrigal, or canzona before him at all times and therefore he can divert little attention to the keyboard.

Here he adds, in passing, that since most German organists are accustomed to playing from tablature, they should first write out the score to see how thorough-bass works.

3. He has to have a good ear and be able to follow the singers.

Since we are seeing the thorough-bass practice at its birth, at least so far as Praetorius knows, it is interesting to find that the Italian composers were at yet only sporadically using the numeric symbols. Praetorius is quick to say that if this system is going to work, the numbers must be used all the time. To illustrate the potential problem, Praetorius quotes from a new score he has just received by Bernardo Strozzi:

> Therefore I must not fail to demonstrate clearly and conclusively that such figures are absolutely necessary, no matter what others may say, especially since no organist can know or guess the intentions of the composer. For when the organist would assume the composer had put a fifth in a certain place, it might well have been a sixth ... Anyone with a discriminating ear can reflect how pleasant a performance will sound when the organist decides to play a fifth while the singer sings a sixth ...
>
> Some say indeed, that one should indulge one's ear and move one's fingers according to what one hears. To those I reply that this will bring no good results. For once the keyboard is struck, a sound is immediately produced, and though one may want to remove one's finger quickly, it has accomplished its task and the dissonance has been heard.

To this Praetorius adds,

> If he were deaf or would not hear very well and had to be constantly afraid of playing a fifth instead of a sixth ... he would with all his fear hardly be able to pay much attention to the thorough-bass. While looking for the sixths and sevenths which he hears, he would skip notes and get off the track completely.

Interestingly, he also has observed that organists, who had not yet mastered reading this new notation, and thus encountered problems in performance, would simply begin improvising to hide the problems!

> But when they heard their own mistakes, they would quickly start with diminutions and runs until finally they managed to calm down. But in this way they would often disturb the [improvisation] of the singers.

In the end, as Praetorius sees it, the real value of the thorough-bass numbers is to help the organist, to prevent errors which might embarrass him.

> Without these figures one would rather have to regard him as a fool whose lot it is, among other things, to have to guess

all kinds of foolishness and stupidity. When the organist thus dares to guess and anticipate the ideas in the composer's mind, he will come to grief and appear like a clumsy idiot. Therefore one immediately says that the organist is crazy and has lost his head.

Another advantage of this new invention, especially to Praetorius, an organist himself, was that one only had to keep the thorough-bass parts themselves and not the entire scores. Why, he says, if one had to keep in books of tablature just the music played in one church in Rome during a single year, "the organist would have to have a bigger library than a doctor at laws."

The most extraordinary discussion of all, in Volume III of the *Syntagma Musicum*, is Praetorius' description of the new church concerto in its practical application. If one thinks of one of the Gabrieli works for two choirs of voices and two choirs of instruments, for example, it is stunning to read the suggestion by Praetorius that such a work was not intended to be played as it appears on paper, but rather what appears on paper can serve as a kind of "source material" from which more vocal and instrumental parts are extracted to form more choirs. What he is talking about, in effect, is freedom in doubling and he suggests that this should come as no surprise since this kind of doubling of church singers by instrumentalists has been practiced for some time, a fact almost never admitted by music history texts.

> This will hardly annoy anyone who has had experience in princely and other chapels, nor town musicians, if they stop to consider that in their own church choirs they put a cornett or trombone player next to the choir boys with whom they play in unison and octaves.[29]

[29] Ibid., 138 (118).

We see this freedom in application distinctly when he defines *capella*, or one of the choirs which make up a polychoral composition in the Italian style.

> In my opinion the Italians originally used *capella* to designate an additional separate choir, extracted from several different choirs with various kinds of instruments and voices, as they

are employed at the larger imperial, Austrian or other Catholic musical establishments ... In every concerto one, two or three such *capellae* can be extracted and set up in different parts of the church, each of them consisting only of four persons, or more if available. In case there is a lack of performers, they can be left out entirely.[30]

[30] Ibid., 133 (113).

Praetorius, an experienced Church conductor, devotes a significant portion of this volume to explaining the perimeters, possibilities and problems in such reassembling and re-orchestrating of the original music. While our purpose here will be to simply outline his major suggestions, it will soon become apparent to the reader how pale in comparison are our performances today of the polychoral works of composers such as Giovanni Gabrieli.

Praetorius begins with some observations regarding the vocal parts alone.[31] The reader must keep in mind that Praetorius is thinking here of a work, let us say, which appears on paper for *two* four-voice choirs, one of four voices of singers and one of four voices of instruments, which might be performed as *five or more* four-voice choirs, spread throughout the church. The additional, newly created choirs, consist of material taken from the original version of the composition.

[31] Ibid., 91ff.

The soprano part, "sung by light and delicate voices of small boys,"' he recommends doubling to the extent that it can be heard by all the other choirs. We get our first indication of what Praetorius means by "doubling" when he speaks in general of the middle vocal parts.

> The middle voices, such as alto and tenor, may similarly move in unison in all choirs. For in such a case it sounds no different than when eight, nine or ten boys—if there are enough singers available—are put on a single part next to one another, sometimes along with an instrumentalist, on trombone, cornett or violin. When one separates the various choirs and puts one here, one there, the third still further off, and so on, it is surely best if all the middle parts in each choir continue throughout a composition. This will allow the harmony to resound more fully and to be more clearly heard throughout the entire church.

The handling of the bass part was a very sensitive issue with Praetorius, for purposes of harmony and acoustics. There is what he calls a "foundation bass" in every composition, which would be the true bass line in a modern analytical sense. But in polychoral compositions this is (on paper) found at the bottom of only one choir, the remaining or other choirs having parts labeled "bass," but which are not in fact the true bass. These other basses, Praetorius calls middle basses. The problem is that if a given listener in the church happens to be seated near a choir which does not have the true bass, and is seated too far away to hear the true, or foundation, bass, wherever that choir is located, the listener hears harmonies in incorrect inversions, etc. There are two immediate solutions. If the church has an organ, then the organist plays "the lowest bass for a foundation," presumably loud enough to serve as the true bass for the listener. If there is no organ, the conductor or choir master extracts the true bass and spreads it around to the other choirs, thus,

> making the foundation bass heard everywhere and therefore doubling it in each choir is particularly necessary in schools and municipal churches, where one cannot have an organist, regal or positive with every choir as in princely and other chapels.[32]

[32] Ibid., 92.

Having made these suggestions regarding the vocal parts, Praetorius turns to the production at large. He begins by stating that from his experience in the performances he has heard, there are "three general kinds of flaws frequently heard in concerti." The first objection is directed toward those who perform the composition as it is written.

1. The discrimination of the performers does not always go far enough to explore and grasp the potential of the artfulness of the written composition.

2. That the instruments are not selected according to the type of concerto, or do not agree with the voices and form discords with them.

3. They put the lowest bass in one choir only.

With regard to the third "flaw," Praetorius again recommends that in tuttis the forces be rearranged so that *all* the basses are given the true bass in unison. He quotes an unnamed musician in this regard:

> When the choirs are far separated, the real bass or lowest voice in motets of eight, ten, twelve, sixteen, or more voices should be retained in all choirs whenever they sing together; particularly at the end it should be heard clearly above all others. Otherwise, with no foundation underneath, cacophony results, as both [score] and experience prove.[33]

[33] Ibid., 94ff.

Now, regarding the distribution of the music in the "new" choirs which one might create, Praetorius offers some general rules. This discussion,[34] which includes creating new doublings several octaves higher and lower than the original music, is so enlightening we feel obligated to quote it in full.

[34] Ibid., 95ff.

> Unison doubling can be used throughout a composition without hesitation in high, low and middle voices as well as by instruments.
>
> Octave doubling can be permitted in all voices, provided one part is sung while the other part is played. In arranging a concerto it is quite customary in the case of a low choir, in which the soprano is to be sung by an alto with three trombones or three bassoons, to double the alto with a violin. The instrumentalist then must play the alto part an octave higher. In tuttis—also when only a few choirs join in together—one can quite fittingly have the alto part of the vocal choir transposed one octave higher and use it with the instrumental choir.
>
> The same thing may be done in all voices, and it does not offend the ear when the part of the singer in a choir is played an octave higher or lower by cornetts, violins, recorders, trombones, or bassoons. For some melody instruments, especially recorders are to be played one or two octaves higher than written. This compares with the practice of combining many different stops on an organ in unisons, octaves, superoctaves and sub-octaves and contrabasses.
>
> Provided enough players are available, quite a splendid sound is produced in tuttis if one assigns to a bass part—at the regular pitch—a common or a bass trombone, a choristbassoon, or pommer; in addition a double bass trombone, double bassoon, or large double pommer, and double bass,

which all sound an octave lower, like the sub-basses on organs. This is particularly common in contemporary Italian concerti and can be sufficiently justified.

After giving several more examples of doubling, taken from his own experience, Praetorius addresses the principal objection which one might have to this freedom of doubling, which is that it creates parallel octaves. For Praetorius this was a question not of theory but rather a question of the ear responding to the acoustics of the specific performance.

> If someone should have a concerto with only two choirs—one high and one low, positioned at opposite ends—performed at a church or a large hall and should remain standing with the higher choir, he will scarcely hear the lower choir in tuttis when both choirs join in together. He will find then that he can hear no foundation with the higher choir; but in absence of the lower fifths—formed by the foundation bass against the bassett or tenor of the higher choir—dissonant fourths will be heard for the most part, especially if there is no fundamental instrument present, such as a positive or regal. Someone wrote me recently from Venice that,
>
>> the leading musicians in Italy make frequent use of unisons and octaves in tuttis. For they know from their own experience that in large churches, where the choirs are far apart, a much fuller sound is achieved in tuttis when the choirs move in unison or octaves with one another than when they are arranged in such a way that unisons and octaves are carefully avoided, with the result that a perfect and full harmony can no longer be heard.
>
> I could name a number of very excellent older theorists and practical musicians who would not allow me to do this at first. But later, when they had tried it themselves and further reflected upon the matter they had to approve of it and agree with me that having previously considered it very bad, almost like a deadly sin, they themselves now found that unisons as well as octaves in the basses could not be avoided if in all choirs a complete harmony were to be maintained.

Praetorius also quotes the Italian composer Viadana in this regard.

> In concerti for several choirs one can without danger of confusion extract various capellae at one's pleasure. It does no damage then if there are octaves and unisons between the choirs, since one can hardly hear them, the choirs being placed far apart from one another.[35]

After arguing for freedom in unisons and octaves, Praetorius adds that parallel fifths are not allowed in any circumstances. He says, however, that he sees frequent diminished fifths in Italian music as well as improvisation [diminution] which "helps to excuse and cover up a great deal."[36]

Praetorius devotes extensive discussion to the possible choirs of instruments which may be used to augment concerti. Perhaps the most interesting of his review of these consorts is his discussion of one evidently new, the string consort.[37]

> I have come to the conclusion that there is some need for such a capella. For some among us Germans are still unaccustomed to the new Italian invention, according to which sometimes only one, sometimes two or three *Concertat-Stimen* sing to the accompaniment of organ or regal, and do not like this style very well; they are of the opinion that it sounds too empty and is not particularly pleasing and agreeable to those who know nothing about music. Therefore I have had to think of a way to add a choir in four parts which could at all times join in with trombones or *Geigen*.
>
> Since such an ensemble, when used in church, makes for a richer sound, I soon achieved public acclaim ...
>
> It is to be noted here that this capella I have called *fidicinia* because it is better to have it made up of string instruments such as *Geigen*, lutes, harps, and especially viola da gamba, where these are available, and viols da braccio. For the sound of viols and *Geigen* has particular delicacy and is continuous, without the breathing necessary on trombones and other wind instruments.[38]

But, he admits, the idea of a string consort is a new one and not everyone will like it.

> But it is up to anyone's pleasure to use this capella, or leave it out. For, as mentioned above, I have only added it because of the approbation of certain listeners and would not otherwise have deemed it very important.

---

[35] Ibid., 99.

[36] Ibid., 100.

[37] The reader is reminded that, in general, the "professional" player was a wind player until after the middle of the sixteenth century.

[38] Ibid., 136 (116) ff.

But if one would wish to compose or arrange for such a *capella fidicinia*...one would attract those listeners in Germany who still do not know what to make of the new style, and once having roused their interest one would undoubtedly succeed in giving them great pleasure and satisfaction.

Praetorius mentions the string choir again in association with the cornett choir,[39] both being recommended for high choirs. If the part is very high, he prefers the violin,[40] "unless a good cornett player having complete control of his instrument is available." For the lower parts he recommends a trombone or a *Tenorgiege*, since the lower cornetts sound "as unpleasant as a cowhorn."

He makes his recommendations on the basis of the clef seen in the original music, but also on the basis of mode. Thus for the transverse flute choir we read,

> On the transverse flute one generally plays the tenth mode, Hypoaeolian, one tone lower. None of the modes are better fitted for these instruments than Dorian, Hypodorian and Hypoaeolian taken down a tone.[41]

He mentions that the lower parts of such a flute choir can not be heard well on flute and recommends trombone or *Tenorgeige*. However, he says, such a part could be played by a flute an octave higher, "along with all kinds of other instruments, if no other transverse flutes are involved."

The recorder choir is of such a range that Praetorius points out such parts can be just as effective with voices or viols da gamba.[42] In the case of a vocal choir, he mentions that boys can learn to sing high A "provided one would take the pains with them and not mind the trouble to teach them." He adds that it is sometimes nice if a boy sings the tenor part an octave higher. If a choir of recorders is used, "I find it better to give the bass part to a bass trombone, or even better a bassoon." In general, he recommends,

> If one wishes to use recorders alone without any other instruments, in a canzona, motet or concerto for several choirs, one can effectively use the entire consort of recorders, particularly the five sizes beginning with the largest—because the small

[39] Ibid., 154.

[40] Praetorius always uses *Geigen*.

[41] Ibid., 156.

[42] Ibid., 157.

ones make too much noise—which produce a very pleasant, soft and delicate harmony. They are especially effective in smaller rooms; in the church, however, the large bassett and bass recorders cannot be heard very well.

Regarding the trombone and bassoon choirs, Praetorius is primarily concerned with warning the reader of their limited upper ranges.[43] No trombonist, he says, can play a high G, and bassoons and pommer should be limited to the D above middle C, although "some players are getting to the point now where they can play four, five and more tones higher with good intonation, provided they are quite skillful and have particularly good reeds." He concludes with a comment on modes.

[43] Ibid., 159ff.

> It should be noted here that for such large and low bass instruments as pommers, bassoons or dulcians, and trombones, no compositions are better fitted than those written in Hypodorian (in our usage the second mode) and Hypoionian, which we call the twelfth mode, otherwise called the fifth or sixth mode.

The crumhorn choir presented a difficulty in the fact that the instrument known to Praetorius had a very limited range.[44] For them he recommends Mixolydian transposed down a fourth or Hypomixolydian.

[44] Ibid., 165.

Although the shawm choir was a basic sixteenth century consort, Praetorius finds them difficult to use as an optional choir in a concerto because they are constructed a fifth apart and hence exceed the ranges of the music.[45] He warns that the higher, or smaller, the shawms are, the more intonation problems there are. In particular, it is best "to leave the squeakey discant shawm alone."

[45] Ibid., 166.

The final consort Praetorius discusses is the lute choir, by which he means an ensemble consisting of harpsichords or spinets, theorbos, lutes, pandoras, *Orphoreon*, cithers, a large bass lyra, or "whatever fundamental instruments of this kind one may be able to gather together," a mixture he associates with the English.[46] He adds an interesting example from his own experience.

[46] Ibid., 168.

> I once arranged to have the magnificent, immeasurably beautiful motet by de Wert, "Egressus Jesus," in seven voices, performed by 2 theorbos, 3 lutes, 2 cithers, 4 harpsichords and spinets, 7 viols, 2 transverse flutes, two boys and an alto singer and large bass viol. This produced a brilliant and magnificent resonance.

In addition to this discussion of the various consorts use in concerti, Praetorius also comments on the proper style of playing the fundamental organ part. This discussion is very important because it reveals, in passing, the extent to which improvisation was also a part of the performance tradition of such works as the familiar concerti of Gabrieli. He begins by quoting Viadana.[47]

[47] Ibid., 137ff.

> The organist should play from the thorough-bass part, or score, in a very plain style and as cleanly and correctly as possible just as the notes follow one another, without using many runs, especially in the left hand which carries the foundation. But if he wishes to employ some faster movement in the right hand, as in agreeable cadences or similar figures, he has to do this with particular moderation and restraint. Otherwise the singers are impeded and confused, and their voices covered up and drowned out.

Praetorius, in adding his own observations, reveals that the voices as well were engaging in improvisation.

> I have been told by discriminating music lovers of high and noble rank that there are outstanding organists in Italy and elsewhere who, in such concerti, use neither diminutions, nor groppi in cadences, nor mordents. They simply play one chord after another as indicated in the thorough-bass so that the motion of the hands is hardly noticeable.
>
> I rather like the idea that no black notes are used. [But] it does not seem so inappropriate to me if in some concerti the organist observes carefully where the singer makes his diminutions and passaggi and then plays in a plain style, moving stepwise from one key to the next. But as the singer, after completing many varied passaggi, beautiful diminutions, groppi, tremoletti, and trilli, becomes tired and sings the following notes without elaboration, the organist may introduce agreeable diminutions, etc., but only in the right hand—and attempt to imitate the singer's figures, diminutions, variations,

etc. Thus the two collaborate, as it were, in producing an echo, until the singer recovers and again proceeds to display his artful embellishments. In my humble opinion, one should not omit all mordents and tremoletti when no diminution or similar figures are employed; for they will not disturb the singer's voice at all, or not nearly as much as all sorts of runs and diminution.

Moving to new points, Praetorius says it is not possible for the organist to perform all concerti bass parts at sight. Therefore he should look over the composition, to determine the style and to plan his progressions more perfectly. During tuttis in concerti, the organist should "use both manual and pedal simultaneously." However, Praetorius advises, that is enough.

> But one should not add other stops, for the delicate and soft tone of the singers would otherwise be smothered by the heavy noise of the many organ stops and then the organ would be more prominent than the singers.

Praetorius also mentions the well-known tradition of having one or more string instruments double the fundamental organ line. In his discussion of the various instruments appropriate to this function, we are most interested in his reference once again to frequency of improvisation. Here, as in all cases Praetorius has mentioned, he means by "improvisation" what the player does with the part in front of him. In this light the following is rather extraordinary.

> He who plays the lute (which is the noblest instrument of them all) must play it nobly, with much invention and variety, not as is done by those who, because they have a ready hand, do nothing but play runs and diminution from beginning to end, especially when playing with other instruments which do the same, in all of which nothing is heard but babel and confusion, displeasing and disagreeable to the listener. Sometimes, therefore, he must use gentle strokes and repercussions, sometimes slow *passaggi*, sometimes rapid and repeated ones, sometimes something played on the bass strings, sometimes beautiful conceits, repeating and bringing out these figures at different pitches and in different places; he must, in short, so weave the voices together with long

> *Gruppen*, trills, and accents, each in its turn, that he gives grace to the consort and enjoyment and delight to the listeners, judiciously preventing these embellishments from conflicting with one another and allowing time for each.[48]

[48] Ibid., 146ff.

The new violin also appears on the scene playing in the same fashion.

> The discant Geige, known as Violono, must also play beautiful *passaggi*, distinct and long, with playful figures and little echoes and imitations repeated in several places, passionate accents, mute strokes of the bow *Gruppi*, trills, etc.[49]

[49] Ibid., 148.

Having given the reader his views on the individual characteristics of the various consorts which might serve as additional choirs in the performance of the Church concerti, he now devotes a lengthy section to the art of doing this in practice, with particular reference to his own compositions.[50] Again, we can only briefly outline his extensive proposals.

[50] Ibid., 169ff.

The First Art he calls *Tubiciniae and Tympanistriae*, in which one employs the aristocratic trumpet corps.[51] The problem here is that these trumpet corps often did not read music and performed only memorized "concert" works, such as sonatas. But Praetorius found that if the trumpets were, let us say, in D, if he wrote a Church concerto in D they could simply join in, playing their memorized pieces, and it would sound OK—provided the Church choir master took their tempo!

[51] At the end of this volume [Ibid., 224] Praetorius lists his books. Among these is a now lost work entitled, *Instruction in the use of trumpets and timpani with full ensemble in electoral and princely chapels, also in other churches, depending on time and place, without producing confusion or drowning out the other vocal and instrumental parts.*

> One thing should be remembered here: since the trumpeters are in the habit of rushing, because the trumpet requires a good deal of breath which cannot be sustained very well at a slow pace, one should accelerate the beat when the trumpeters enter, otherwise they always finish their sonatas too soon. Later the beat may be lengthened, until the trumpeters start in again.

And if, due to some greater need by the duke, the trumpeters do not show up, you can perform the composition anyway.

> But if one cannot, will not, or must not use the trumpeters and timpanists, such compositions can nevertheless be performed quite well in town churches without trumpeters.

The Second Art consists of having four boys placed in separate locations in the church, with three of the boys joined by various instruments and the fourth by the full choir. The special effect occurs with,

> each of them singing what is found in his part, cleanly and with animation, clearly and distinctly as if reciting the notes. Thereupon the entire vocal and instrumental ensemble and organ respond, in a style which the Italians call *concerti ripiani* ...
>
> It is also quite delightful, and the words of the text can be heard better, if at the beginning the first verse is sung by the boys alone to the accompaniment of a soft and delicate stop on the organ, the *Geigen* and lutes being omitted entirely ...
>
> If one or two discant parts are blown on instruments and not sung, one can nevertheless easily guess the preceding texts and rhymes of the first and third discants from the parts of the second and fourth discants which respond to the former like an echo.
>
> On some organs there are *Cymbel-Glucklein* which, added to the full choir, sound quite delightful and attractive. If they are not too loud, they may sometimes be used even when the boys sing alone.

The Third Art is what we would call today a small church concerto,[52] familiar in such compositions by Schütz, for example, for one singer and three trombones. In a word, it was a kind of chamber concerto. Praetorius discusses this type extensively, with respect to instrumentation and placement. One may have two, three or four singers standing with or apart from an organ; or one may have choirs with solo singers and instruments; or one can alternate singers and instruments, as in the case of a psalm. Another "manner," as he calls it, is to have choirs with the discant parts improvising.

One may have a string choir double the organ, "good for inexperienced organists." The reader gains the impression here that the current string playing must have been rather robust, for Praetorius warns,

> It must be noted here that in small churches, chapels, and rooms, when one, two or a few more voices alone are singing and a regal or other fundamental instrument is available, the

[52] Although music history texts do not discuss it, there were at this time four general kinds of concerti: a large and small church concerto and a large and small concerto da camera.

string choir must play quite delicately and softly or must be omitted entirely. Otherwise the voices cannot be heard properly because of the sound of the instruments. But in large churches, where the string choir can be separated a little further from the voices and placed by itself, it must not be left out; on the contrary it is highly necessary in order to provide a richer sound.

Another manner of the Third Art is to have a full chorus, with instruments, which enters in the middle or at the end of a composition. An alternative manner is to have two instrumental choirs, carrying the inner parts, but positioned in a separate location. He adds that the further away the instruments are from the singers, the better the individual voices can be heard. Another manner related to these is to have the two discants improvising, with instrumental choirs used in alternation.

The Fourth Art is a polychoral work in which an entirely different chorale is sung between the verses of the original composition, with the penultimate verse sung in unison with the congregation. Similarly, the Fifth Art is the insertion of an independent "Hallelujah" or "Gloria" fragment "at the beginning, in the middle and at the end of a composition." This, he says, may be thought of as a kind of ritornello and he mentions that he got the idea from an Italian composition, by Fattorini, in which the composer had inserted some Latin phrases in this manner. Praetorius found this style to be very pleasing[53] and he mentions that he thought of writing out a separate Hallelujah or Gloria in every mode so they could be published and made available for this purpose. But, he moans, in his previous efforts which have been published there were "so many errors that the mere thought of it makes me break out in a cold sweat."

The Sixth Art follows in the same manner, but with an instrumental sinfonia played as a kind of prelude at the beginning of the choral work. An alternative might be to perform a "pavan, mascherada, or ballet in place of the sinfonia," but one must make sure the piece has a full harmony. Here

[53] The repeating ritornello was one of the important steps toward later "architectural forms," which are found pleasing by the right hemisphere of the brain.

again, ritornelli may be inserted in the middle of the choral work and astonishingly he recommends,

> a galliard, saltarello, courante, volta, or similarly gay canzonette, which, however, must not be too long. I have found that quite a few people have liked this very well.[54]

In the Seventh Art,

> The chorale is sung by one voice while the other parts, be it two, three, four, five or more, play on instruments alone, producing harmony, but also fantasies and imitations against the chorale.

Four more "Arts" follow which involve various combinations of the previous recommendations. The Twelfth Art, and final one, involves the use of echo effects.

Praetorius, at the end of this volume, lists a number of his own compositions which demonstrate these varied concerti techniques. Some of these have as many as thirty-five separate voices in nine choirs! We can only say again, how pale in comparison are our performances today of the Italian polychoral compositions.

Finally, putting everything together, Praetorius deals with an essential problem in the performance of large-scale concerti, and that is tuning. His first suggestion is that it would be nice if the organist could play a little prelude to the concerto, for then the players could simultaneously be tuning.

> In conclusion I must kindly suggest to all organists that they should generally make use of an appropriate introduction when attempting to perform a concerto with several choirs in church or at a banquet. Although it may not belong to the main work, it would serve to make the audience favorably disposed, receptive and attentive, and thus entertain them better—just as excellent orators do who intend to hold forth extensively on important matters. Using their preludes at the beginning they should thus call the listeners and the entire ensemble of musicians together, as it were, so that they may look for their parts and tune their instruments properly and that way prepare themselves for the start of a good and well-sounding performance.[55]

---

[54] This recalls the famous Gossec *Te Deum*, of 1790, the first large band work of the French Revolution, which has two internal dance movements, which are completely out of character with the somber *Te Deum*.

[55] Ibid., 151.

That is theory; practice is something else! Praetorius suddenly remembers his own experience, when, as he was playing an organ prelude, the instruments suddenly ruined his performance by beginning to tune for the following concerto. Being an organist, he cannot understand why all those players can't tune their instruments and "warm-up" at home, before they come to perform!

> But it creates great confusion and din if the instrumentalists tune their bassoons, trombones, and cornetts during the organist's prelude and carry on loudly and noisily so that it hurts one's ears and gives one the jitters. For it sounds so dreadful and makes such a commotion that one wonders what kind of mayhem is being committed. Therefore everyone should carefully tune the cornett or trombone in his lodging before presenting himself at the church or elsewhere for performance and he should work up a good embouchure with his mouthpiece [at home] in order that he may delight the ears and hearts of the listeners rather than offend them with such cacophony.

Praetorius returns to the problem of pitch in the performance of concerti, now as it is affected by personalities of the performers.

> This point above all must be carefully kept in mind in all concerti, by instrumentalists as well as singers. No one must cover up and outshout the other with his instrument or voice, though this happens very frequently, causing much splendid music to be spoiled and ruined. When one thus tries to outdo the other, the instrumentalists, particularly cornett players with their blaring, but also singers through their screaming, they cause the pitch to rise so much that the organist playing along is forced to stop entirely. At the end it happens then that the whole ensemble through excessive blowing and shouting has gone sharp by a half, often indeed a whole tone and more.[56]

[56] Ibid., 148ff.

8
Mattheson on Performance Practice

JOHANN MATTHESON (1681–1764) was one of the most valuable observers we have left to us from the Baroque Period. Among his numerous observations of the music of his time are some very interesting comments on performance. He tends to think of performance in terms of the separate venues of church, chamber and theater, as do many of his contemporaries.

He describes the old chant style and notation, adding an interesting observation confirmed in other sources but rarely mentioned in general history texts, that in this style there was "ever so many embellishments and artificialities used therewith."[1] He next turns to the motet style, in which he specifies that the accompanying instruments do *not* improvise. He mentions that he particularly appreciates the older motets by Hammerschmidt, whom he says "has done more for the glory of God than a 1,000 opera composers." In general, however, such works in the old polyphonic style may be "the greatest art," nevertheless,

> art is not nature. If this could succeed in expressing the passions and the true sense of words, then there would be nothing which compares with it, and the half-educated would soon burn their fingers on it.[2]

The previous two forms Mattheson finds used only in the church, but one which is found in church, theater and

[1] Johann Mattheson, *Der vollkommene Capellmeister* (1739), trans. Ernest Harriss (Ann Arbor: UMI Research Press, 1981), I, x, 37.

[2] Ibid., I, x, 50.

the chamber is the madrigal. With regard to the reference to the church here, Mattheson has in mind the cantata, oratorios and passions which he regards as having "the true madrigal's nature in them." Regarding the madrigal in the chamber, Mattheson points to the great polyphonic examples of the sixteenth century, which he associates with "concertizing" but "seem very strange to us: since they do not conform to present-day tastes at all."[3]

[3] Ibid.,I, x, 56.

Mattheson, in his *Neu-Eröffnete Orchestre*, points out that in his time many more styles are now possible in church music, including arias and recitatives. In the case of the latter, however, more restraint, seriousness and *solidite* is required than when these forms are used in the theater.[4]

[4] Johann Mattheson, *Das Neu-Eröffnete Orchestre* (Hamburg, 1713), 155.

Regarding the instrumental style, Mattheson first defines instrumental music as nothing other than "speech in tones or oratory in sound."[5] Instrumental music, he suggests, must be "always based on one specific emotion." Another very interesting observation, especially for this early period, suggests that only certain emotions can be associated with certain instruments.

[5] *Der vollkommene Capellmeister*, I, x, 63ff.

> Just as every instrument has its own nature, this style is divided into about as many secondary styles as there are instruments. One for example composes completely differently for violins than for flutes; not in the same way for lutes as for trumpets, etc., for which insight, labor and experience is required.

Regarding the use of the instrumental style in the church, Mattheson cautions that such music must have "a special solemnity and a serious quality ... lest it smack of a loosely-united overture." But he does not mean by this that instrumental church music must be dark in mood. On the contrary joyful instrumental music can contribute to the atmosphere for devotion.

> Yet one should not indiscriminately abandon all vivacity in the sacred service, especially since the style of writing under discussion often naturally requires more joyousness and cheerfulness than any other, namely according to the subject and circumstance giving occasion for it. Indeed, the

instrumental style serves primarily for presenting those very things for which voices are not always appropriate or suited ... Joy does not contradict seriousness; for then all mirth would have to consist of jesting. A cheerful disposition is best disposed for devotion; where such is not to be done mechanically or simply in a trance.

One type of instrumental music in the church which Mattheson cautions the composer about is the canon. If the composer wants to bring such works "out of the classroom, as out of its true element," it should be done "cautiously and seldom."

The theatrical style, says Mattheson, requires more skill in composition than either church or chamber music because it must be "the most natural and have nothing constrained or farfetched."[6] Even in an instrumental overture for the theater, Mattheson contends, neither the "opulence nor inner depth, which is characteristic of this very style in the church" is required. In fact, he continues, profundity itself is contrary to the character of stage plays,

[6] Ibid., I, x, 72ff.

> whose mark of distinction is always something of the playful and fictitious, which is not supposed to produce any profound, serious impression; but only a serviceable and hence more diverting, incidental presentation rather than a durable, engaging one: with which in fact emotions are touched and moved, through the perception of the vision and hearing, yet are not greatly disturbed by seriousness, and various untoward passions are not often presented. The feelings imparted by the stage are sometimes not unpleasant; but they last only a moment and produce no lasting impression: since everyone knows that the thing is artificial.[7]

[7] Ibid., I, x, 79.

But it is in opera, Mattheson finds, that the composer has the opportunity to freely express emotions in music.

> [Opera is the best medium of all for expressing] each and every *Affectus* since there the composer has the grand opportunity to give free rein to his invention. With many surprises and with as much grace he there can, most naturally and diversely, portray love, jealousy, hatred, gentleness, impatience, lust, indifference, fear, vengeance, fortitude, timidity, magnanimity, horror, dignity, baseness, splendor, indigence,

pride, humility, joy, laughter, weeping, mirth, pain, happiness, despair, storm, tranquility, even heaven and earth, sea and hell, together with all the actions in which men participate …

Through the skill of composer and singer each and every *Affectus* can be expressed beautifully and naturally better than in an Oratorio, better than in painting or sculpture, for not only are Operas expressed in words, but they are helped along by appropriate actions and above all interpreted by heart-moving music.[8]

[8] *Das Neu-Eröffnete Orchestre*, 167ff.

In two different books Mattheson writes that the purpose of opera is not only pleasure, but that it has a definite didactic role. First, speaking of the general value an opera house has for a city, he notes,

Scholars, artists, artisans come along too, and the city takes on the kind of eminence with a good opera as it has with good banks. For the latter are for service, the former give pleasure; the latter serve to give security; the former to instruct.[9]

[9] Johann Mattheson, *Der musicalische Patriot* (Hamburg, 1744), 176.

......

A good opera theater is nothing less than an advanced school of many of the fine arts, including together and simultaneously architecture, scenography, painting, mechanics, dancing, acting, moral philosophy, poetry and most especially music, united most pleasantly and always giving new demonstrations for the edification and pleasure of distinguished and sensible spectators.[10]

[10] Johann Mattheson, *Die neueste Untersuchung der Singspiele* (Hamburg, 1744), 84.

Dance music is associated primarily with the theater and here Mattheson recommends French music, for France "remains the true school of dance."[11] The style of composition for dance, Mattheson calls *hyporchematic*, the components of which he identifies as "strict metrical division; a slow rhythm in the proper pattern; a uniform, serious yet lively movement; an appropriate length; and unity among the parts," together, of course, with correspondence between melody and dance steps.

[11] *Der vollkommene Capellmeister*, I, x, 80ff.

Regarding the chamber style, Mattheson first turns to instrumental music which he says has a completely different character than instrumental music in the church and theater style.[12] The chamber style "requires far more diligence and

[12] Ibid., I, x, 104ff.

perfection than elsewhere, and must have pleasant, clear interior parts," by which he apparently meant that everything was more exposed to the listener. Instrumental music "clearly asserts superiority in the chamber style; indeed, even if the melody should occasionally suffer a little thereby, it is still embellished, ornamented and effervescent. That is its distinctiveness."

Under the subject of the chamber, Mattheson also discusses several kinds of popular songs and canons, etc., as well as dance music. Regarding the latter, he mentions in particular the Polish dance style, *a la Polonoise*, which he says is so interesting that there is no hesitation to provide "serious words and lyrics." This style, he says, "often has a quite strange and pleasant effect."

Mattheson writes that discussion of types of chamber forms could be extended considerably if one wanted to continue into the secondary branches. Among these forms which deserve study, he finds,

> especially the field or martial style would be of no small consideration. For although marches and such manly melodies belong to the hyporchematic style; still the martial music itself has, in many respects, things which are somewhat peculiar to it which might be worth investigating.

On Singing

On the subject of vocal music, Mattheson first offers an interesting review of his perception of national differences.

> If we turn from playing to singing, oh! that is when the misery really begins. Look at the fervor with which the French men and women singers present their pieces, and how they almost always seem really to feel what they are singing. Hence the reason that they strongly stir the emotions of the listeners, particularly their countrymen, and replace through gesticulation and mannerisms what they lack in thorough instruction, in strength, or in vocal ability.
>
> The Italians carry this even further than the French; indeed, sometimes they even go a little too far: As in almost all their undertakings they frequently overstep the limits and love the

extremes. Meanwhile they frequently have tears in their eyes when they perform something that is melancholy; and on the other hand, their heart is overjoyed when there is something enjoyable: for they are very emotional by nature ...

Only the cool Germans, although they have revealed to the Italians their great musical abilities through the three great H's, namely Handel, Heinichen and Hasse, on the one hand place their greatest merit in the fact that they look just as stiff and unemotional with the sad as well as the cheerful affections with which their music deals ... they sing very decently and rigidly, as if they had no interest in the content, and are not in the least concerned with the consideration of the proper expression or meaning of the words ... as is demonstrated daily by teachers and students. On the other hand, it is quite a favor if they do not gossip with, trifle with or ridicule their neighbors during rests; even if the things of which they sing would be worthy of the highest attention.[13]

[13] Ibid., I, vi, 18ff.

While the medieval theorists used to write that "to sing well" meant understanding the mathematics-based theories of music, Mattheson says that the expression, "to sing *properly*," has to do with "the emotions, as well as the styles, words, melody, harmony, etc."[14] Because of these close relationships, Mattheson expresses the belief that only one who can sing himself can write well for singers. It is, he says, much better if ability, knowledge, consideration and execution stand together.

[14] Ibid., I, i, 7.

From among his many recommendations for training the voice,[15] we found particularly interesting his conviction that early in the training a certain amount of loud singing is necessary, for which he recommends singing in church "as must necessarily be done, but also to hide the errors which occur among the multitude of fellow singers." If one cannot thus practice in church, then,

[15] Ibid., II, i.

> one could go to a lonely place in the field, dig a small yet deep hole in the ground, place his mouth over it, and shout into it as loudly and as long as can be done, yet always without forcing.

We are also interested to see a reference to what we call the "pyramid" principle, a performance adjustment required

by the fact that the brain genetically exaggerates the perception of higher pitches for the purpose of ease in understanding speech. Mattheson refers to the adjustment for this when he observes that experience for the past 200 years teaches,

> that each singing voice, the higher it goes, should be produced increasingly temperately and lightly; however in the low notes, according to the same rule, the voice should be strengthened, filled out, and invigorated.[16]

[16] Ibid., II, iii, 15.

On Improvisation

Improvisation is mentioned frequently by nearly all writers of the Renaissance and Baroque, but unfortunately with very few details other than the general rules for specific ornaments. Because it is so unusual, therefore, that Mattheson provides a broader view of the importance and the aesthetic role in performance practice in church, theater and chamber performance, we will quote him at some length.[17] Curiously, Mattheson uses the term "fantasy" for improvisation.

[17] Ibid., I, x, 88ff.

> The name fantasy is normally detested; although we do have a style of writing with this name which is a favorite and which maintains its place *mainly* with the orchestra and on the stage, not only for instruments but also for vocalists. It actually consists not so much in the writing or composing with the pen, as in the singing and playing that occurs spontaneously, or as is said, *extempore* ... Though the so-called *Fantasie, Capriccie, Toccate, Ricercare,* etc., may be written down or printed, they really belong [in this classification], not to mention the *boutades* and preludes.
>
> Italian musicians very often take the opportunity to show off their ideas thus, and avail themselves of this style to the special pleasures of the connoisseur; whether or not the fantasy were actually written down and the vocalist or the instrumentalist were thus saved the trouble; or which is always better, the composer were to do nothing further than to note the appropriate place where such spontaneity could be employed as one wishes. Such commonly occurs at a cadence, be it at the end or anywhere else. But this takes clever minds which are stock full of inventions and are rich in all sorts of figures (sometimes overly so).

Not to mention other artists, the famous Handel often composed accompaniments in his operas in which the clavier alone was performed, according to the player's whim and ability, without direction in its style: which requires a special person, and the few others who have tried to imitate him had a great deal of trouble with it; though they were otherwise rather firm in the saddle.

We have stated above that this fanciful style has its place in the operas; though, with the qualification: *mainly*; since nothing keeps it from also being heard in churches and chambers. In this respect it is peculiar in that it is *one and the same* everywhere; whereas when the other writing styles are used in the other main types they are in many respects subject to a different arrangement. What would the organists do if they could not improvise spontaneously in their preludes and postludes? [Otherwise] this would indeed only yield something awkward, memorized, and inflexible.

How often does not a skilled violinist (not to mention other instrumentalists) amuse himself and his listeners in the most agreeable way when he merely improvises and quite alone? That which occurs every day on the clavier, as the most appropriate instrument for this, on the lute, the viol da gamba, flute and so on, is familiar; if one only thinks on it and puts it in its proper class: and does it as the skilled throats of the prima donnas do it, especially the Italians. One can best perceive such among those who are endowed with similar skill at the court and on the stage. Only it is a pity that there are no rules available for such art of improvisation!

For this style is the freest and least restricted style which one can devise for composing, singing, and playing, since one sometimes uses one idea and sometimes another, since one is restricted by neither words nor melody, but only by harmony, so that the singers' or players' skill can be revealed; since all sorts of otherwise unusual passages, obscure ornaments, ingenious turns and embellishments are produced, without close observation of the beat and pitch, though these do occur on paper; without a regular principal motif and melody, without theme and subject which would be performed; sometimes fast sometimes slow; sometimes with one sometimes with many voice parts; also sometimes a little behind the beat; without meter; yet not without a view to pleasing, to dazzling and to astonishing. Those are the essential characteristics of the fantasy style.

One is restricted in this style of writing only to the rules of harmony, to no others. Whoever can bring to bear the most artistic embellishments and the rarest inventions does the best. And if occasionally a rather fast type of beat slips in, it only lasts a moment; if no other follows, then the meter ceases. The principal motifs and subjects cannot be completely ignored just because of the improvisatory nature; they may however not be done in sequence, much less be regularly performed: hence those composers who work out formal fugues in their fantasias or toccatas do not maintain the integrity of this style, for nothing is so very contrary to it as order and constraint.

On Ornaments

Mattheson does not engage in extensive explanation of the performance of specific ornaments in his *Der vollkommene Capellmeister*, because, he says, even if he did, his comments would soon be out of date anyway. Also, he admits, this is an art in which it is much easier to point to what is bad than to teach what is good. He calls the art of adding ornaments to a melodic line, *Modulatoria*,[18] and presents a discussion of the academic terms used to represent the elements of oratory, which he wants to suggest might form the foundation for possible ornamentation.[19]

Mattheson also makes a few important observations which touch on aesthetics. First, he points out that ornamentation "depends more on the skillfulness and sound judgment of a singer or player than on the actual prescription by the composer of the melody."[20] He is quick to point out that ornamentation can spoil a beautiful melody, a tendency toward which "I can never pardon the French musicians." In his conclusion, he provides some hints regarding his sense of aesthetics in this form of improvisation.

> This does not mean we despise ornaments. Well-used embellishments are not to be despised at all, whether the composer himself designs them, if he is a skilled singer and player; or whether the performer produces them extemporaneously. We however most severely criticize the misuse, and also the insolence of the singers and players who at the wrong time and without discretion presume to use such excessive orna-

[18] Ibid., II, iii.

[19] Ibid., II, xiv. These parts of speech are introduction, report, discourse, corroboration, confutation and conclusion.

[20] Ibid., II, xiv, 40.

ments, from lack of good taste, indeed, good sense; as well as the annoying fanaticisms of some much too fantastic composers with their insane ideas, which they consider as jewels and pearls regardless of the fact that they are usually only polished and coated glass.[21]

[21] Ibid., II, xiv, 43.

By this he means that if the original contribution by the composer is lacking, ornaments cannot disguise this. In another place he makes this more clear.

> To say, however, that the most miserable melodies should be beautiful to the hearing if they are performed well, is not in accord with nature and truth. Many a connoisseur of colorful notes and embellishments considers any unornamented melody as miserable; though it is so only in miserable eyes and not fundamentally. A rotten tree cannot bear fruit, no matter where one transplants it. The shrewdest ornamentation accomplishes only as much here as the skilled gardener who can improve a sound plant by diligent nursing, but if it is worth nothing he can never achieve anything proper. Some instrumentalists and singers know how to find ways to destroy quickly the most beautiful melody; but it is impossible for them, and even all of the artists of the world, to make beautiful the most wretched.[22]

[22] Ibid., I, x, 32.

On the Conductor

Finally, we find in the *Der vollkommene Capellmeister* a rather rare early description of the qualities needed in a good conductor.[23] He begins by placing the greatest emphasis on the integrity and character of the conductor and points to examples he has known of conductors who had cheated their singers out of money due them. But in general,

[23] Ibid., III, xxvi.

> He should in no way be offensive or scandalous in his living and conduct, for commonly the greatest contempt arises from that. A good reputation and esteem are such delicate things that with a single false step everything one has gained for oneself in many years through great assiduousness can be destroyed.

A central challenge for the conductor, in Mattheson's view, is the need to balance being friendly as a person with the necessary authority in rehearsal.

A director of the choir must not be lazy with unconstrained words of praise, but must copiously employ them, even if he finds only scant cause for them among his students. But if he is to and must admonish and contradict someone, then he should do it quite seriously, yet as gently and politely as is possible. Affability is considered a most favored and rewarding virtue by people in all ranks: a director then should of course also strive for it, and should be very gregarious, sociable and obliging: especially when he is not performing his official tasks. In his official duties, becoming seriousness and precise observation of them probably does more service than too great familiarity.[24]

As for conducting itself, while some "pound with sticks, keys and feet," he has found "that a little sign, not only with the hand but merely with the eyes and gestures, could accomplish most of this; if only the performers would assiduously keep their eyes on the director."

The personal accomplishments which Mattheson believed were important for a conductor included ability to sing, to play the clavier, knowledge of tuning, knowledge of principles of seating plans and "the greatest difficulty" of all: having the discernment required to succeed in divining the sense and meaning of another composer's thoughts.

He stresses the importance of rehearsals and points out that the conductor often needs the rehearsal as much as the players.[25] Reminding us that most Baroque performances were also premieres, Mattheson adds that one important purpose of the rehearsal is to make the necessary corrections.

> It is no disgrace but rather an honor to improve that which has not turned out well. How then can one know or perceive it without rehearsal?

With regard to the rehearsal, he cannot help but add that some responsibility lies with the attitudes of the individual musicians as well.

> The director as well as the performers should set their heart and soul on nothing other than the service of God ... [they] must certainly put away all other, dissolute thoughts, and must direct their mind, from reverence, only on the holy work

[24] Ibid., III, xxvi, 7. He points to the ideal example of J. S. Cousser, formerly Kapellmeister at Wolffenbüttel, who so charmed and helped his singers cordially in his home that they all loved him. However, in rehearsal, the musicians,

> almost all had fear and trembling before him, not only in the orchestra but also on the stage: for he knew how to reproach a person for his errors in such a sharp manner that often the eyes of the latter filled with tears. On the other hand, he calmed down again immediately, and diligently sought an opportunity to bind the thus-produced wounds through extraordinary politeness.

[25] Ibid., III, xxvi, 23.

at hand. If this occurs, then the execution will proceed well: for all mistakes which are made derive from inattentiveness and from such a disposition wherewith one is at another place with his thoughts.[26]

[26] Ibid., III, xxvi, 25.

A final requirement for the successful conductor or composer contains some timeless advice.

> A composer and director of music must be of a vigorous, high-spirited, indefatigable, diligent, and energetic nature; yet also orderly: yet most often the most active are deficient in this last. Idleness must be hated as a devil, because it is his place of repose ...
>
> Neither impatience nor a sudden flush of emotion serves any purpose here. If one does not have enough desire or deep-felt love for the thing so that he can suppress many a displeasure over it and so that adversity cannot alienate him from his noble plan; then he is not well suited for the exercise of this discipline and its sphere of duties.
>
> Indeed, with music and its pursuit very few roses are strewn in the path; moreover persons of authority and in high esteem seek, though it is unfair, to suppress and disparage everything about it as much as possible ... A master must have the heart in such circumstances to set a cheerful example for others, and must know how to create in himself so many pleasures from this noble pursuit that he would always be in the position, all obstacles notwithstanding, of finding his greatest peace in harmony and of reviving his spirit.[27]

[27] Ibid., II, ii, 55ff.

In his *Der vollkommene Capellmeister*, Mattheson, in passing, gives a rather impressive list of topics which must be taught if the "essence of music" is to be understood.[28] While he does not say specifically that he associates this curriculum with conductors, or Kapellmeisters, it seems implied since this is the subject of his book. The list includes all the elements of what we would call theory and composition today, plus organ building. Included as well are acoustics, music history,[29] a study of how music functions in society and the training of the voice as well as various instruments.[30] Among the interesting specific topics we find *a*) the special qualities of a conductor; *b*) expression in singing; *c*) the difference between vocal and instrumental melodies; and *d*) how to direct, produce and execute music.

[28] Ibid., I, i, 9ff.

[29] Ibid., I, iv, 6ff, divides the field of music history into Chronology, Biography and the study of instruments. He divides the history of music into three eras: the beginning of time until the sixth century AD (a total of 4,000 years!), the sixth century until 1600, and 1600 until the present (1739). This last period, he says, contains so much material that the first two periods seem only trifling by comparison.

[30] Ibid., III, xxiv, discusses the need for someone to write an up-to-date treatise on instruments. He mentions the fine work by Praetorius [of 1619], but points out that "all musical instruments have changed a great deal since then." The topics which he recommends for such a book range from a technical description and how to actually play each instrument to discussion of their use in churches, theaters and chambers.

In another place,[31] Matheson focuses specifically on the education and skills needed by the Kapellmeister and composer. Without education, he says, a musician can exercise his trade, but he cannot be an artist. This education need not be found at a university, but can be gained at home under "clever leadership."

[31] Ibid., II, iiff.

The specific requirements of this education begin with languages: Greek, Latin, French and Italian, the language of the theater. Without these languages, how can the Kapellmeister ever be a *galant homme*? He must also have considerable knowledge in poetry and, in an emergency, be able to write good verse himself.

Matheson considered music to be a "substantial part of erudition and one of the disciplines which is closest to theology." Perhaps this explains his following statement that "whoever advances in music and goes backwards in morals walks like a crab and misses the proper goal."

For the composer, in addition to the usual studies in the klavier, counterpoint and harmony, Matheson gives the highest priority to being able to sing, which he clearly believed was an essential key to understanding the emotions in a composition.

> If the stirring of the emotions and passions of the soul depends on something quite different, namely upon the skillful composition of an intelligible, clear, and expressive melody; then no one who is not well experienced in the art of singing can reach this goal.[32]

[32] Ibid., II, ii, 40, 44.

But, for composition, not everything can be learned, in particular, "a good natural ability or innate instinct and spirit." To find if he has this, Matheson recommends his looking into his own heart to see,

> whether he would be satisfied with mere patchwork and pieces from diverse sources, which were toilsomely collected by begging?

It is not necessary, when one composes a dirge or lamentation, to begin to cry, "yet it is absolutely necessary that he open his mind and heart to the affection at hand." For how, Mattheson asks, will he be able to excite a passion in other people's feelings if he has not experienced it himself?[33] Here Mattheson, remarkably, adds a precise comment on the nature of the communication of emotions in music, that they are both universal and personal at the same time.

[33] Ibid., II, ii, 64ff.

> He must also study the affective disposition of his listeners as much as possible. For although it is true: Each head has its own mind; still a certain propensity, a certain taste, usually predominates with wise and attentive listeners.[34]

[34] Ibid., II, ii, 66.

Mattheson would have probably acknowledged that composers are "born, not made," but he found that in some cases Nature has left the requisite qualities incomplete.

> One sometimes encounters fine minds without true desire and love for it; thus one encounters nothing more seldom than the required diligence and necessary, untiring industry, joined together with these two things, natural ability and real desire: because commonly not a little laziness and idleness, lasciviousness, comfortableness, and the like, tend to go side by side with innate gifts and inclinations.
> A so-called natural disposition without ambition or love is like a buried treasure ... Desire and diligence without natural ability is really the worst of all.[35]

[35] Ibid., II, ii, 59ff.

This role which Nature plays, led Mattheson, in another place, to comment on the treatment of students.

> Natural stupidity or innate simplicity is among the failures of the intellect which no one can rightfully punish, though it can be deplored or at best ridiculed. Desiring to make youngsters intelligent with thrashing is not only futile, but godless. Many examples verify that beatings make heads ten times more dumb than they were previously. This is and remains abysmally characteristic of education in almost every guild and apprenticeship.[36]

[36] Ibid., II, ii, 30. Mattheson specifically was thinking, in the last statement, of Turmblaser guilds.

Finally, we noticed an interesting passage in the *Der vollkommene Capellmeister* in which he seems to have a nostalgic fondness for the old cornett and trombone consorts which were also so much associated with church music. It is interesting here, however, that the cornett, which was so praised for its beautiful sound during the sixteenth century, he now thinks of as penetrating and harsh.

> Here this question occurs to me: why then do the good cornetts and trombones, which were formerly closely related and were highly esteemed as staples by the expert civic musicians as well as the composers, seem to be banished now so completely from the churches, at least from the ones here, as if they had been discovered to be incompetent? For the former instrument is still very penetrating, with all its harshness; whereas the other sounds very majestic, and fills a large church beautifully. Whoever wants to may answer this question.[37]

[37] Ibid., III, xxv, 7.

9
Mattheson on the Composition of Good Melody

> The nature and character of each key,
> namely whether it is happy, sad, lovely, devout, etc.,
> are actually matters of the science of melody.[1]
> *Johann Mattheson (1681–1764)*

[1] Johann Mattheson, *Der vollkommene Capellmeister* [1739], trans. Ernest Harriss (Ann Arbor: UMI Research Press, 1981), I, ix, 47.

JOHANN MATTHESON (1681–1764), was one of the earliest theorists or philosophers to come to the correct conclusion that emotions are communicated to the listener through melody, and not through harmony. It appears to us that it was this realization which led to his careful study of melody, itself the most extensive ever done by its time.

Before presenting his discussion of the characteristics of melody, Mattheson makes some introductory remarks. First, he observes that it is not sufficient to define music as simply playing or singing well (which was a basic definition of music in the latter Middle Ages) for "the noblest part of music [is] composing."[2] Indeed, he points out that in Italy a singer is called *Musico*, an instrumentalist, *Suonatore*, but only the composer, "who often has the least to say about his work," is called *Maestro*! The correct, basic definition of music, therefore, is:

[2] Ibid., I, ii, 11ff.

> Music is a science and an art of placing proper and pleasing sounds prudently, uniting them correctly with one another, and presenting them sweetly, to promote God's honor and all virtue through their euphony.[3]

[3] Ibid., I, ii, 15.

He follows this by observing that "nothing is accomplished by science alone; art is required as well." By this he means you cannot speak of music without speaking of performance.

Next Mattheson turns to the classifications of music and begins with a review of the medieval classifications of "universal music" (music of the spheres, etc.), "human music" (having to do with the soul, etc.) and "actual music." Since the first two classifications cannot be actually heard, he explains he will discuss only "actual music."[4] The goal of actual music, he says, is that

> which would through the instrument of the ears please the sense of hearing which dwells in the soul, and would thoroughly move or stir the heart or soul.[5]

Regarding such performance, Mattheson gives the highest aesthetic value to singing.[6] Although he observes that singing is almost always done with instruments ("singing without instruments has mostly been done away with"), such music is still called *vocal* music. Indeed, he says, even if the instruments play as skillfully and charmingly as possible, as soon as the voices enter they get all the attention.

After Baroque composers generally won the victory of establishing for music the role of expressing emotions, replacing the old mathematics based concepts, a new question became the subject of debate: are the emotions expressed by melody or by harmony? While Mattheson believed that it was melody which expressed emotions, others, in particular Rameau, seemed to argue for harmony. Johann Scheibe wrote a letter praising Mattheson for understanding that melody was based in Nature, while harmony was merely the product of art—of which he points to J. S. Bach as a tiresome example.[7]

For Mattheson, his entire understanding of the definition of music was centered in his conviction that melody was the primary element in music which communicates feeling.[8] This was, of course, a philosophy which would become even more clearly understood in the following Classical Period.

[4] Ibid., I, ii, 21ff.

[5] Ibid., I, ii, 24.

[6] Ibid., I, ii, 38ff.

[7] Quoted in Cannon Beekman, *Johann Mattheson, Spectator in Music* (Archon Books, 1968), 89.

[8] *Der vollkommene Capellmeister*, II, iv. Recent clinical research confirms his deduction.

The growing emphasis on melody had its roots both in the abandonment of the old polyphonic style and in the new emphasis on feelings, as confirmed in the popularity and influence of opera.

Mattheson begins his lengthy discussion of the art of writing good melodies with a discussion of the *loci topici*, which represent a conceptual attempt to organize an explanation of music after the model of rhetoric. These he intends as tools for the composer in the invention of melody, as for example *causa efficiens* refers to the way a story might suggest the design or nature of a prospective melody. Another is *Materia circa quam*, which refers to the actual thoughts a composer has while writing, and here Mattheson highly recommends thinking of a beautiful female.[9] One of the most important of these is *locus descriptionis*, for it is here that the emotions might inspire the writing of a melody. Mattheson observes that one must not think that words are the only source of the communication of emotions in music, but even,

> in purely instrumental music, always and with every melody, the purpose must be to present the governing affection so that the instruments, by means of sound, present it almost verbally and perceptibly.[10]

Other *loci* take into consideration the type of listener who will hear the melody and the acoustics of the hall in which the melody will be heard [*locus effectorum*]. When you borrow a melody from someone [*locus exemplorum*] you should develop it or do something nice with it, or as Mattheson puts it, pay back what you have borrowed with interest.

The above represent points of inspiration or starting points. A discussion of actually writing the melody, for which he uses the Greek verb *Melopoie*, together with the characteristics of a good melody come next.[11] In his introduction to these characteristics, Mattheson stresses his most basic beliefs about melody: that melody communicates the emotions; that Art is the servant of Nature (too much art obscures the beauty of Nature); and that harmony must be taken from melody and not the other way around as in earlier polyphony.

[9] Ibid., II, iv, 62.

[10] Ibid., II, iv, 45. In another place [Ibid., II, v, 40], without explanation, he recounts hearing a French singer sing an unaccompanied song on stage which had such charm that "it enraptured the listeners," but when this same actor later played this melody on an alto flute the result was "truth so plaintive and touching that it caused real sorrow among the listeners."

[11] Ibid., II, vff.

With this foundation, Mattheson now discusses at some length the four basic qualities which a good melody must have.[12] The first quality is that it be *facile*, a concept which Mattheson associated with its ability to communicate, for he stipulates, "we cannot have pleasure in a thing in which we do not participate." His seven characteristics of *facility* are,

[12] Ibid., II, v, 48ff.

1. There must be something in all melodies with which almost everyone is familiar.

This is something which, according to Mattheson, the ear demands. We might add that modern clinical research in brain function appears to confirm this.

2. Everything of a forced, farfetched, and difficult nature must be avoided.

What he means by this, he says, can been seen in the works of "mannered composers" easier than being described in words. Errors of this nature tend to result from lack of intelligence or ability in invention, whereby "loss of natural fertility is replaced with wondrous curiosities." In this regard, Mattheson quotes a fine composer who observed that only with the greatest diligence and practice could he achieve what those with only half his ability could.

3. One must follow nature for the most part, practice to some degree.

Mattheson's thought here is rather interesting. "Practice," here, includes tradition and academic concepts with its artificial constraints. Therefore the one least experienced in the "science" of composition will be the one most likely to compose something natural. The experienced composer must act as a "dilettante" if he hopes to capture the natural quality of great art.[13] "Nature never lacks beauty, naked beauty, only sometimes it buries it under a discreet disguise or a theatrical mask. Our gem cutters can polish the diamond; but they cannot give it any other luster or purity than that which nature has already given it." Thus, it follows,

[13] Schumann once observed that when he first began to compose he had to "unlearn" everything he had learned in school.

4. One should avoid great artifice, or hide it well.

Artifice, observes Mattheson, should never be confused with great art. If the composer must embellish his melody, he should imitate the fencer with his feints.

5. In this the French are more to be imitated than the Italians.

This, he says, because the French taste requires a cheerful, lively spirit, which is a friend of decorous pleasantry, and an enemy of all of that which reeks of trouble and toil. Also, Mattheson quotes a French treatise which suggests that the French considered their art closer to Nature than that of the Italians.

> If we find Italian music to be a rival, then we must not forthwith banish it to misery; but also must not quote it foolishly, but avoid all of the most superficial and enrich ourselves with its beauty. For although we French occasionally adopt Italian teachings on the high art, the Italians on the other hand, as regards grace and charm, are also frequently inclined to consult the harmony of our land in order to be so much closer to charming Nature: which is always simple, always sincere, and finds no beauty where constraint reigns, no tenderness where artifice plays the master.[14]

[14] Ibid., II, v, 63, quoting Jean Baptiste Gresset, *Discours sur l'harmonie* (Paris, 1737).

6. Melody must have certain limits which everyone can attain.

Mattheson advises that to encourage performance opportunities, the range of the melody should not exceed an octave.

7. Brevity is preferred to prolixity.

Here Mattheson is thinking primarily of retention by the listener.

THE SECOND BASIC QUALITY which a good melody must have is *clarity*, for which Mattheson gives ten characteristics.[15]

[15] Ibid., II, v, 50 and 72ff.

1. The *caesuras* and divisions should be observed precisely: not just in vocal but also in instrumental pieces.

   Mattheson observes that he is amazed that everyone thinks such phrasing points are not needed in instrumental music. But without them, he says, there can be no clarity.

2. One must always aim at one specific passion.

   In general, he says every melody should express one primary emotion. Without this the listener can make nothing of it but "idle singing and playing." Here Mattheson suddenly turns to education and expresses his amazement that music composed for educational purposes emphasizes various theories but is devoid of emotion.[16] And while using this emotionless music, what do the teachers do?

[16] Ibid., II, v, 79ff.

> Do they not become angry, do they not perspire, do they not rejoice; do they not cry; do they not clap their hands; do they not threaten? Who wants to say that this would pertain more to mere, cold instructions, than to the vivid affections?.... If one wants to enhance strong ideas and theories and wants to make a worthy contribution to them, then such cannot take place halfheartedly.

   In short, he says, "everything which happens without praiseworthy emotions, is nothing, does nothing, signifies nothing: be it where, how and when it may...." The most simple child's game is never without passion, not only incidentally, but by preference: no infant can be said to be free of it.

3. A meter must not be altered without reason, without need, nor without intermission.

   Mattheson criticizes the French recitative for constant changes in meter, which results in seeming to have none at all. He says meter must be uniform, for it is "the soul of melody."

4. The number of beats should be proportionate.

He prefers an even number of pulses in even the slowest Adagio and states that fast movements should never have an odd number of beats in the bar.

5. No cadence should appear contrary to the usual division of the beat.

6. The accent of the words should be closely observed.

Here Mattheson's concern was that the melody be composed in such a way that the melodic accent falls on the most important word of the sung sentence.

7. One must very carefully avoid embellishment.

"Daily experience," says Mattheson, "shows us what kind of terrible patchworks are pasted together from neglecting this commandment of melodic beauty." By way of illustration, he quotes an anonymous observer:

> The arias are so varied and intricate that one becomes impatient before the end comes. The composer is satisfied if he writes only nonsensical notes, which the singers, through thousands of contortions, make even more absurd. They laugh during the saddest performance, and their Italian excesses always appear at the wrong place.[17]

[17] Ibid., II, v, 101.

As for himself, Mattheson thinks,

> Such embellishment, whether produced by a composer lacking in taste or an arrogant vocalist, reminds me of nothing more than a far too opulent livery for pages or trumpeters, where all is completely covered with gold and silver lacing to such an extent that one can perceive neither the cloth nor its color.

This comparison, he sighs, is still too kind.

8. One must aim at a noble simplicity in expression.

"Sensible simplicity ... must not be understood as something stupid, absurd, or vulgar; but rather as something noble, unembellished and quite singular." This is evident, Mattheson finds, in many other areas.

Simplicity constitutes the most important point in writing and reading as well as in singing and playing, indeed in the whole of human affairs: and if ever innate characteristics were to occur, this certainly would be the right place.

This much is beyond dispute, that men, some more than others, also excel in this matter according to how the physique and the orderly or disorderly mixing of the humors are fit or unfit for sensation. Noble thoughts always have a certain simplicity, something of the unaffected, and only a single aim. Whoever presents such without any constraint, according to the simple laws of nature, will be succeed.[18]

[18] Ibid., II, v, 104ff.

9. One must precisely examine and differentiate the writing style.

Here he is thinking of not confusing the appropriate styles for church, theater and chamber, as well as those styles appropriate for specific instruments ("one should not set military pieces for lutes").

10. One must not base the aim on words, but on their sense and meaning: not look to sparkling notes, but to expressive sounds.

Though last, Mattheson warns, this is the most important, and equally so for instrumental music.

For the fact that not a single melody should be without meaning, without aim, or without emotion—even though without words—is established by this, and through the laws of nature.

THE THIRD BASIC QUALITY which a good melody must have is that it must be *flowing*. For this he provides eight rules.[19]

[19] Ibid., II, v, 51 and 110ff.

1. One should pay careful attention to the uniformity of the meters or rhythms.

2. Also, preserve precisely the geometrical proportion of certain similar phrases, namely the *numerum musicum*, i.e., the measurement of melody by numbers.

In the first of these Mattheson is concerned with some basic order of the rhythms at the level of the beat, although an unvarying beat would "cause impropriety and disgust." In the second, Mattheson is looking for a kind of sequential metric form, based on the internal rhythms within the measure.

3. The fewer formal cadences which a melody has, the more flowing it most certainly is.

4. Cadences must be selected and the voices for these managed well before one proceeds to the pauses.

Aside from the obvious concern with the interruption of the melody, Mattheson was also bored by the lack of variety he heard in cadences.

5. In the course of melody, the little intervening resting places must have a certain connection with that which follows.

6. The overly staccato style is to be avoided in singing; unless a special circumstance requires it.

7. Do not take the passages through many sharp jolts, through little chromatic steps.

8. A theme must not impede or interrupt the melody in its natural course.

THE FOURTH QUALITY which a good melody must have is the most important, *charm*. Here Mattheson supplied eight rules:

1. Steps and small intervals are preferred to large leaps.

2. One should cleverly vary such small steps.

3. Collect all sorts of unsingable phrases, in order to avoid them.

4. On the other hand, select and amass ones which sound good as models.

In illustrating these four rules, Mattheson provides for the most part melodic idioms of the sixteenth century style.

5. Observe well the relationship of all parts, members and limbs.

This refers to aesthetic correspondence of the internal melodic parts of a form such as the da capo aria form.

6. Employ good repetitions, yet not too often.

7. Begin with sounds which are pure, related to the key.

8. Employ reasonable runs or colorful figures.

Following this, Mattheson discusses the rhythmic notation of melody, in particular as it relates to accompanying a text. It is here that he revisits the ancient Greek poetry rhythms.

10
On Court Music in the German Baroque

WHEN ONE CONSIDERS the long period of war which began with the Thirty Years' War, it sometimes seems a wonder that culture developed at all in central Europe. But, while the progress rose and fell with the fortunes of individual courts, the German-speaking countries eventually made extraordinary progress in their musical life. Ironically, the driving force behind this great development in German culture came from the outside, from Italy and from France. From France came the Hautboisten wind band, which begins to appear in German courts in around 1690, and was based on a model in the court of Louis XIV, the *Les Grands Hautbois*. Aside from a vast repertoire of original works which are still extant, there were two important facets of the Hautboisten development. First, it was the Hautboisten movement which also introduced the modern oboe to Germany, the first of the modern winds which replaced the old Medieval and Renaissance ones beginning in c. 1675. There were, nevertheless, a few courts who maintained for some time the older Renaissance consorts. We see an example in an engraving from Halle of 1676 of the "Hof-Schalmey-Pfeiffer." One sees here twelve players of shawms all dressed in their uniform of green coats.[1]

Second, it was the forms of the Hautboisten which became the symphony and divertimento of the Classic Period. This story will be told in the following chapter.

[1] W. Seraunky, *Musikgeschichte der Stadt Halle* (Halle-Berlin, 1939), II, 423.

The other national influence on German court music came from Italy. Following on the heels of Italian opera, numerous Italian composers and musicians moved North to the German-speaking countries during the seventeenth and eighteenth centuries, bringing the seeds from which the German Baroque in music grew. The Germans managed to give some things a new life, such as the many Italian instrumental forms, the Intrada, Sinfonia, Concerto, Aria, Canzona, etc. These had been Church forms in sixteenth century Italy but became secular court forms in seventeenth century Germany.

A typical example of a great noble who wanted the status symbol of Italian musicians was Friedrich August I (1694–1733) of Dresden. Speaking of his interest in Italian opera, one contemporary wrote,

> All the arts and sciences seem to have been united in this breath of air. The extraordinary payments which the king grants the players have attracted the best and most excellent masters of this art to Dresden from Italy, the great school of music.[2]

[2] G. Pietzsch, *Sachsen als Musikland* (Dresden, 1938), 52.

After Ferdinand II became emperor in 1619, the strong Italian influence in the Austrian court can already be seen in the fact that such famous Italian composers as Viadana and Grillo,[3] not to mention Victoria, dedicated works to him. Although Italian opera arrived in Vienna in 1627, in the courts of Germany it is the next decade before this form would begin to become popular. A letter by Heinrich Schütz of 1633, reflecting on his trip to Italy in 1628–1629, reveals Italian opera was yet unknown in Dresden.

[3] Even at the end of the eighteenth century Mozart had to confront the official Italian composers in Vienna.

> During my recent journey to Italy I engaged myself in a singular manner of composition, namely how a comedy of diverse voices can be translated into declamatory style and be brought to the stage and enacted in song—things that to the best of my knowledge ... are still completely unknown in Germany.[4]

Italian opera would not appear in the court at Munich until 1653. But so pervasive would Italian opera become

[4] Quoted in Gina Spagnoli, "Dresden at the Time of Heinrich Schütz," in *The Early Baroque Era* (Englewood Cliffs: Prentice Hall, 1994), 176. In 1671, Bontempi and Peranda of this court produced the earliest extant German opera.

that the first great German opera composer, Reinhard Keiser (1674–1739), whom Mattheson called "the greatest opera composer of the world,"[5] remained little known, then or today.

[5] J. Mattheson, *Das neu-eröffnete Orchestre* (Hamburg, 1713), 217.

The great influx of Italian musicians during the seventeenth century did not occur without difficult adjustment. The resident German musicians must have often resented these foreign celebrities,[6] as we can see in a letter of Heinrich Schütz complaining that he was being blamed for importing them.

[6] Roger North, in England, expresses similar frustration with foreign musicians.

> More and more each day (regarding Your Highness's Italian musicians and those installed in the electoral court ensemble) not only repeatedly unpleasant judgment is passed against me by various ecclesiastics and lay persons but, furthermore, to my particular astonishment, I have learned that I am considered, and slandered as, the cause and instigator of the change.[7]

> Now it is set up dressed in superlatives brought from I know not where, at immense charges in profuse salary, pensions, subscriptions, and promiscuous courtship and flattery in the bargain. These far fetched and dearly bought gentlemen return home rich, buy fine houses and gardens, and live in admiration of the English wealth.

[Quoted in John Wilson, *Roger North on Music* (London: Novello, 1959), 250]

[7] Quoted in Spagnoli, "Dresden at the Time of Heinrich Schütz," 168.

[8] Quoted in Ibid., 169.

A senior chaplain in this court wondered if before long there would be any German musicians left to sing "a German *Our Father* in church."[8] In addition, the resident musicians must have felt that the monies being expended on foreign musicians was money much needed for their own support.

Finally, since the Italian musicians were Catholic, their desire to observe the Mass in Protestant areas caused concern. In Dresden, in 1673, they were forbidden to practice their faith. But such problems did not succeed in slowing the influence of Italian music in Germany.

In Northern Germany one finds an occasional noble who was also an active musician, such as Johann Georg II, in Dresden, who is presumed to have studied with Heinrich Schütz and was a composer of large-scale church works. Telemann, in his autobiography, relates a visit to Berlin where he secretly attended a private opera performance in which all the roles were sung by people of high rank.[9]

[9] The passage is quoted in Bernd Baselt, "Brandenburg-Prussia and the Central German Courts," in *The Late Baroque Era* (Englewood Cliffs: Prentice Hall, 1994), 234.

But, it is in the Catholic areas of the German-speaking nations that one especially finds nobles who were musicians and composers. Being Catholic, their ties with Italy were much closer than the courts of the North who regarded their

Italian musicians as visiting celebrities. But the closer ties in the Catholic regions must have also made them more sympathetic to the ideals of Italian humanism and the model of the noble given by Castiglione as a man who values and can perform music.[10]

In Munich, the Elector Maximilian II Emanuel (1679–1726) listened to music every evening and was a talented performer on the viola da gamba. His son, Carl Albrecht (1726–1745), was a great patron of Italian opera composed by musicians of his household. He himself attended and directed rehearsals. He was succeeded by Maximilian III Joseph, a virtuoso on the viola da gamba and a composer of church music and concerti. He unfortunately reigned during the War of the Austrian Succession, the economic results of which forced a decline in the musical activities of this court.

It is in Vienna, of course, where the association with both Italy and the influence of Italian humanism was most strongly felt. The personal involvement of the nobles in music there,[11] together with their influence on Bohemia and Hungarian musical activities, would create an environment which would in time produce a Mozart and a Beethoven.

The emperors Ferdinand III (1637–1657), and Leopold I (1658–1705), were active composers whose music still exists.[12] The music establishment of Leopold seems suspended between the Renaissance and the Baroque, with both a Renaissance consort of trombones and cornetts for the church and a more modern Hautboisten band for secular use. The later patronage of music by the court in Vienna can be measured by the growth of the strings in the Hofkapelle. There were approximately fifteen in 1690, twenty-nine in 1705 and forty-one in 1728. Maria Theresa, who bridges into the Classical Period, although a singer herself, was forced to reduce the musical establishment for economic reasons.

Court musicians performed for a wide variety of entertainment events, including allegorical pageants, festivals, balls, banquets and fireworks. Such functional music, with new German names such as *Aufzug*, *Ritterspiel* and *Tanzspiel*, still exists in many libraries. Philipp Hainhofer, a visitor to

[10] Baldassare Castiglione (1478–1529), as a diplomat for the Duke of Urbino and Popes Leo X and Clement VII, in one of the most famous books of the Renaissance, *Il Cortigiano* (The Courtier), which attempts to describe the attributes of the perfect gentleman and lady from the sixteenth century aristocratic perspective.

[11] Metastasio complains in a letter of 1734 of having to hurriedly compose a theatrical work for two archduchesses to sing. [See Charles Burney, *Memoirs of the Life and Writings of the Abate Metastasio* (New York: Da Capo Press, 1971), I, 156]

[12] Including an "Hymnus de Nativitate" (c. 1649) for SATB and ten winds by Ferdinand III and a "Beatus vir," for voices and winds by Leopold I.

the court in Dresden in 1629, has left us an account of how elaborate the music could be for a meal in the royal garden house.

> The space behind every portrait is hollow and set up in such a way that one can perform a certain kind of music. When one dines in this upper hall, the musicians are also positioned in the lower hall with the doors closed so that the resonance ascends delightfully through the ventilators. Above, under the ceiling, there is also an arrangement for hidden music, so that one can hear such music from 32 different locations, each separated.[13]

He also describes the instrument collection on the third floor of the Dresden palace. Here he lists a number of Renaissance instruments, including consorts, as well as portraits of fourteen famous composers, and the reader will notice how many of them are Italian, including Andrea and Giovanni Gabrieli, de Rore, Monteverdi, de Lassus, Striggio, Willaert, Croce, Merulo, Orologgio and Sweelinck. Hainhofer adds the reflection,

> A number of these Kapellmeisters prospered; others, however, despite all their art, remained poor. Some among them indeed committed suicide.[14]

Finally, Hainhofer describes a banquet in which the music, in the Renaissance tradition, was varied in instrumentation with each composition. He reports vocal ensembles, a wide variety of string instruments and some novelty performances: a performer who fiddled with one hand and piped with the other, a trombonist who imitated figures played by cornetts and violins and music by "several glasses blown into."[15] Curiously, he concludes by commenting that he enjoyed everything, "in spite of the saying 'There is no song so good but that one tires of it'."[16]

On the occasion of the noble's birthday, all the components of his musical establishment would participate in the celebration. Sometimes this involved the commissioning of poets and composers to produce great allegorical productions similar to those of the Renaissance. For the birthday of the Duke

[13] O. Doering, *Des Augsburger Patriciers Philipp Hainhofer Reisen nach Innsbruck und Dresden* (Vienna, 1901), 217. Charles Ogier, a French representative to a Danish wedding in Copenhagen in 1634, reports being surprised by a concert of vocal and instrumental "invisible music." "It came to us through various openings and resounded now near, now far." As the diplomats got into their carriages to leave, again "subterranean and invisible music" was heard. See Hans Moser, *Heinrich Schütz* (St. Louis: Concordia, 1936), 149.

[14] Hans Moser, *Heinrich Schütz*, 138.

[15] Ibid., 138ff.

[16] Ibid., 139.

of Saxony (March 5, 1621), for example, Schütz wrote "Felicitation of Apollo and the nine Muses," performed by "His Electoral Grace's Collegium Musicum with 12 cornetts and as many living voices beside trumpets and timpani."[17] When Schütz traveled to Copenhagen in 1634 for a Danish royal wedding, immediately upon his arrival, he was assigned the duty of creating music for two plays, a ballet and a masked ball![18] The ballet, based on Orpheus and other Greek gods, was given after a lavish banquet. A contemporary descriptions speaks of Orpheus singing while accompanying himself on a violin, "in a voice that was a pleasing and charming as it was plaintive."[19] When the devil's wives appeared, the "noise of their cymbals and tongs" drowned out the song of Orpheus. Later, another singer, a eunuch, appeared who "knew how to use his voice so skillfully that he was listened to with amazement by all present." The summary by the eyewitness reads,

> Thus we find vivid and varied problems for musical treatment: soli in song form, recitatives in the new opera style, soli with obbligato instruments, different ensemble sections varied with duets, terzets, soli and choruses, and finally the introductory and closing choruses. But one sees at once that the music should be called concert music rather than dramatic music. It serves a purely decorative purpose and has no organic relationship to the content of the action.

For the birthday of Duke Christian of Weissenfels (1712–1736), a contemporary describes the performances by a number of ensembles. The celebration began with the Duke's eight trumpets playing "Feldstücke" from a castle tower while both his and the civic militia fired canon salvos. When the shooting ended, the trumpets played "morning songs." During a procession to the church, the trumpets and timpani played intradas until all the nobility and visiting guests were in their places.[20] The civic trombones played from the city hall tower followed by a performance by the Duke's wind band [*Hautboisten und Waldhornisten*].[21]

The great allegorical pageants of the sixteenth century become more rare during the Baroque. One noble who enjoyed

---

[17] Ibid., 114ff.

[18] Ibid., 147.

[19] Ibid., 150ff.

[20] A. Werner, *Stadtische und fürstliche Musikpflege in Weissenfels* (Leipzig, 1911), 55.
[21] Ibid.

this kind of extravagant display was Friedrich August I (1694–1733) of Dresden.[22] For the carnival season of 1695 he had organized a great procession of the gods, each accompanied by an ensemble of musicians. First came Jupiter and Juno with thirty-two musicians, followed by Mars and Bellona with shawms, trumpets, timpani and drums. Then Neptune with an Hautboisten band dressed as satyrs followed by Apollo with twelve musicians playing oboes, bagpipes, guitars and violins. His mistress appeared as Aurora and she had eight musicians. Interestingly, the Nine Muses were accompanied by women musicians.[23]

One of the Baroque entertainments which developed out of the Renaissance-style pageants were the so-called horse ballets,[24] which were first imported from Italy by Ferdinand III (1637–1657), for his marriage to Maria Anna, daughter to Philip III of Spain. On this occasion the names of Ferdinand and his bride were spelled out by vast numbers of cavalry on the floor of the arena. In the case of international weddings, such as this, part of the purpose was a political show of force, a symbolic demonstration of the importance of the emperor and the empire. The political aspirations were enhanced by the publication of the official programs and descriptions which were sent to courts throughout Europe.

We see the same political overtones, as well as another great horse ballet, in the entertainments—covering two years—associated with the wedding of Leopold I and Margareta Theresa of Spain. In July 1666, five months before she arrived in Vienna, her birthday was celebrated there with a grand ballet composed by the court ballet composer, Schmelzer.[25] The following November there was another ballet, *Concorso dell' allegrezza universale*, as well as a *dramma per musica* by the Venetian composer, Ziani, given in honor of the birthday of the emperor's mother.

In January 1667, another great horse ballet was given for which rehearsals began six months earlier! For the some 1,000 participants involved, a special stadium was constructed by the Burghof and the theme, "The Contest between Air and Water," was expressed through various gods

[22] Aside from his interest in music, poetry, theater and traveling throughout Europe, he also found time to father 354 children!

[23] George Buelow, "Dresden in the Age of Absolutism," in *The Late Baroque Era* (Englewood Cliffs: Prentice Hall, 1994), 220.

[24] A form of this still exists today in Vienna in the so-called "Spanish Riding School."

[25] Several compositions for this horse ballet are extant.

debating on behalf of air and water. A published account of another horse ballet, with music by Cesti, given by Leopold[26] tells us that the event began with the emperor leading the first dance, mounted on a richly decorated horse. Then the Duke of Lorraine entered with his party, while one heard *"a strepitosa armonia da un pianissimo concerto di Timpani e Trombe guerriere."* Next was an elaborate procession, centering on the allegorical figure, "Germania," followed by a tilting contest with the targets being sea-monsters and savages. Finally, in the horse ballet proper, to the music of a *corrente*, one saw the emperor, with Counts Dietrichstein and Preiner and the Duke of Lorraine,

[26] *La Germania esultante, Festa a Cavallo* . . . (Vienna, 1677).

> execute the first figure of the ballet in the greatest variety of curvets and volts; after which the ballet is ridden—first by four, then by six, and finally by eight knights, the figures changing as the music changes. Thereupon the riders are seen to press forward to the strains of the fiery *giga*, taking the barrier by twos—a magnificent feat never before seen at festivals of this sort. Then some gallop to the center of the field, while the rest are performing their volts and curvets. Their ballet is now carried on by threes in the four corners of the arena, while two others execute new figures in the center. Around these two the twelve entwine the round dance *treccia* (or, as it is known in Vienna, *Trezza*), which has its counterpart in another winding dance by eight riders. The two convolutions uncoil themselves, the knights reappear in the center and thence betake themselves toward the spectator's seats, making way for nine knights who execute the figures of the *sarabanda*. They form a crescent, in the center of which the emperor and the Duke of Lorraine take their stand. Again we behold the knights confronting each other in pairs, executing elaborate steps, at first on the spot and then in motion. The two groups part and stride across the arena, greeted by the tumultuous applause.

The horse ballet of 1667 was followed by more ballets during Carnival. In June, Cesti's opera *La Semirami* was performed for the emperor's birthday, followed by another *balletto a cavallo* by Schmelzer in July for the birthday of the empress. More operas were given the next winter and finally in July 1668, for the wedding itself, the *Il pomo d'oro* by

Cesti. This opera in five acts, to which were added six ballets, twenty-three scene changes and thirty-eight singing roles required two days for its performance.

Leopold was followed in Vienna by Karl VI (1711–1740), who maintained a large Hautboisten band of some fifteen players, a consort of trombones and cornets and a large trumpet choir, who are now listed in court records as "musical," meaning we presume that they could read music. Next comes Maria Theresia, who helped create the environment which made Vienna, by the end of the century, the center of the musical world. It was under her reign that the composer Dittersdorf visited the court and recorded an eye-witness description of one of the very last great allegorical displays in the old Renaissance tradition.

> [The artificial lake] was 80 feet broad and 100 feet long. From bank to bank, in the center of the lake, two galleries were thrown across; on each of these were seated a number of trumpeters and drummers, with other players on wind instruments; they were heard playing alternate strains.
>
> In the lake itself, at a little distance from the shore, there stood, at regular intervals on each side, 8 pedestals, painted so as to look like stone, and adorned with bronzed grotesques. On the first 2 pedestals, 2 live bears stood opposite each other, dressed as clowns; on the second pair, 2 wild boars, dressed as columbines; on the third, 2 big goats, dressed as harlequins; and on the fourth were 2 huge bulldogs.
>
> You may fancy the noise made by growling bears, grunting pigs, bleating goats, howling dogs, and the music going on at the same time!
>
> After allowing his guests an interval in which to enjoy the scene, the Prince waved his handkerchief as a signal, and the show began.
>
> Two gondolas emerged at either end of the gallery, and made towards the cottage; each was manned by 4 gondoliers, dressed in Venetian fashion. One of them sat on the beak of the vessel, with a bundle of spears, lances, and similar weapons, laid crosswise before him; two others rowed, and the steerer, turning the gondola wherever he chose, sat behind them. These two gondolas advanced, circling in different ways round the pedestals; there were afterward joined by two others, then by two more, and then the last two. The

eight went through their manoeuvres with such accuracy, that no ballet master, marshalling his *danseuse*s, could have improved upon them. When they had gone their rounds, they were ranged face to face, and a tournament began, in which each water-knight, seated on the beak, broke from 4 to 5 lances; then they went once more round the pedestals on which the comic actors stood. At one and the same moment, each knight, armed with a staff, struck at one of the grotesque masks, a spring gave way under the blow, and a trap door fell. Numbers of white ducks and geese, and one swan as well, were concealed in each of the hollow pedestals, and you may fancy the alacrity with which these winged creatures took to their native element, though a marionette rode upon each of them. These marionettes were various figures, proportioned to the size of the birds, which they bestrode—clowns. Harlequins, Anselmos, Doctors, Leanders, Pasquins, Scaramouches and other Carnival mummers.

A fray ensued, and the knights seized their clubs and threatened one another. Gondolas darted about in studied disorder. When one collided with another, the knights dipped their clubs, which were hand-syringes, into the lake, and squirted the enemies. Whenever they neared a pedestal, the creature on it got the whole benefit of a shower bath, and the animals loudly resented the rudeness of the whole proceedings. The effect on the audience may be imagined, for orders had been given to the musicians in either band to blow in any key they chose. Directly after the skirmish had begun one trumpeter blew a shrill blast in D, whilst another, with the aid of a crook, did the same in C, and another in E *la fa*. Some of the drummers had tuned up. Others had tuned down; oboists, clarinetists, bassoonists followed suit. What an infernal discord it was! The beasts growled, the ducks and geese quacked and spluttered, coming into collusion with the moving gondolas every moment, and the 3,000 spectators roared with laughter. Show me the hypochondriac who could remain unmoved by such a spectacle![27]

[27] *The Autobiography of Karl von Dittersdorf*, trans. A. D. Coleride (London, 1896), 64ff.

This rapidly growing support of music by the nobles in the German-speaking lands had the somewhat adverse result of making the court musicians increasingly busy. No longer merely the producers of music for meals and church, they were now, as Heinrich Schütz pointed out to his patron, involved with, many diverse festivities ... which occurred during this time at imperial, royal, electoral, and princely gatherings, in this country and abroad, but particularly at each and every one of your own royal children's weddings, and no less at the receiving of their sacred christenings as well.[28]

And with the increasing appreciation by the nobles, higher demands followed. Before the visit of the Emperor Matthias in 1617, Schütz was instructed that his ensemble must "acquit itself with honor and glory before the visitors."

We may be sure that, as servants of the court, the pay of these musicians did not keep pace with the growing demands for their service. One reason for their financial difficulties was that the court musicians were often paid mostly in commodities, rather than actual money which they could save to purchase such things as clothes. A record of a court bassoonist in Weissenfels, for example, specifies as part of his yearly allowance, "20 pounds of beef, 9 portions of bread, 9 portions of wine and 18 portions of beer."[29]

It is no wonder that the court musician often looked with envy on the life of the civic musician. Even Schütz, in the letter just mentioned, complained,

> God knows that I would prefer with all my heart to be a cantor or an organist in a small town to remaining longer amid conditions in which my dear profession disgusts me and I am deprived of sustenance and of courage.[30]

Another court musician who served in Weissenfels, Johann Beer, also dreamed of an easier life as a civic musician.

> With the court you've got to be in one place today, tomorrow in another. Day and night, unfortunately, makes no difference. Tempest, rain, sunshine—it's all the same. Today you've got to go into church, tomorrow to the dining hall, the day after tomorrow to the theater. Compared to all this disturbance, life is somewhat more peaceful in the towns ...
>
> Many princely musicians long for the city, because the service in the court is so insecure and he must be ready to move if the support for music by the noble fails or if he decides to cut back. What good are riches without stability? I say continued poverty could be called better luck than

[28] Memorandum of January 14, 1651 to the elector Johann Georg I, quoted in Spagnoli, "Dresden at the Time of Heinrich Schütz," 164.

[29] Werner, *Stadtische und fürstliche Musikpflege in Weissenfels*, 74.

[30] Quoted in Moser, *Heinrich Schütz*, 196ff.

irregular riches, where one may go from a horse to an ass and from the ass even to sit in the dust ...

In the city one can hope for quicker advancement ... this has the civic musician, but at court even if he had a doctorate in all three faculties he waits without hope. The more excellent he is, the more he will remain in his station which he once accepted, to remain used, all feathers plucked from his wings so he can not hope to soar higher.[31]

[31] Johann Beer, *Musicalische Diskurse* (Nürnberg, 1710), 18ff. Beer (1655–1700) was a native of Upper Austria.

A further complaint which Beer could have mentioned was the dangers of accompanying the noble in his hunting. Beer, in fact, was accidentally shot and killed while on a hunt in 1700. Metastasio, in a letter of 1732,[32] relates some details of a similar accident in which the emperor of Austria accidentally shot and killed Prince Schwaisemberg during a hunt.

[32] Charles Burney, *Memoirs of the Life and Writings of the Abate Metastasio* (New York: Da Capo Press, 1971), I, 87.

But, as they say, "the grass is always greener on the other side of the fence." Bach, in 1730, submitted a memorandum to the Leipzig Councilmen complaining about the difficulties of life as a German civic musician. Quite the reverse of Beer, Bach contemplates how nice it would be to be a court musician, as for example in Dresden.

It is somewhat strange that German musicians are expected to be capable of performing at once and *ex tempore* all kinds of music, whether it comes from Italy or France, England or Poland, just as may be done, say, by those virtuosos for whom the music is written and who have studied it long beforehand, indeed, know it almost by heart, and who, *quod notandum*, receive good salaries besides, so that their work and industry thus is richly rewarded; while, on the other hand, this is not taken into consideration, but the German musicians are left to look out for their own wants, so that many a one, for worry about his bread, cannot think of improving—let alone distinguishing—himself. To illustrate this statement with an example one need only go to Dresden and see how the musicians there are paid by His Royal Majesty; it cannot fail, since the musicians are relieved of all concern for their living, free from *chagrin*, and obliged each to master but a single instrument: it must be something choice and excellent to hear.[33]

[33] Quoted in Hans T. David and Arthur Mendel, *The Bach Reader* (New York: Norton, 1966), 123.

One observer, writing of Hamburg at the end of the Baroque, leaves the impression that the long hardships of war had permanently affected the culture. He noted that although the town had a certain pride in having Telemann in residence, "the taste for music had totally vanished: people were more interested in educating their children to make money than to make or appreciate music."[34]

[34] Griesheim, *Die Stadt Hamburg* (1760), 194ff.

11
On the Hautboisten

ONE MEDIUM which played a prominent role in late Baroque German court music, yet which is almost never mentioned in general music history texts, was the Hautboisten band. Lack of information by previous scholars caused this ensemble to be written off as simply a military band attached to the court. But it was never anything of the kind, as the very large body of original concert music extant in German libraries and court accounts make quite clear. The Hautboisten also plays a pivotal figure in the development of the forms of the Classical period, for the *concerto da camera* of the Hautboisten became the symphony and partita of the Classical Period and the *Ouverture* became the divertimento. Quite separate from this, the Hautboisten as a medium naturally transformed itself into the *Harmoniemusik* of the Classical Period; only the name and the style of composition changed.

At a time when Italian style had such a strong influence, the instrumentation came from France and with it the modern oboe, as is reflected in the Germanized French name, "Hautboisten." The influence of the court of Louis XIV on the rest of Western Europe is well documented. Frederick the Great complained in 1750,

> Everyone in Germany goes there ... The French taste rules our food, our furniture, and our clothes.[1]

[1] Frederick II von Brandenburg, *Memoires pour servir a l'histoire de Brandenbourg* (1750), II, 771.

It should be no surprise, then, that one of the fundamental ensembles of the court of Louis XIV, the *Les Grands Hautbois*, a twelve-member oboe and bassoon band, should be imitated in the courts of Germany. It began to arrive in German courts during the final two decades of the seventeenth century, as can be documented by its appearance in Stuttgart (1680), Weissenfels (1695),[2] Dresden and Gotha (1697) and Gottorf (1699). Some German ensembles, in imitation of *Les Grands Hautbois*, even carefully had exactly twelve players. Twelve-member Hautboisten bands can be documented in Halle (1676),[3] Jena,[4] and Eisenberg, where the ensemble was known as the "Apostles."[5] Like the French version, the Germans at first divided the parts of the ensemble (regardless of the number of players on a part) into two soprano oboe parts, tenor oboe (taille) and bassoon, while in the second generation horns were added. A leading scholar of this field finds that by 1700 virtually every major court in Germany possessed one of the new Hautboisten bands.[6]

Furthermore, the appearance of names in German court records at this time suggest that the new French oboe came to Germany in the hands of French players. Their French names can be documented in court records of Celle (1681), Bonn (1697), Dresden (1699, "François le Riche") and in Berlin (Dec. 22, 1681, "Pierre Potot and François Beauregard").[7] The modern French oboe differed with the shawm primarily in the fact that it was cylindrical, whereas the shawm was conical. No one has been able to prove what stimulated the invention of this new instrument in Paris just after the middle of the seventeenth century. Our supposition has always been that the new cylindrical sound had been suggested to Parisian ears by their interest in the musette, a small bagpipe. The cantor of this instrument could be, and was, sometimes performed without the bag, in which case it was for all practical purposes a little (cylindrical) oboe. The association we assume between this "little oboe" and the new modern French oboe is strengthened by the fact that the court oboists played the musette as well, as we can see in a contemporary observation,

[2] According to A. Werner, *Stadtische und fürstliche Musikpflege in Weissenfels* (Leipzig, 1911), 95. The elector was apparently dissatisfied with the Hautboisten he engaged in this year, for two years later he replaced them by hiring an entire band [*Kammerpfeifer*] in Vienna.

[3] W. Serauky, *Musikgeschichte der Stadt Halle* (Halle-Berlin, 1939), II, 423.

[4] Werner Braun, "Entwurf fur ein Typologie der 'Hautboisten'," in *Der Sozialstatus des Berufsmusikers vom 17. bis 10. Jahrhundert* (Kassel, 1971), 47.

[5] Werner, *Stadtische und fürstliche Musikpflege in Weissenfels*, 96.

[6] Braun, "Entwurf fur ein Typologie der 'Hautboisten'."

[7] Curt Sachs, *Musik und Oper am kurbrandenburgischen Hof* (Berlin, 1910), 61.

> When one has heard the musette in the hands of those who play it perfectly, as does M. des Touches, one of the Royal Oboists, it must be admitted that it yields to none of the other instruments, and that there is a singular pleasure in hearing it.[8]

It appears that by the seventeenth century in both France and in Germany the bassoon had come to be identified as the bass of the oboe. Mersenne wrote, in 1635,

> I treat of these species of basses because they can be joined in the concert of oboes, and are different from the preceding bass (oboe) only in that they break into two parts to be able to be managed and carried more easily; that is why they are called Fagots, because they resemble pieces of wood.[9]

Johann Mattheson, of Germany, calls the bassoon "the ordinary bass" of the oboe.[10]

It is not clear if the bassoonists also came from Paris, but the instrument begins to appear in Germany at the same time as the Hautboisten ensemble. Indeed, a reference in the Weissenfels court records to a musician in 1698 calls him "an oboist who plays the bassoon." The bassoon is mentioned in court records in Saxony in 1666 and 1680[11] and in Wissenfels by 1667.[12] The Berlin court had four bassoons by 1708, who, together with four oboes, constituted the Hauboisten.[13]

We might pause to add that music for bassoon ensemble enjoyed a brief fashion in the late Baroque. Gottfried Pepusch composed, c. 1700–1713, a work for six bassoons which was much liked by Friedrich Wilhelm I.[14] The Kapellemeister of the Württemberg court in Stuttgart, Reinhard Keiser, wrote a work in 1720 for eight bassoons, which he describes in a letter to the prince:

> There are two suites which I have composed in all respect for your majesty a few days ago. When the players had practiced them on their instruments they produced harmony of a special effect. The two bassoonists of your bande have expressed the greatest satisfaction with them … The "La Chasse" and the "Granadier-Marsch" produced good humor … The King of Denmark had 8 such bassoons and "bassonetten" in his Granadier-Guarde which were ceremonious and pleasant to hear.[15]

[8] Martin Mersenne, *Harmonie Universelle* [1635], trans. Roger Chapman (The Hague, 1957), 359.

[9] Ibid., 372.

[10] Johann Mattheson, *Das neu-eröffnete Orchestre* (Hamburg, 1713), 269.

[11] Peter Panoff, *Militarmusik* (Berlin, 1944), 84.

[12] Werner, *Stadtische und fürstliche Musikpflege in Weissenfels*, 57ff.

[13] Sachs, *Musik und Oper*, 66. One of these oboists, Peter Glosch, had a work dedicated to him by Telemann in 1716.

[14] G. Thouret, *Friedrich der Grosse als Musikfreund und Musiker* (Leipzig, 1898).

[15] J. Sittard, *Zur Geschichte der Musik und des Theaters am Württembergischen Hofe* (Stuttgart, 1891), II, 13.

The composer Johann Trost has left a composition for six bassoons (two octavo, two quarto and two normal instruments) and two horns.[16] Also one finds in London in 1744 a reference to a work performed by twenty-four bassoons and four contrabassoons.

The important point to be made about the first generation of the Hautboisten in Germany, the ensemble made up of oboes, tenor oboes and bassoons, is that the extant repertoire is that of a concert medium, not a military one. The repertoire consists of major, multi-movement, works which are serious in tone. These characteristics hold true for such works as an entire "band library" at BRD-HRD-Fü, the twelve *Sonatas* by Johann Müller (printed in Amsterdam c. 1709)[17] and the several *Ouvertures* (suites) by Venturini, composed in 1723. There is an extant work for two Hautboisten bands in DDR-ROu, although we have not seen it.

The second, and last, generation of the Hautboisten ensemble begins just after the dawn of the eighteenth century and continues until the Classical style retires the Baroque. The new characteristic of this second period was the addition of the horns. Before the eighteenth century horns are very rarely found at court in indoor venues. They are nowhere mentioned, for example, in either the Chapelle Musique or the Grand Écurie of Louis XIV in France. Even as late as 1717, in Vienna, an aristocratic lady wrote, in describing a court ball,

> ... the music good, if they had not that detestable custom of mixing hunting horns with it, that almost deafen the company.[18]

A long tradition has assigned credit for the idea of moving the horns from the hunting lodge to the palace in Germany to a cultured Bohemian aristocrat and supporter of the arts, Franz Anton, Count von Sporck. The best account was written in 1792:

> In the year 1680 he set out upon a tour of foreign countries, according to the custom of Bohemian nobility. He visited the foremost royal and princely courts, where he noted everything

[16] The manuscript is in DDR-Z.

[17] Now available at maximesmusic.com.

[18] Lady Mary Wortley Montagu, quoted in R. Morley-Pegge, *The French Horn* (London: Ernest Benn), 16.

which struck him as beautiful, artistic, or useful; and brought them back with him for the ornament and benefit of his native land. In this connection we must not omit mention of an incident which forms a proper part of the history of music in Bohemia. In Paris he heard the hunting horn for the first time, an instrument which had been invented there a short time before. He found this instrument so agreeable that he caused two men from his retinue to be instructed in the art of playing it. Which they brought shortly to the highest degree of perfection, and upon their return to Bohemia taught it to others.[19]

It does appear that the idea came to Germany from the East and one of the earliest references to the subsequent expanded Hautboisten speaks of the "Sachsische Variante."[20] The important thing is that with the addition of the horns, we now have a Classical *Harmoniemusik* in everything but the name. We find the new Hautboisten with horns mentioned in Zeitz in 1715,[21] the "Sachsische Variante" in c. 1730,[22] a performance for the Nurnberg Carpenter's Guild in 1731 by three such expanded bands[23] and even in the Bavarian military by 1722.[24] In addition, we have important extant repertoire for the Hautboisten with horns, including works by Handel and Telemann.

Before we turn to the second important aspect of the Hautboisten story, the role its forms played in creating the forms of the Classical Period, we must first conclude these brief remarks about the medium itself by mentioning that these German Hautboisten bands also made concert tours. One of these was the Hautboisten of the Brandenburg court in Berlin, led by an oboist-director named "Lubuissiere" (and sometimes "Lapuisier" or "La Bassire"), whose tours can be documented between 1693 and 1700.[25] The next leader of this Hautboisten, Gottfried Pepusch, took the band on a tour to London in 1704, where a review in the *Daily Courant* (April 4) mentions that they performed some music by his brother, "that Eminent Master, Mr. John Christopher Pepusch" [Johann Christoph Pepusch].

Gottfried Pepusch seems to have been considered an important teacher of this new medium, for in 1703 an entire

[19] Quoted in Hirsching, *Historische-Litterarisches Handbuch Beruhmter und Denkwurdiger Personen* (Leipzig, 1792), xiii, 146.

[20] Braun, "Entwurf fur ein Typologie der 'Hautboisten," 59.

[21] Werner, *Weissenfels*, 96.
[22] Braun, "Entwurf fur ein Typologie der 'Hautboisten," 59.
[23] Ibid., 54.
[24] Johannes Reschke, "Zur Geschichte der Deutschen Militarmusik des 17. und 18. Jahrhunderts," in *Deutsche Musik-Kultur* (1937), Nr. 2, 15.

[25] Braun, "Entwurf fur ein Typologie der 'Hautboisten," 46.

Hautboisten band came from Ansbach to study with him.[26] Six of his students were hired as a Hautboisten band in Hannover in 1705 and when Johann Mattheson visited Hannover the following year he was astonished by the "Virtuosen," especially the "exquisite Bande Hoboisten."[27]

Aside from the important development of the seventeenth century French *Les Grands Hautbois* into the German *Hautboisten* and finally into the *Harmoniemusik* of the Classical Period, there is also a very important role played by the German Hautboisten bands in developing the Classic Period forms. Most of the Hautboisten music found in German libraries fall into two forms, one of which is the "Ouverture." Because of the French spelling usually found, some later scholars have renamed this form the "French-Overture-Suite." In these works the first movement usually begins in a slow 3/4, followed by a fast polyphonic movement of major proportions for the period, often of about six minutes. What follows are usually four or five short dance movements, the last of which is sometimes a minuet. Exactly such a work is the well-known Handel *Fireworks Music*, which also ends with a minuet.

The majority of the extant scores are called simply, "Concerto." The reader should remember that this word first appears in music as the name of an ensemble, such as "Concerto di Palazzo" of Sienna (1559) or in the civic wind band Girolamo Dalla Casa conducted (c. 1584), "*Concerti delli stromenti di fiato della Illustriss. Signoria di Venetia.*" By the late sixteenth century the word had become transformed to be associated with a style, representing a dialog or polychoral style as we see in Bottrigari's famous definition,

> If you inquire into the word Concerto you will find that it signifies "contention" or "contrast."[28]

Praetorius, in his *Syntagma Musicum*, Book III, confirmed this in observing that "concerto" derived from *concertare*, to compete, and not from *conserere*, to consort. It is only later in the seventeenth century that the word, concerto, is used generally to mean a form.

[26] G. Schmidt, *Die Musik am Hofe der Markgrafen von Brandenburg-Ansbach* (Kassel, 1956), 72.

[27] Johann Mattheson, *Ehren-Pforte* (Hamburg, 1740), 195.

[28] Bottrigari, *Il desiderio ovvero De' concerti de varii stromenti musicali* (1594).

All music history teachers tell students about the "sinfonia da chiesa" and the "sinfonia da camera," the church and chamber symphonies. But there was also a "concerto da chiesa," which came in two sizes, the large church concerto, such as the works of Gabrieli, and the small church concerto, as in such works as Viadana's *Cento concerti ecclesiastici* (1602) and Felice dall' Abaco's *Concerti da chiesa*, Op. 2. And let us not forget, the familiar Italian canzona is also a concerto da chiesa.

Curiously, very few books mention the companion form, the "concerto da camera," although it is a very important form. The concerto da camera, like the church concerti, came in two sizes. The smaller concerto da camera is what is represented by numerous extant works for Hautboisten. The large concerto da camera is first seen in compositions for multiple ensembles, such as Stölzel's composition for three wind bands and strings. It soon became the practice to use several separate ensembles of a particular court in a single composition and it was this practice of using the wind band in the *concertino* and the strings in the *ripieno* which was the first stage of the *concerto grosso*. There are a number of such works extant by Torelli and Vivaldi. This tradition also appears later in Germany, as for example in the case of the composer Fasch who wrote some twenty *concerti grossi* with wind bands in the *concertino*.[29] And then there is Handel, who wrote concerti for Hautboisten with and without horns in the concertino, as if he was hedging his bets and wasn't quite sure which wind band instrumentation would win out. Finally, Muffat suggests that a wind band could substitute for strings in the concertino.

> Should there be among your musicians some who can play and modulate the French oboe or shawm agreeably, you may with the best effect use two of these instead of the two violins, and a good bassoon player instead of the French bass, to form the concertino.[30]

According to Hutchings, composers used the term "concerto grosso" to designate the work as being for a larger number of players and not a "concerto da camera."[31]

[29] Grove, *Dictionary of Music* (1980), VI, 414.

[30] Georg Muffat, *Ausserlesene Instrumental-Music* of 1701, quoted in Oliver Strunk, *Source Readings in Music History* (New York, 1950), 449ff.

[31] Arthur Hutchings, *The Baroque Concerto* (New York: Scribner's Sons), 21.

While the Italians used the full name, as in examples such as Torelli's *Concerto da camera* of 1686 and Manfredini's *Concerti per camera* of 1704, the extant German scores for Hautboisten are always called just "Concerto," dropping the Italian "da camera." At a time when words such as sinfonia and sonata still lacked specific definition in Germany, other than just meaning a larger composition for instruments, the label "Concerto" in Germany did seem to carry the understanding that it meant a work intended for concert performance. This point is made as well by one of the very few scholars who have discussed the concerto da camera:

> In 1730 a symphony might still be an Italian overture, a passage for organ in an English anthem, a march, battle, storm or pastoral piece in an opera or oratorio, or a ripieno concerto served under another name; but if a work were called concerto it was intended for 'absolute' listening, for use at a concert.[32]

[32] Ibid., 29.

This view is confirmed by Georg Muffat in the foreword of his *Ausserlesene Instrumetal-Music* of 1701:

> These concerti, suited neither to the church ... nor for dancing ... [are] composed only for the express refreshment of the ear.[33]

[33] Muffat, *Ausserlesene Instrumetal-Music*.

This distinction, expressed in actual performance, contributed to the concerto da camera becoming the symphony (for strings) and partita (for winds) of the Classical Period. It is in the wind ensemble repertoire of the mid eighteenth century that one can clearly see the transformation of the concerto into the partita and the ouverture into the divertimento. Among the many wind ensemble compositions by Georg Wagenseil (1715–1777) of Vienna, for example, there is a *Divertimento in F* which is really an old Hautboisten eight movement Ouverture under a new name. Another *Divertimento in F*, however, is in four movements (Allegro, Minuetto, Andantino, Chase) which seems much closer to the old concerto form, or the new symphony/partita form.[34] In addition one sees the transformation in the style of the music itself. In the last mentioned divertimento, for example, three

[34] The partita for wind band is really a "concerto da camera," with the "da camera," as in the Baroque, meaning music to be played *inside* the palace. In the first generation or so of the new Harmoniemusik there were only a few works called "Partita di Campagna," for use in the field, but they soon die out.

movements are in the Classical style, but the slow movement sounds very Baroque in character. This, of course, only reflects the cross currents of style at this the borderline between the Baroque and the Classical Periods.

The Baroque Hautboisten, with its concerti and ouvertures, then, become the Harmoniemusik, with its partitas and divertimenti, of the Classical Period. It is important, therefore, to understand that the pure wind band played a continuous and important role in the culture of both the Baroque and Classical Periods.

12
On the Golden Age of the Trumpet in Germany

ANOTHER ENSEMBLE which was at the center of seventeenth century court life, yet receives only cursory mention in scholarly books on music, was the aristocratic trumpet choir. The trumpet had been associated with the noble since antiquity, as for example the high priests of the Old Testament, and this symbolism was not lost on the Baroque German noble. Many German aristocrats began expanding the size of their trumpet choir in the early years of the seventeenth century and in many cases they were organized into a double choir. A look at a few courts will enable the reader to visualize this expansion.[1]

[1] Detlef Altenburg, *Untersuchungen zur Geschichte der Trompete im Zeitalter der Clarinblaskunst* (Regensburg, 1973), I, 24.

Wolfenbuttel	1553:	2 trumpets	1622:	14 trumpets
Darmstadt	1569:	1 trumpet	1629:	6 trumpets
Dresden	1548:	10 trumpets	1629:	14 trumpets
Graz	1567:	8 trumpets	1611:	13 trumpets
Kassel	1538:	8 trumpets	1613:	12 trumpets
Schwerin	1550:	1 trumpet	1609:	7 trumpets
Stuttgart	1550:	6 trumpets	1610:	16 trumpets

These choirs served as an aural coat-of-arms, announcing the noble when he traveled, serving as his ambassador, performing for his meals and entertaining his guests.

Because the trumpet is thus associated with the highest level of society, it is praised throughout seventeenth century literature. For example, Andreas Werckmeister, to whom Bach was indebted for equal-tuning, wrote in 1691,

> God should be praised with them. Yes, the trumpet contains the correct order of all the consonances in itself and is the foremost instrument.[2]

No wonder one of these trumpeters looking back at the end of his life observed,

> A sovereign may have ever so good an orchestra, venery, royal stables, and other such ministrations, but if he does not retain at least one choir of trumpeters and timpani, there is, in my opinion, something lacking in the perfection of his household.[3]

These trumpeters formed their own guilds, in part as an attempt to maintain the standards of their profession. Thus, in a document of 1620, one Caspar Hentzschel comments on the performance of their memorized "Toccetten, Sonaden and Serosoneten." These, he warns his brothers, must be performed in an "artful" manner and never in beer houses. He also recognized a "correct musical art," which interestingly enough he identifies as an "ancient art which was used by the Jews and was communicated to me by an old Jew from Padua."[4] This, apparently, was to suggest he possessed a tradition handed down directly from the Old Testament players.

The trumpeter guilds were also eager to protect their domain from infringement by other musicians and during the seventeenth century they frequently called upon the aristocracy to confirm these "rights" in legal documents. One of these, by the Emperor Ferdinand II, in 1623, states,

> No honorable trumpeter or timpanist shall allow himself to be employed with his instrument in any way other than for religious services, emperors, kings, electors and princes, counts, lords and knights and nobility, or other persons of high quality. It shall also be forbidden altogether to use a trumpet or a timpani at despicable occasions; likewise the excessive nocturnal improper carousing in the streets and alleys, in wine- and beer-houses. He who transgresses in this way shall be punished.[5]

[2] Quoted in Wilhelm Ehmann, *Tibilustrium* (Kassel, 1950), 56.

[3] Ernst Altenburg, *Versuch einer Anleitung zur heroischmusikalischen Trompeter- und Pauker-Kunst* ... (Halle, 1795).

[4] Quoted in Johannes Reschke, *Studie zur Geschichte der brandenburgisch-preussischen Heeresmusik* (Berlin, 1936), 5.

[5] Quoted in Don Smithers, *The Music and History of the Baroque Trumpet* (London: Dent), 115.

In 1653 a new edict by the Emperor Ferdinand III was issued, due to "various difficulties, errors and abuses" relative to the edict of 1623 by his father. The new edict deals at length with the apprentice system, after first stipulating that a prospective student must first present information relative to his "honorable ancestry and birth."[6] In this regard the aristocratic trumpeter is warned that if he "behaves dishonorably toward a widow or an honest man's daughter and makes her pregnant," even though he acknowledges the child, he may not instruct him in trumpet playing. A strong hint is given that if one marries "a person of public ill repute" he will no longer be permitted to be a trumpeter. He would be immediately thrown out of the profession, should he,

[6] Antonium Fabrum, *Europaischer Staats-Kantzley* (Leipzig, 1700), IV, 848ff.

> lose his skill at the trumpet, play in the company of jugglers, court mimes, town watches or at lotteries and the like ... [or] give up his art to become a watchman on a tower, or join the jugglers or comedians.

The student must study with the noble trumpeter for two years, after which a final exam is given.

> Each master shall instruct his apprentice very diligently in his art, and shall not send him into the field until he knows his Feldstücke perfectly. In order to test this, the apprentice must present himself beforehand to the highest and oldest trumpeter and play his test piece for him. If this is not done, then as a bungler he will not be allowed to go into the field.

It is also interesting that the edict places strict limitations on how many students one trumpeter could teach, and how often, which was an attempt to guard against overcrowding the profession. If a trumpeter gives up his art for a higher position, he also gives up the right to teach. If, however, he retires to become a farmer, he may continue to teach - as long as he is not caught "making the boy work in the fields or the wine cellar and not at his music."

The 1653 edict again addresses the standard of behavior expected of the noble trumpeter.

> No honorable trumpeter shall let himself be heard or play the trumpet at night after the curfew hour in the alleys or cross

roads, nor in public houses or wine bars, nor anywhere else, except in the houses of princely lords and noble families.

As for the trumpeters, their principal fear was that their duties might be taken over by the much more accomplished civic musicians, who, for one thing, could read music. The repeated attempts by the noble trumpeters to define the areas of performance which belonged to them suggest these efforts were not respected. Failing in this, they next attempted to restrict the instrument itself to their profession, leaving the old S-trumpet and the cornett to the civic musicians. Their concern in this regard was so paranoid that a document of 1630 suggests they wanted to prevent other musicians, especially trombonists, from even *sounding* like a trumpet.[7] In 1671, the court trumpeters from Altenburg, having heard something of this nature at a local carnival, lodged a complaint with their prince. In this case the city fathers made a strong defense of the civic players, pointing to the civic players' reading from the page, as opposed to the aristocratic trumpeters' tradition of performing only memorized repertoire.

[7] A. Werner, *Stadtische und furstliche Musikpflege in Zeitz* (Buckeburg & Leipzig, 1922), 42.

> The civic players used their instruments, such as trombones, cornets, also strings, according to the music, as well as they could in all places for celebrations, weddings, and other honorable gatherings. It is also customary everywhere that they perform, from the music set down, on the instruments discussed here, and if town's people and other music lovers requested a tune in the manner of trumpets on trombones, cornets, or strings, they could not help but oblige them in this way the best they could. All of which has been customary here and in other places according to their art for countless years.[8]

[8] Quoted in Smithers, *The Music and History of the Baroque Trumpet*, 115.

For a while the aristocratic trumpet guild was thus able to restrict for themselves the use of the trumpet. One finds, for example, that the city council in Leipzig had to make a formal report to the elector explaining why their music director, J. H. Schein, used trumpets in a performance in St. Thomas Church. In response, Schein was directed to use the cornett in the future![9] One famous incident in Hannover makes clear how serious this issue was perceived at the time.

[9] Gottfried Viet, *Die Blasmusik* (Innsbruck, 1972), 24.

At the end of the seventeenth century in Hannover, the elector's trumpeters once broke into the house of the chief Stadtpfeifer, with whom they were at loggerheads, took his trumpet on which he was practicing and knocked out several of his front teeth with it. And what is more, these worthy Kameraden contended that they had only asserted their just right—and escaped all punishment.[10]

[10] Werner Menke, *History of the Trumpet of Bach and Handel* (London, 1934), 26ff.

Along with everything else, the aristocratic trumpeters also were a colorful addition to court life with their uniforms and banners. When Duke Johann von Sachsen-Halle visited Leipzig in 1671 one heard forty-seven trumpets.[11] An eyewitness described the trumpeters of the Duke of Württemberg when he visited England in 1603:

[11] Arnold Schering, *Musikgeschichte Leipzigs von 1650–1723* (Leipzig, 1926), 298.

> As to the order of the proceeding, it was in this manner: first went two trumpeters belonging to the troops of horse, whose trumpets were adorned with silk banners, painted with the arms of Wirtemberg in their proper colours, and after them ten other trumpeters in the same equipage.[12]

[12] Quoted in John Nichols, *The Progresses of King James the First* (London, 1828), 286. An anonymous engraving of the same ceremony showing twelve trumpets is in the Nürnberg Germanisches Nationalmuseum (Sign. HB 116).

Another interesting eyewitness account describes the arrival of the Count of Palatine of Germany, as part of his marriage celebrations to Elizabeth, daughter to James I, in the Winter of 1612. This account is all the more interesting for its attempt to describe the actual playing of the aristocratic trumpets.

> Before the Palsegrave, at his return from the Chappel, went six of his owne country gallants, clad in crimson velvet, laide exceedingly thick with gold lace, bearing in their hand six silver trumpets, who no sooner coming into the Banquetting-house, but they presented him with a melodious sound of the same, flourishing so delightfully that it greatly rejoiced the whole Court, and caused thousands to say at that instant time, "God give them joy!"[13]

[13] Ibid., 548.

As is well known, the aristocratic trumpeters also played a fundamental diplomatic role, as any court official was granted safe passage in foreign nations, or behind enemy lines, if accompanied by a trumpet. Even a high ranking official traveling without one risked imprisonment.

... the Earl of Feversham the general of the forces; who going without Trumpet or passeport is detained prisoner by the Prince ...[14]

[14] *The Diary of John Evelyn* [1673–1689] (Oxford, 1955), IV, 610.

The German aristocratic trumpeters also played a vital role in the standing military bands which were beginning to be formed for the first time during the Baroque Period. We shall include the trumpeters' military duties in an essay on the military which follows.

13
On Civic Music of the German Baroque

IN THE LIVES of the ordinary citizens throughout seventeenth century Germany, the most conspicuous and most important musical organization was the *Stadtpfeifers*, the civic musicians—an institution which was now at its musical peak. For nearly all of their five hundred year tradition these were civic wind bands. The members were specialists until the sixteenth century, when the favored consort principle required them all to be proficient on a number of instruments. Late in the sixteenth century they began to use string instruments as well, but there remained a definite hierarchy with cornetts and trombones at the top, followed by strings and then the lowly bagpipe and percussion.[1]

By the beginning of the seventeenth century these were still small ensembles, which should not cause us to minimize the societal importance of this step forward in having regularly employed musicians paid by the town. In many small towns, such as Marburg, Radkersburg and Graz, there might be only four civic band members.[2] In the larger and more prosperous cities these groups were larger: Augsburg began the century with six, but soon added a seventh; Leipzig had seven and Hamburg had eight in its principal wind band, but also had a relationship with seven bands of five players each, organized as associated civic bands, who could help out in great celebrations.[3] One occasion for such larger festivals was the visit of a high noble. When the emperor visited Dresden

[1] Wilhelm Ehmann, *Tibilustrium* (Kassel, 1950), 23, 30.

[2] Eugen Brixel and Wolfgang Suppan, *Das Grosse Steirische Blasmusikbuch* (Vienna, 1981), 36.

[3] Liselotte Kruger, *Die Hamburgische Musikorganisation in XVII Jahrhundert* (Leipzig, 1933), 188ff and Ehmann, *Tibilustrium*, 21.

in 1662, the civic band was joined by similar bands from Meissen, Pirna and Freiberg.[4]

As with the use of consorts in the sixteenth century, instrumental variety and color was achieved by changing instruments for each composition. Thus an account of a concert by the Nürnberg Stadtpfeifers in 1643 states that they performed on strings; then on silver trumpets and clarions; a "Greek military composition" with trumpets, drums and timpani; on bassoons and bombards in accompanying a chorus; [unnamed] winds in the instrumental performance of a motet and finally a funeral composition for male chorus and trombones.[5]

This required, of course, that each member of the Stadtpfeifers be proficient on all the basic instruments. Accordingly, when an opening occurred the applicant had to audition on many instruments. Often a local composer would be engaged to write compositions for the applicants to read at the audition. When, for example, in 1743, the Zeitz Stadtpfeifers had an opening, they paid Johann Gorner, music director of Leipzig University, twelve Thalers to compose works for trumpet, trombone, cornett, horn, and two each for strings and oboe.[6]

It should perhaps be mentioned that while the Stadtpfeifer positions were generally filled by audition, other civic positions were often obtainable by bribe. In fact, when J. S. Bach applied for an organist position in Hamburg in 1720, he was passed over in favor of a candidate named Heitmann who made a gift of 4000 marks to the town council. Perhaps more surprising than the result is the fact that the town actually advertised their openness to such a bribe.

> The question was raised whether it was desired that money should be given for the organist's post; on which point it was decided that:
> There were many reasons not to introduce the sale of an organist's post, because it was part of the ministry of God; accordingly the choice should be free, and the capacity of the candidates should be more considered than the money. But if, after the selection had been made, the chosen candidate of his own free will wished to give a token of his gratitude ...[7]

[4] Grove, *Dictionary of Music* (1980), V, 615.

[5] Elisabeth Kruckeberg, "Ein historisches Konzert zu Nürnberg im Jahre 1643," in *Archiv für Musikwissenschaft* (1918–1919), 590ff.

[6] Arnold Schering, *Musikgeschichte Leipzigs* (Leipzig, 1941), III, 151.

[7] Quoted in Hans T. David and Arthur Mendel, *The Bach Reader* (New York: Norton, 1966), 80ff.

Bach served on one of these Stadtpfeifer audition panels in 1745 and wrote the following report to the Leipzig Town Council after the examination of the applicant, Carl Friedrich Pfaffe.

> At the command of A Most Noble and Most Worthy Council, Carl Friedrich Pfaffe, hitherto apprentice to Your Honors' Stadtpfeifers, has taken his trial examination in the presence of the other Stadtpfeifers; whereupon it was found that he performed quite well and to the applause of all those present on all the instruments that are customarily employed by the Stadtpfeifers, namely: Violin, Hautbois, Flute Travers., Trompette, Waldhorn, and the remaining bass instruments, and he was found quite suited to the post of assistant which he seeks.[8]

But, human nature being what it is, we must not assume that all Stadtpfeifers were equally fine musicians. When Bach arrived in Leipzig he found some of the Stadtpfeifers at his disposal somewhat lacking. He tactfully observed,

> Discretion forbids me to speak of their quality and musical knowledge, but it should be mentioned that some of them are *emeriti* and others are not in as good *exercitio* as they should be.[9]

But surely his predecessor at St. Thomas, Kuhnau, was exaggerating when he observed that in a hundred Stadtpfeifers there was scarcely one who could write ten words on paper, even if his life depended on it.[10]

We can see how serious this hiring process was in a case which happened early in the eighteenth century in Altenburg, when the mayor, without consultation or audition hired a man named Rossest to play in the town band. While the chief Stadtpfeifer, Stöckel, had not been consulted, he nevertheless was blamed and received contempt from colleagues for allowing this "bungler" to be hired. For example, this incident came to the attention of a former member of the Altenburg civic band, one Hans Christian Biedermann, who had gone on to become a court trumpeter in Weimar. He wrote a letter of condemnation to Stöckel, which read in part,

[8] Quoted in Arnold Schering, "The Leipziger Ratsmusik von 1650 bis 1775," in *Archiv für Musikwissenschaft* (1921), 44.

[9] Quoted in E. H. Muller von Asow, *Johann Sebastian Bach Briefe* (Regensburg, 1950), 112.

[10] Kuhnau, *Musicus vexatus* (1690).

> I must report that a bad *Aestim* of you and your *collegen* has resulted even so far away as Leipzig, Jena and here in Weimar ... [As a result of your actions] all bunglers will now travel to Altenburg (and the words will go out) that all bunglers and "fellows of the road" who have been cut off from other employment can be engaged in Altenburg ... I say freely, that you have bound yourself to this Rosselt and you must look out for evil. You should not have let him draw a single stroke on a violin before consulting with the guild ... and formalizing the contract with a *Notario*.[11]

[11] The entire letter is quoted in Arno Werner, *Stadtische und fürstliche Musikpflege in Zeitz* (Buckenburg, 1922), 41ff.

In view of these expectations, the reader might find interesting a letter of recommendation, written by a father in support of his son's application for a music position in Stettin in 1607. Particularly astonishing here is the large number of instruments the young man owned!

> My son has arrived at a point in his art where he has studied and learned diligently all the musical instruments. First, he is a good trumpeter and secondly a good cornett player and plays well the discant violin, Querpfeife, dulcian, quart-, tenor- and alto-trombone. In summary: all perfect instruments, although without proclaiming his fame—for as one says, "Self praise stinks." But he can prove himself where it matters, in what the ear hears and the eye sees. To cover the subject, he doesn't quarrel or criticize, and can use the instruments I have given him in praise of God: trombones, cornetts, a good quart-trombone; a dulcian consort; a large and small bombard consort; a large cornett consort; a crumhorn consort; a Querpfeiffen consort; a flute consort; and a violin consort. He can play all parts and use the fifth, sixth, or eighth voices [i.e., read the various clefs], comes from a good home ... and is twenty-six years old.

The regular duties of the typical Stadtpfeifer were quite varied, as we see in a contract for one Christoph Schumann in 1726. The reader will note here in particular the participation in the well-known tower music, known as *Abblasen*; the surrogate clock duty and the regular service accompanying singers in the church.

> He should at 3:00 AM, 9:00 AM and 9:00 PM play with diligence a spiritual Psalm, to the honor of the Almighty God and to

inspire Christian prayer and to sustain the goodwill of the citizens and the entire community. Further, at night he should faithfully watch and take heed that with his assistant the horn player they mark every quarter hour with the usual horn playing. He should keep his quarters in the tower clean. He must volunteer to play in church with his instrument and assist the civic musicians with weddings, operas, and official banquets, although not permit himself, though helping, to actually take part in the ceremonies.[12]

[12] Quoted in Ehmann, *Tibilustrium*, 32.

The tower music, or Abblasen, played several times a day from a tower as indicated above, was a very important part of German civic life and deserves far greater attention by music historians. Far from performing mere chorales, the musicians played chorale canzonas, chorale fantasies, free canzonas, sonatas and suites.[13] In the quality of their performance as musicians, there was a certain "public relations" aspect to this music, as is indicated in an ordinance from Zeitz in 1701, which speaks of the performance of Abblasen to "better ornament the town for visitors."[14] More important, however, was the spiritual and psychological impact of this music, which Johann Pezel called "a friendly and peaceful sound,"[15] on the ordinary citizen. The trombones, on which the Abblasen were most frequently performed, had themselves become symbols of God and Christian music. Thus, Kuhnau, Bach's predecessor in Leipzig, reflected,

[13] Ibid., 34.

[14] A. Werner, *Vier Jahrhunderte im Dienste der Kirchenmusik* (Leipzig: Merseburger), 218.
[15] Ibid., 217.

> When our civic musicians at Festival time blow a spiritual song on the loud trombones, every measure stirs the image of angels singing.

No other instruments, but wind instruments, he says are played in Heaven by the angels![16]

[16] Quoted in Ehmann, *Tibilustrium*, 55ff.

Regarding the impact of this music on the citizen, one must first remember that there was no noise level comparable to modern towns and that the loudest sound most people would hear in their entire life was a small church organ, Therefore, it is reasonable to assume that most people in the village could hear this tower music. What then might be the effect of this spiritual music, floating down from on high, played by instruments which were themselves symbols of

God and heard by the citizen several times a day throughout his entire life? We have heard distinguished musicians in Europe contend that this music, played continuously from the late sixteenth through the eighteenth centuries, was more responsible than any other factor for the development of the German character as we know it today.

An eloquent summary of the duties of the tower musician is given in a 1679 poem by Jacob Lottich.

> When Titan's high course is about to bring midday, the clock strikes ten;
> Then the musicians meet with all their odds and ends,
> Form a group and let us have a tune for lunch on their trombones.
> The midday music can be heard from the town hall tower,
> Almost high up in the open air; it sounds for the honor of God and to inform the people,
> So that everyone knows each day at this time it is the tenth hour.
> When Latous has departed from us with his never tiring horses
> And when we no longer see any light or any rays from him on earth,
> Then a bell is rung so that its sweet sound entices us to vespers.
> A cornettist then takes the best of his Zinken,
> Chooses a Psalm which he considers just suitable, and he pipes in an artful manner;
> He does his duty, stays on the church tower and remains awake for the rest of the night.
> In the streets guards who have been appointed for this purpose walk up and down and see
> To it that the streets are safe; they seize the trespasser against law and order;
> They prevent fire and turmoil so that everyone shall be safe while they rest.
> As often as the clock strikes, the hours are called out.
> There is no shortage of clocks: hardly anywhere would you find such ingenious clock works.
> Anyone who does not believe this should come here and see for himself that one weight alone propels two big clocks.

As soon as Aurora gleams in gold and red hues the watchman
  still awake takes his trumpet, alerts and wakes up the town
  with a morning song.
After that he retires and makes up for his lost sleep.[17]

As the above poem points out, the worker's "noon break" came at 10:00 AM at a time when work in the fields had to begin with first light. It was for these concerts that the collection of sonatas by Johann Pezel (1639–1694), known as *Hora decima* ("Ten o'clock hour") was published in 1670. Among his many publications were a collection of two-part works intended for the recreational music by the musicians in the tower during their long and lonely hours on duty.[18] Yet another publication of dance movements, *Fünff-stimmigte blasende Music*, a massive collection of seventy-six works, may have been used for public concerts from a balcony of the city hall building. Several important published collections by Pezel are lost and these include two collections of Intradas (Leipzig, 1669 and 1676) for cornett and three trombones and a collection of six-part works for cornets and trombones called *Decas Sonatarum* (Leipzig, 1669).

Pezel, who is probably the best known of the German civic musicians to musicians today, appears to have enjoyed a university education and was also the musical director of the collegium musicum of the University of Leipzig from 1673 to 1682. In 1677 he applied for the position of cantor at St. Thomas Church, the position J. S. Bach would later hold, but he was considered not acceptable as he had been a Catholic.

Another important published collection associated with Leipzig is the *Vier und zwantzig Neue Quatricinia* by Gottfried Reiche. Reiche's dedication is a testimonial to the importance of these civic wind players.

> Nothing in all art can claim finer qualities than Noble Music. My pen is much too weak either to repeat here, or to say better what professional and highly-learned men have affirmed so competently. As this matchless art spreads its charms in many ways, we find in most cities the praise-worthy custom of having the so-called Abblasen sounded from churches and town halls. This is always a sign of joy and peace; because,

[17] Quoted in Don Smithers, *The Music and History of the Baroque Trumpet* (London: Dent), 121ff.

[18] *Bicinia variorum instrumentorum, ut a Violinis, Cornettis, Flautis, Clarinis et Fagottis com apprendice a 2 Bombardinis vulgo Schalmeyen* (Leipzig, 1675).

wherever such music must be discontinued there must be national mourning, war, or other misfortune.

Regarding Reiche's final sentence, Kuhnau once observed, "Nobody will pray more devoutly for the long life of his sovereign than the instrumentalists!" And one measure of Reiche's reputation can be seen in the fact that during the year-long period of mourning in 1694, when musical performances were not permitted, the city council voted a special monetary "Gratifikation" to Reiche to make sure he was not tempted to leave town.[19]

The continuation of the introduction to Reiche's *Neue Quatricinia* also mentions some five-part sonatas which are lost. The implication of his remarks is that the art of publishing in Leipzig did not permit these particular works to be set in type. One can only presume that they must have contained more ligatures, that is faster note values than his previous work. For those interested in early wind repertoire, it is in any case a great loss.

> In my own small way, I am also willing, for the honor of God and the useful pleasure of my fellow men, to publish some five-part pieces. I have already written 40 five-part Sonatas for the musicians here in Leipzig, with whom I have now been associated for 8 years, but because of the difficulties their appearance presents to the technique of printing, I have had to put them aside. I have taken care with the [present] Quatricinia to make them easy on the eyes and to write something using slower notes. One more thing must be understood: the Alle breve is performed with a fast moving beat. Although this reminder is not for the musically enlightened, it is added for the benefit of those who know less about the art.[20]

His estate, following his death in 1734, listed five books of chorales for the tower musicians which are also lost.

Reiche was the senior Stadtpfeifer in Leipzig at the time of Bach and, judging by Mattheson's *Ehren-Pforte* (1740), was better known than Bach. Mattheson adds that you can see in an engraving of Reiche that "he resembles an honest man as closely as one drop of water does another." He died

[19] Smithers, *The Music and History of the Baroque Trumpet*, 126ff.

[20] The original German text is given in Mary Rasmussen, "Gottfried Reiche..." *Brass Quarterly* (1960), IV, I, 10, fn. 30.

in service, after a parade honoring a visit by the elector of Saxony in 1734 (an occasion for which Bach contributed his "Preise dein Glück, gesegnetes Sachsen"). One present wrote,

> On October 6th the skilled and experienced musician and Stadtpfeifer, Gottfried Reiche, ... and senior member of the local musician's guild, suffered a stroke not far from his lodging in the Stadtpfeifer- gasschen, as he was on his way home, so that he collapsed and was brought dead into the house. And this is said to have occurred because on the previous day he had been greatly fatigued by playing in the royal music and had suffered severely from the smoke of the torches.[21]

Several additional collections of German Stadtpfeifer music which survive are by Daniel Speer, who served during the late seventeenth century in Breslau. Speer, who was also highly educated, has left an education treatise, *Musicalisches Kleeblatt*, which contains ensemble music with his own comments on instrumental technique. In this work, for example, he finds five indispensable qualities for good trumpet playing: good health, good breath control, a fast moving tongue, willingness for constant practice and good, long trills made with the chin. He discusses the embouchure in detail, concluding with,

> Above all, an incipient shall accustom himself to draw in his cheeks, not blow them out, for this is not only unseemly, but hinders the breath from having its due outlet and causes a man pains at the temples, so that true teachers are accustomed to box the ears of their pupils to cure them of this bad habit.

Speer is perhaps better known for another collection, his *Neugebachene Taffel-Schnitz* (1685), which must be translated as meaning something like "newly baked table goodies" and contains seven sonatas for wind band. Another publication, *Musicalisch-Türckischer Eulen-Spiegel* (1688) contains six five-part sonatas for wind band and is dedicated to several civic wind band musicians:

> To those well-honored and highly regarded ones who so well practice and perform the noble free art of music; Herr Johann

[21] Quoted in G. Wustmann, *Quellen zur Geschichte Leipzig* (Leipzig), I, 436.

Gotthard Heinrich Strenz, well-deserving instrumentalist of the Holy Romas Imperial city of Heilbronn; and Herr Georg Gottfried Blinzing, commissioned city musician at the princely Württemberg capital city, Tübingen; his especially highly honored, worth and well-loved gentlemen and friends.[22]

Two additional published collections of civic wind band music appear to be lost, a collection of dance movements, *Joco-seria* (after 1688) and another *Klee-Blatt* volume published after 1697.

In addition to the tower music, the Stadpfeifer bands also performed evening "concerts," which are also usually associated with the city hall. They performed for a wide variety of other civic occasions, including official civic banquets, for university functions, public and trade guild celebrations and even for courts which did not maintain their own musicians. As is more generally known, they also performed in church when needed and participated in the performances of the collegium musica. It appears that through their guilds they continued their entitlement to be the "first call" musicians for private weddings. Indeed, one guild ordinance in Zeitz allowed a bride and groom to bring in outside musicians only after they had "come to terms" with the local Stadtpfeifers.[23]

The music guilds of Baroque Germany are worthy of much more study. They may have begun to represent a wide number of players, as do the "band associations" of Germany today. According to Ehmann,[24] for example, the guild in Strassburg consisted of 751 members. We have the regulations for one of the guilds, the *Confrerie des Joueurs d'Instruments d'Alsace*, for 1606,[25] which helps give us a sense of what these civic music guilds were like, as well as their values. We have to explain that the use of "king" for the player who served as the leader of the guild only refers to the fact that they followed the only social structure they knew, the monarchy.

1. No wind player, string player or other musician may play by day or night, in the street or in a house for dances or dinners, nor may he receive money or gifts, unless he

---

[22] Quoted in Mitchel Sirman, *The Wind Sonatas in Daniel Speer's Musicalisch-Türkischer Eulen-Spiegel* (Unpublished dissertation, University of Wisconsin, 1972), 32.

[23] Werner, *Zeitz*.

[24] Ehmann, *Tibilustrium*, 28.

[25] M. B. Bernhard, "Notice sur la Confrerie des Joueurs d'Instruments d'Alsace," in *La Revue historique de la Noblesse* (Paris, 1844), 8ff.

is first admitted to the fraternity of musicians of Alsace, under the penalty of confiscation of his instrument; the same is true for minstrels ...

2. Each new member must swear to be obedient to the king and the brotherhood statutes.

3. Each member when in uniform must wear a silver medal showing the Queen Mother of God.

4. Upon entering the fraternity he must show his birth certificate and have a signed authorization by the noble of the area he comes from.

5. To be admitted a player in the city, a minstrel must have served two years apprenticeship.

6. The right to join as an apprentice, or to resign an apprenticeship, costs 12 Strasbourg *schellings*.

7. To become a fraternity member, or to resign, costs two *ecus d'Empire*.

8. All the members will assist with the annual musicians day festival (*Pfeiffertag*) and are exempt from annual taxes.

9. On the day of this celebration, the entire fraternity must meet at the church, then to the castle to give homage to the noble. Each of them has to take part in the fraternity meal and take his turn at the dance which the king will have arranged with the host. The king is exempt from [playing the dance] along with two colleagues; the four masters, or jurists, do only half.

10. If a member, through illness or by order of the noble, can not take part in this festival, he must justify it with good evidence and send his annual tax.

11. Each member has to pay to the sergeant who announces him.

12. Each year, at the time of this festival, the members must renew their certification that they are on the roles of the fraternity. Without this certificate they are prevented from playing their instruments ...

13. If a member leaves the fraternity and wishes to return he must pay one *ecu d'Empire*.

14. Upon the death of a member, his best musical instrument and his medal belong to the king of the fraternity.

15. A member does not have to have apprentices.

16. None will play instruments at dinners, dances, festivals day or night, indoor or out without being contracted through the fraternity.

17. If someone makes a contract with a musician after he has made a contract with a first one, the former does not have to play unless the latter receives a salary equal as if he had played.

18. No musician has to play with a musician who is not a member of the fraternity.

19. One does not play instruments for the wedding of a Jew who has not paid a golden *guilden*, which must be given to the king.

20. All difficulties relative to the profession, contracts contrary to the statutes and injuries between members, etc., are settled by a tribunal of the fraternity and the king.

21. On the day of the annual festival no player has to play elsewhere than the place of the festival.

22. All infractions of the statutes are judged by the king or in combination with a tribunal of the fraternity. Fines, according to the nature of the infraction, will be paid in money which goes to the chapelle de Notre-Dame...

23. A member can appeal the judgment of the king or the tribunal to the court.

24. This fraternity having been founded in the glory of God and in particular in honor of his very saintly mother, each member must annually say a Mass, and not just to help with the annual festival, to help honor all the festivities of Notre-Dame...

25. The Noble reserves the right to change these ordinances according to the needs of the time.

In terms of the future development of music, perhaps the most important civic institutions were the *collegium musica*, meetings of students and local musicians who met, sometimes in coffee houses, for the performance and enjoyment of music. The Leipzig collegium musicum had existed periodically during the seventeenth century but became more influential after 1702 when it was reorganized by Telemann. Under Telemann the group began to meet on a regular weekly basis and gave concerts for the citizens.

Bach began to become involved with the Leipzig collegium musicum after 1729, when he seems to have become more interested in secular music in general and a number of his secular cantatas and instrumental works appear to have been composed for these performances. There is extant an announcement for his public concerts in 1736 which includes several interesting details.

> Both the public musical Concerts or Assemblies that are held here weekly are still flourishing steadily. The one is conduced by Mr. Johann Sebastian Bach, Kapellmeister to the Court of Weissenfels and Music Director at the Thomas-Kirche and Nicolai-Kirche in this city, and is held, except during the Fair, once a week in Zimmerman's coffeehouse in the Cather-strasse, on Friday evenings from 8 to 10 o'clock ...
>
> The participants in these musical concerts are chiefly students here, and there are always good musicians among them, so that sometimes they become, as is known, famous virtuosos. Any musician is permitted to make himself publicly heard at these musical concerts, and most often, too, there are such listeners as know how to judge the qualities of an able musician.[26]

[26] Quoted in Hans T. David and Arthur Mendel, *The Bach Reader,* 149.

A collegium musicum was also active in Hamburg beginning in 1660 and its emphasis was in giving concerts of new works composed in other major cities. The group, composed of local professional and amateur musicians, became widely known and after his arrival in 1721, Telemann became associated with its concerts. Expanding the scope of their repertoire, Telemann began repeating performances of works he had composed for the local church. This brought an immediate complaint from the town council.

> Because the current Kantor Telemann has thought to perform for money his music in a public inn where all manner of disorder is possible; and moreover he makes free to perform operas, comedies, and similar entertainments likely to arouse bawdiness ... and all without the consent of this most excellent Council and Citizenry; so the Oberalten of the Council seek a decree that for such music the Kantor shall be most earnestly disciplined and forbidden further such performances.[27]

[27] Quoted in J. Sittard, *Geschichte des Musik- und Concertwesens in Hamburg* (Altona and Leipzig, 1890), 61.

In 1678 Hamburg also had the distinction of becoming the first German city to build a public opera house. It had seating for two thousand and its more than ninety performances a year was the beginning of repertory opera in the modern sense. Although some nobles were enthusiastic over Italian opera, the climate after the period of war left many people more inclined toward religious music. It was in this context that Rector Biedermann of the Freyberg Gymnasium expressed his extreme disapproval of virtually any form of music in his school's curriculum following a performance by the students of a *Singspiel* in 1748.[28] In any case, opera was slower in developing in Germany and one must assume that this explains, at least in part, why so gifted a native composer as Reinhard Keiser (1673–1739) never received the credit he deserved.

With the arrival of Telemann in Hamburg in 1721, public concerts became a vital part of civic life. In a letter to a friend, he is enthusiastic to find strong support for concerts among the leaders of the city.

> A great advantage is added to this by the fact that, besides the presence of many persons of rank here, also the most prominent men of the city—including the entire city council—do not absent themselves from public concerts. Likewise the reasoned judgment of so many connoisseurs and intelligent people give opportunity for concerts.[29]

We imagine that such works as his concerti for Hautboisten must have been written for concerts at this time, combining as they do a direct galant style and programmatic references to Hamburg geographical features which would be familiar to that public. By the early eighteenth century there were public concerts with the public buying tickets.

During the late years of the seventeenth century another town famous for its public concerts was Lübeck. Its *Abendmusiken*, given in the Marienkirche, were even advertised by the city fathers for the purpose of attracting visitors.

In Leipzig soon after the beginning of the eighteenth century local publishers began to print music expressly intended for amateur performance by the middle class.

[28] Beekman Cannon, *Johann Mattheson, Spectator in Music* (Archon Books, 1968), 96. Mattheson's book of 1750, *Matthesons bewahrte Panacea...*, was written in response and presents his reasons why music should be part of the curriculum of every school.

[29] H. Grosse and H. R. Jung, ed., *Georg Philipp Telemann Briefwechsel* (Leipzig, 1972), 213.

The growing appeal of this market was not lost on Bach, whose first *Clavier-Übung* of dance music admits in its title, "Composed for Music Lovers, to Refresh Their Spirits."

In his autobiography, submitted for Mattheson's *Ehrenpforte* in 1740, Telemann provides a rare first-hand account of peasant music.

> In Pless, a dominion of the Court of Promnitz in upper Silesia, where the Court used to repair for six months, as well as in Cracow, I became familiar with Polish and Hanakian music in their true, barbaric beauty. In the public taverns the band would consist of a fiddle strapped to the body, a Polish bagpipe, a bass trombone and a regal. The fiddle was tuned a third higher than usual, and could thus outscream any six ordinary violins. At places of better repute the regal was omitted, but the number of fiddles and bagpipes was augmented. Indeed, once I found thirty-six bagpipes and eight fiddles together. One can hardly believe with what inspiration bagpipers and fiddlers improvise while the dancers rest. An observant person could pick up enough ideas from them in a week to last a lifetime. In short, this music contains much valuable material, if it is properly treated.[30]

By the end of the Baroque there must have been much musical activity among the upper middle-class merchants in Germany, although this topic, with the exception of the Fugger family of Munich, has received little scholarly interest to date. The reader will recall that the great Giovanni Gabrieli of Venice had dedicated his *Concerti* of 1587 to Jakob Fugger.

[30] Quoted in Sam Morgenstern, *Composers on Music* (New York: Pantheon, 1956), 40.

14
On Church Music in Baroque Germany

CHURCH MUSIC IN GERMANY during the Baroque suffered greatly from the Thirty Years' War (1618–1648). This epic battle between the Protestants and Catholics not only was very destructive of the church buildings themselves, but, of course, drained the various states of available funds. There was very little left to support professional musicians who formerly made their career in the church. It is hard to imagine Heinrich Schütz having to write this plea in 1652 to the secretary of the Elector of Saxony on behalf of a court chapel singer.

> But now I can no longer conceal from you that the bass singer who some time ago had to pawn his clothes again, and ever since has been living at his house like a wild beast of the woods, has informed me through his wife that he now must and wishes to leave us.[1]

After thirty years of war it then took a number of years for the necessary economic recovery which would make possible renewed spending on large-scale musical productions. Thus even by 1661, Schütz cannot yet see any improvement in the city where he has been employed, as he writes the elector:

> In conclusion, so far as I am personally concerned, I must protest that, after promising practically everything but the blood from my veins, actually advancing a part of my means to suffering musicians, it will be altogether impossible for

[1] Letter to Christian Reichbrodt, May 28, 1652, quoted in Gertrude Norman and Miriam Shrifte, *Letters of Composers* (New York: Knopf, 1946), 14ff.

me to continue here in Dresden any longer. With regard to this place I am not merely announcing but stating positively that I would prefer death to living under such harassing conditions.[2]

And let us not fail to contemplate on the loss to musical literature the war caused in the case of this one single man, one of the most talented composers of the seventeenth century. What great church concerti this man, a student of Gabrieli, might have composed!

Early seventeenth century accounts of church music in Germany also reflect the generally unstable climate caused by the Thirty Years' War. One cantor in Dresden complains in 1619, that as a result of the daily assemblies, of drinking bouts, and of serenades, the voices were ruined, and that they changed before their time; that there were actually few good voices at hand; that the pupils spent too much time drinking toasts, and that the choir rehearsal times were often otherwise occupied.[3]

Surviving music, together with extant documents, suggest a close association between the Stadtpfeifers and the churches of Germany. In the case of smaller towns, who might not be able to afford their own regular Stadtpfeifers, the civic wind bands of other towns were imported for important church festivities. Thus the Kantor in Walkheim brought in the Stadtpfeifers from Rochlitz in 1603 and the Kunstpfeifers from Liebenwerda helped out in Finsterwalde in 1612.[4] It is only in the context of this ancient association between town and church that one can understand the somewhat amusing sentence in Bach's certificate of appointment in Mühlhausen, in 1707, which requires him to "defend our common city from all harm."[5]

For most of the seventeenth century, "Stadtpfeifer" meant mostly wind instruments.[6] Of course, the Stadtpfeifer already had their repertoire for "Instrumentalkonzert," some of which was suitable for performance during Communion in the Protestant Church or for the Offertory in the Catholic Church.[7] They were used sometimes to help singers hold their pitch,[8] or in the case of a Rothenburg o.T. document,

[2] Quoted in Hans Moser, *Heinrich Schütz* (St. Louis: Concordia, 1936), 209.

[3] Ibid., 156.

[4] Arno Werner, *Vier Jahrhunderte im Dienste der Kirchenmusik* (Leipzig: Merseburger), 219.

[5] Quoted in Hans T. David and Arthur Mendel, *The Bach Reader* (New York: Norton, 1966), 55.

[6] Werner, *Vier Jahrhunderte im Dienste der Kirchenmusik,* 220, says *only* wind instruments, as the strings were still considered amateur [burger] instruments. An exception was the court Kapelle in Dresden, which had violins during the seventeenth century, according to George J. Buelow, "Dresden in the Age of Absolutism," in *The Late Baroque Era* (Englewood Cliffs: Prentice Hall, 1994), 217.

[7] Arnold Schering, "Einleitung," *Denkmaler Deutscher Tonkunst* (Wiesbaden, 1958), XXIX–XXX, ix. Actually, original compositions for winds for Communion and Offertory exist in great numbers through the nineteenth century.

[8] Josef Sittard, *Zur Geschichte der Musik . . . am Wurttembergischen hofe* (Stuttgart, 1890), I, 302,
   . . . *und von den Instrumentisten zu [bessern] erhaltung des Toni, mit Zincken und Posannen ihr Assistenz darbei gelaistet werden.*

just to help the rehearsal process.

> The Stadtpfeifer should appear with their instruments as early as Vesper prayer time, on Sundays and Festival days, but also during the week as the Kantor requires, to help rehearse the music to be used the following Sunday.[9]

Beginning about 1620 one finds even stronger co-operation between the civic Stadtpfeifers and the Church. One reads of four Stadtpfeifers engaged in the cathedral in Madeburg in 1619 and a statement from the cathedral in Naumburg in 1626 mentions the service by the Stadtpfeifers, with their instruments, on fourteen Feast days.[10] Even in such small villages as Falkenhain, Mügeln and Thallwitz one finds Stadtpfeifers playing for the same Feast days.[11]

In the Protestant churches they made possible performances of the polychoral concerti of the Italian tradition, as described by Mattheson.

> There one uses works with three or four choirs, distributed in general as follows: In one choir very good trumpets and timpani are heard; one part of timpani for six trumpets and two pair for twelve trumpets. In another choir are trombones, cornetts and other wind instruments. In a third choir are singers, of an accompanied nature called Capella ... A fourth choir, yet again singers, is the main choir ... all will be conducted by the director.[12]

On occasions of special celebration rich instrumental resources were employed, as we read, for example, in an account of the celebration of the Centennial of the Reformation in 1617. The eyewitness reports an interlude performed by five choirs of trumpets, in addition to works with voices and trumpets.

> The musicians of the elector of Saxony, our Gracious Lord, performed this music: eleven instrumental players, eleven singers, four organists, four lutanists, one theorbo player, three organ choir boys, five discant singers, alternating with various kinds of magnificent instruments, also with two organs, two regals, three clavicymbals, and in addition eighteen trumpeters and two timpani, all presented with appropriate solemnity under the direction of Heinrich Schütz from Weissenfels.[13]

[9] Quoted in Wilhelm Ehmann, *Tibilustrium* (Kassel, 1950), 41.

[10] Werner, *Vier Jahrhunderte im Dienste der Kirchenmusik*, 219.

[11] Ibid.

[12] Quoted in Arnold Schering, *Musikgeschichte Leipzigs* (Leipzig, 1941), xx. Marpurg, in *Kritische Briefe uber die Tonkunst* (1760), I, 17, gives a similar description of a large concerto for voices and winds he heard in a dream.

[13] Matthias Hoe von Hoenegg, "Parasceve ad solemnitatem evangelicam" [1617], quoted in Carol MacClintock, *Readings in the History of Music in Performance* (Bloomington: Indiana University Press, 1979), 139.

Not only were a broad variety of instruments available for use in the Protestant Church, but the choir conductor had broad freedom with regard to substitution, as suggested in a note in the collection, *Geistliche Harmonien* by Johann Horn (c. 1630–1685).

> If shawms are not available use flutes, and if there are no trumpets use cornetti, etc., letting the musical director make the most agreeable arrangements.

Another festival, the Naumburg Princes' Day, celebrated in the spring of 1614, included a total of some ninety musicians brought by various nobles. One highpoint was a performance in the church, conducted by Michael Praetorius. He had placed one ensemble in the organ loft, another in the nave, a third by the baptismal and a boy's choir in the choir of the church. The cantor, we are told, was moved to tears.[14]

When the Thirty Years' War concluded with the Peace of 1648, one finds very strong co-operation throughout Germany between churches and the Stadtpfeifers.[15] Now even in the Reform Church winds appear in the service under pressure of public demand, although this service varied from town to town, especially in South German churches. There, for example, one finds Stadtpfeifers were "obligat" in Friedberg, but completely missing in Alsfeld.[16]

To the North, one finds the Stadtpfeifers of Köln a. d. Spree in 1657 playing "Psalmlieder" and other works in the cathedral in Berlin[17] and in Dresden a civic contract for 1675 requires the Stadtpfeifers to perform for a half-hour before the bells are rung on the three High Feast days, to perform the church music in the Sophienkirche and Frauenkirche whenever the superintendent was preaching, and to play once every six weeks in the church at Neustadt.[18] An interesting reference from Hamburg in 1650, describing a Service of Thanksgiving for the peace, gives the instrumentation of the civic band heard in the church as trombones, cornets and dulcians.[19] So rich were the possibilities for accompanied church music because of the availability of the Stadtpfeifers, that when some choir director preferred *a cappella* music he was sometimes fired, as was the case in Wittenberg in 1628.[20]

[14] Moser, *Heinrich Schütz*, 76.

[15] Werner, *Vier Jahrhunderte im Dienste der Kirchenmusik*, 219.

[16] Ibid.

[17] Curt Sachs, *Musik und Oper am Kurbrandenburgischen Hof* (Berlin, 1910), 73.

[18] Grove, *Dictionary of Music* (1980), V, 615.

[19] Liselotte Kruger, *Die Hamburgische Musikorganisation im XVII Jahrhundert* (Leipzig, 1933), 57.

[20] Arno Werner, *Stadtische und fürstliche Musikpflege in Weissenfels* (Leipzig, 1911), 219.

Because the Stadtpfeifers were often required to participate in church by contract, the church was sometimes in a position to involve itself in the affairs of the Stadtpfeifers. In Zeitz, for example, the church had a voice in the audition process for new Stadtpfeifers and in this same town the church was able to prevent the Stadtpfeifers from playing weddings and other outside jobs on Sunday.[21]

Also, since in many cases the instruments the Stadtpfeifers used belonged to the city, there must have been some fear of conflict, for there are numerous extant documents relating to churches purchasing their own instrument collections for the Stadtpfeifers to use. For example, the church music director in Schweinfurt, in 1606, acquired "two new cornets, two trombones, two pair of crumhorns, two *Zezstuck* and two cornets."[22] The St. Wenzel Church in Naumburg in 1657 owned no fewer than sixty instruments, including a consort of eight crumhorns, trumpets, trombones, a consort of Schreyerpfeife and dulcans.[23] Church records in Zeitz mention the possession of shawms until 1689 and the purchase of the new French oboe in 1691.[24] The private chapels in private courts also were collecting instruments, as we see in an inventory of the Württemberg court chapel in 1636 which listed "two Venetian cornets, a quart-trombone, another trombone and three cornets."[25]

Strings rarely appear in the church collections until the beginning of the eighteenth century. One can see the date of arrival of the violin in the St. Thomas Church collection in Leipzig in an inventory which reads,

1 large violin
1 large spinet
1 large Bombard and 4 smaller ones
1 Quart-fagott
6 trumpets and a small one in Eb
3 old trombones (alto, tenor and bass)
2 "new" violins, purchased in 1701.[26]

At about this time Telemann became Kapellmeister of the court at Eisenach and reports that he was ordered to hire singers who could double as violinists.[27] An interesting

[21] Arno Werner, *Stadtische und fürstliche Musikpflege in Zeitz* (Buckeburg, 1922), 40, 43.

[22] Ehmann, *Tibilustrium*, 42.

[23] Arno Werner, "Die alte Musikbibliothek und die Instrumentsammlung an St. Wenzel in Naumberg a. d. S.," in *Archiv fur Musikwissenschaft* (1926), VIII, 390ff.
[24] Werner, *Stadtische und fürstliche Musikpflege in Weissenfels*, 95.

[25] Sittard, *Zur Geschichte der Musik ... am Wurttembergischen hofe*, I, 340.

[26] Arnold Schering, *Musikgeschichte Leipzigs* (Leipzig, 1926), II, 114.

[27] Telemann's autobiography in Mattheson, *Ehrenpforte* (1740), quoted in Sam Morgenstern, *Composers on Music* (New York: Pantheon, 1956), 41.

manuscript, c. 1745, by Johann Schneider require the oboists and hornists to put down their instrument in two movements and play violin.[28] A similar practice can be documented in Salzburg, according to an observation by Marpurg,

> The oboe and the transverse flute are heard rarely, but the waldhorn is never heard in the cathedral. All these gentlemen, therefore, join in playing the violins in the church.[29]

During the Baroque one also finds records indicating that the wind bands belonging to the aristocracy were also required to appear in their private chapels. An order of 1621, for example, by the Württemberg court of Duke Johann Friedrich (1608–1628), requires the trombone and cornett players to appear without fail for the choir rehearsals during the week.[30] It was in these private chapels, in particular, that one heard the aristocratic trumpet choirs joining in church music. This represented a problem for the choir director, for these trumpets usually did not read music and only performed memorized pieces. But since they played natural instruments, consisting of only a triad in a single key, so long as the choir director had a work in the same key, the trumpets could join in with little damage.[31] Another solution was to add them at the end of a composition, such was the case with the *Psalm 136* of Schütz. At the end of the Bass part of this composition, Schütz has written "*Darauff wird stracks eine Intrada zum Final geblasen,*" as a cue for just such a performance. Yet another possibility can be seen in the case of a Te Deum sung in 1604 in Mainz in which one heard alternating verses played by the civic cornets and trombones and the aristocratic trumpets and timpani.[32]

Monasteries also used instruments with their choirs. There is an interesting document dated c. 1720 from the Göttweig Abbey in Austria relative to the negotiations of purchasing either a Hautbois, *Chalimou* or flute consort from the maker Jacob Denner.[33] In this document the instrument maker, Denner, offers the Abbey three possible consorts, of oboe, clarinets and flutes. The bass instrument in each case is called "bassoon," but this seems to mean here only "bass

[28] Schering, *Musikgeschichte Leipzigs,* 100.

[29] Don Smithers, *The Music and History of the Baroque Trumpet* (London: Dent), 181.

[30] J. Sittard, *Geschichte des Musik- und Concertwesens in Hamburg* (Altona and Leipzig, 1890), I, 45.

[31] Praetorius discusses this performance problem at length in his *Syntagma Musicum,* III.

[32] Adam Gottron, *Mainzer Musikgeschichte* (Mainz, 1959), 43.

[33] Horace Fitzpatrick, "Jacob Denner's Woodwinds for Göttweig Abbey," *The Galpin Society Journal* 21 (Mar. 1968), 81ff.

instrument," as a different price is given under each consort. In fact, the scholar Fitzpatrick writes that in the case of the clarinet consort the reference is "unequivocally a bass clarinet ... fifty years before the bass clarinet is thought to have been invented." He also adds that the term "Chalimou" is found for another thirty years in Austrian church bands.[34]

[34] Ibid., XXI, 81ff.

Denner's document reads,

1 Chor Hautbois miet 6 Stimmen alle von buxbaum
3 Primieur Hautbois a 5 fl.	15 fl
1 Taille	9 fl
2 Basson, a 22	44 fl

1 Chor Chalimou mit 6 Stimmen
3 Primieur Chalimou, a 3 fl	9 fl
1 Second Chalimou	7 fl
2 Basson, a 18	36 fl

1 Chor Flauden mit 6 Stimmen
3 Primieur Flauden, a ex 3 fl	9 fl
1 Second Flauden	6 fl
2 Basson, a 15 fl	30 fl
Zu diesen noch 1 Flaud d'Almanq	45 fl

Another document, from the monastery at Melk, deals with the purchase of two English horns and a bassoon in 1748.[35] One document from this monastery describes the performance of an ensemble of four players during the ritual of "Bleeding" [*Phlebotomia*], a health measure practiced twice a year and attended by the public![36] A document for this ceremony in September, 1723 reads,

[35] Robert Freeman, *The Practice of Music at Melk Monastery in the Eighteenth Century* (Dissertation, UCLA, 1971), 103.

[36] Ibid., 151.

> Only *eine kleine music* [the wind band] by some three or at most four persons or instruments is allowed during the afternoons as well as evenings on the first and second days. The other musicians are not to appear either in the cloister or at the table. On the third day, however, *plenior Musica* may be permitted.[37]

[37] See Ehmann, *Tibilustrium*, 38, and Freeman, Ibid., 135, 151.

Freeman also documents an appearance by a wind band made up of students at the monastery, together with the monastery's trumpets and timpani, which performed in a welcome ceremony in 1743 for Maria Theresa.[38]

[38] Freeman, Ibid., 206.

There were some anomalies within this rich practice. One was Hamburg, where toward the end of the seventeenth century the combined effects of a decline in the Stadtpfeifers [*Ratmusikanten*], together with the popularity of opera, resulted in a decline in interest in church music. Local preachers took the opportunity to attack the cantata as being too much like opera, an influence they declared to be unchristian and the work of the Devil.[39] It was also in Hamburg that an incompetent organist obtained a post in competition with Bach, by bribing the audition committee.

> I remember, as will still a large number of parishioners, that some years ago a certain great virtuoso [Bach], whose merits have since earned him an important cantorate [in Leipzig], presented himself as an organist in a town of no small size [Hamburg], performed on many of the finest organs, and aroused the admiration of everyone for his mastery. But there also appeared among other incompetent journeymen, the son of a wealthy artisan [named Heitmann], who could execute preludes better with thalers than with his fingers. It was he (as might easily be guessed), who gained the post, although almost everyone was angered by it.[40]

Another anomaly was the Imperial court in Vienna, which continued to favor the performance of works in the sixteenth century polyphonic style, although music of other styles was also used. This conservative and old-fashioned attitude continued quite late due to the influence of Johann Fux (1660–1741), who was also probably the last person to use the cornett in a German-speaking church. Fux, clearly, was not a man to embrace new ideas. When Mattheson wrote him for biographical details for his book on German musicians, Fux responded, "Suffice it to say that I was considered worthy to be the first Kapellmeister to Charles VI."

A difficult question is why there would be any desire in Vienna at this time to hear music in the old Palestrina style. Vienna was otherwise so influenced by Italian humanists, who had long since argued against polyphonic music. The answer probably lies in the fact that Vienna was a thoroughly Catholic city and because the most influential composers in residence were Italian.

---

[39] George J. Buelow, "Hamburg and Lübeck," in *The Late Baroque Era* (Englewood Cliffs: Prentice Hall, 1994), 201. In the early years of the eighteenth century, there were also disputes at Halle University over the use of music in the church. See Bernd Baselt, "Brandenburg-Prussia and the Central German Courts," in *The Late Baroque Era* (Englewood Cliffs: Prentice Hall, 1994), 238.

[40] Johann Mattheson, *Der musicalische Patriot*, 316.

Among the more progressive composers one finds rather outspoken criticism of the old Renaissance church polyphony. Heinichen finds the Church the appropriate locale for counterpoint and, although he admits it has a value for students and that he was an "ardent champion of it" in his own youth, he nevertheless seems cool to its musical potential.[41] German church music, he says, "tolerates neither too much fire, inspiration, nor gay ideas." In his warning to composers in overusing counterpoint, he reveals a general hostility to the old polyphonic style in a series of specific criticisms. Most counterpoint, he finds, is based on the "lifeless manipulation of notes but not on the actual sound," thus "the more one sinks into the excesses of such stereotyped artifices, the more one necessarily must depart from the Ear." The excessive use of counterpoint, he says, "is the shortest path to musical pedantry, ruining many fine talents that otherwise could have been developed into something worthy." Furthermore, he finds writing counterpoint laborious, on the order of a farmer loading manure onto wheelbarrows! From such study, one can make a dull contrapuntist out of any dumb boy, but one cannot make a composer with good taste.

Another who criticized the polyphony style was Johann Mattheson, who, in quoting the text to Bach's *Cantata* Nr. 21, provides a witty demonstration of the nonsense of this style.

> I, I, I, I had much grief, I had much grief, in my heart, in my heart. I had much grief, etc., in my heart, etc., etc., I had much grief, etc., in my heart, etc., I had much grief, etc., in my heart etc., etc., etc., etc., etc. I had much grief, etc., in my heart, etc., etc.[42]

During the seventeenth century there were some German composers who found it much more difficult to break with the past. The gifted composer, Samuel Scheidt, at one point confessed that he heard nothing which surpassed the old style.

> I am astonished at the foolish music written in these times. It is false and wrong and no longer does anyone pay attention to what our beloved old masters wrote about composition. It

[41] Johann David Heinichen, *General-Bass Treatise* [1711], quoted in George Buelow, *Thorough-Bass Accompaniment according to Johann David Heinichen* (Ann Arbor: UMI Research Press, 1986), 28off. Heinichen (1683-1729) was a prolific composer in Dresden, but is known today only because of this important treatise which deals on many aspects of performance practice.

[42] Quoted in David and Mendel, *The Bach Reader*, 299.

certainly must be a remarkably elevated art when a pile of consonances are thrown together any which way.

I remain faithful to the pure old composition and pure rules. I have often walked out of the church since I could no longer listen to that mountain yodeling. I hope this worthless modern coinage will fall into disuse and that new coins will be forged according to the fine old stamp and standard.[43]

As a matter of fact, Scheidt, in his arrangements for his own funeral, requested his former student, Christoph Bernhard of Hamburg, to compose a funeral motet in the style of Palestrina.[44]

Scheidt's own principal concern, relative to church music, seems to have been in the realm of performance. In a letter describing the church music in Halle, in 1630, where he was director of music, he observes,

> ... unlike the Chapel's [choir] now, whose voices are as the lowing of bullocks, sheep, and calves, their gullets filled with plums besides, so that neither [words nor music] can be understood; yea, they sing so flat that one would rather stop one's ears and flee from the church.[45]

One practice which both progressive and conservative observers could join in opposing was the introduction of popular music into the church service. Martin Geier, in his funeral sermon for Schütz, warned,

> If you will forgive me, gentlemen of the music profession, there now prevails in the church an altogether new kind of song, but one that is prolix, abrupt, fragmentary, dancelike, and not at all reverential. It is better suited to the theater and the dance hall than to the church. In seeking Art, we are losing time-honored devotion to prayer and song.[46]

Another who complained of the influence of the theater was Christian Gerber, who wrote in 1732,

> Although a moderate kind of music may remain in the church, especially since the late Dr. Dannhauer considers it an ornament of divine service (although all theologians do not agree on this point), yet it is well known that excesses often occur, and one might well say with Moses: "Ye take too much upon

[43] Letter to Heinrich Baryphonus, January 26, 1651, quoted in Gertrude Norman and Miriam Shrifte, *Letters of Composers* (New York, Knopf, 1946), 17.

[44] Moser, *Heinrich Schütz*, 221.

[45] Samuel Scheidt, letter to Rector Christian Gueinzius, April 2, 1630, quoted in Piero Weiss, *Letters of Composers Through Six Centuries* (Philadelphia: Chilton, 1967), 40ff.

[46] Moser, *Heinrich Schütz*, 702.

you, ye sons of Levi."[47] For it often sounds so secular and gay, that such music better suits a dance floor or an opera than a divine service. Least suitable of all is it, in the opinion of many pious souls, to the Passion, when the latter is sung.

Fifty and more years ago it was the custom for the organ to remain silent in church on Palm Sunday, and on that day, because it was the beginning of Holy Week, there was no music. But gradually the Passion story, which had formerly been sung in simple plain chant, humbly and reverently, began to be sung with many kinds of instruments in the most elaborate fashion, occasionally mixing in a little setting of a Passion Chorale which the whole congregation joined in singing, and then the mass of instruments fell to again. When in a large town this Passion music was done for the first time, with twelve violins, many oboes, bassoons, and other instruments, many people were astonished and did not know what to make of it. In the pew of a noble family in church, many Ministers and Noble Ladies were present, who sang the first Passion Chorale out of their books with great devotion. But when this theatrical music began, all these people were thrown into the greatest bewilderment, looked at each other, and said: "What will come of this?" An old widow of the nobility said: "God save us, my children! It's just as if one were at an Opera Comedy." But everyone was genuinely displeased by it and voiced just complaints against it. There are, it is true, some people who take pleasure in such idle things, especially if they are of sanguine temperament and inclined to sensual pleasure.[48]

In a letter to the Leipzig town council after his appointment, Bach promised to write music of such a nature,

> that it shall not last too long, and shall be of such a nature as not to make an operatic impression, but rather incite the listeners to devotion.[49]

[47] Numbers 16:7.

[48] Quoted in David and Mendel, *The Bach Reader*, 442, 229ff.

[49] Johann Sebastian Bach, letter to the Leipzig town council, May 5, 1723, quoted in Weiss, *Letters of Composers*, 65.

15
On Military Music in Baroque Germany

DURING THE SEVENTEENTH CENTURY, before the introduction of the new Hautboisten, the movements of the German armies were controlled by the powerful trumpet guilds. These guilds were sufficiently independent that even when serving the army the trumpeters were subject to guild discipline rather than military codes.[1] Indeed, existing under imperial "privileges," the trumpeters expected a level of respect above that of the ordinary soldier, as Altenburg maintains.

> No colonel, cavalry captain, or commanding officer shall willfully treat a trumpeter or military timpanist badly, as was in vogue for some time. [He shall not] shame him, despise or prescribe menial labor for him without good cause, nor throw him out of the service without pay, but rather, as in the custom of old, treat him like an honorable officer.[2]

Altenburg also points out that the trumpeter was entitled to wear the ostrich feather on his hat, which was otherwise reserved for officers. But, he warns, it will be necessary for the trumpeter to augment with his own funds the clothing allowance in order to buy clothes of a better quality—more appropriate to a trumpeter—for it is important that a trumpeter "shall and must live in grand style, especially when he is young and single."

For his quarters, the trumpeter was allowed to have extra lodging money which normally only married men received.

[1] Henry Farmer, *Military Music* (London, 1912), 36.

[2] Ernst Altenburg, *Versuch einer Anleitung zur heroischmusikalischen Trompeter- und Pauker-Kunst . . .*, trans., Edward Tarr (Halle, 1795), 54.

He received his horse from the nobleman who was paying the costs of his particular regiment, but the trumpeter had to pay the regular cavalryman who fed and groomed the horse, took care of the saddle and boots, etc. To do all this on a trumpeter's pay requires budgeting, warns Altenburg!

The primary duty of the trumpeter, of course, was to sound the military signals which transmitted the instructions of the officers to the troops. Altenburg observes that these, being nothing more than "artistic variations" on the major triad, must have been invented by someone with talent and intellect to have brought about such diversity from only the six lowest pitches. This possibility of "artistic variations" was such that Altenburg remembered, and regretted, that the "old calls" had been gradually abbreviated until they had lost their original meaning and were now so "capriciously played that their true purpose and melodiousness have been obscured, especially in the *Feldstucke* played by many instruments together."

> But among them all no *Feldstuck* is more improperly played, by all armies, than the heroic trumpeter march. It should be played slower for the heavy cavalry, in order to express the serious and heroic, and it should be played more briskly for the Hussars because they are the light cavalry.[3]

[3] Ibid., 89.

The cause for this loss of the original style of performance, Altenburg attributes to the modern concept of notating the signals. Art, it seems, always is the loser when it is removed from the experiential and made conceptual.[4] The principal military signals known to Altenburg at the end of the Baroque Period were,

> *Boute-selle*, boots and saddles, sounded two or three hours before riding out of camp. Its real importance is to encourage the troops.
>
> *A Cheval*, to horse. In the field, upon hearing this call the cavalry assembles in order before the commander's quarter.
>
> *Le Marche*
>
> *La Retraite*, retreat, played in the evening after the sun has gone down ... and all is calm.

[4] Actual notated examples of seventeenth century German military signals are very rare, due to the quasi-secret nature of the trumpet guilds. One extant example, the "General Caraffa-Fanfare" (1690) is given by Eugen Brixel, *Das ist Osterreichs Militarmusik* (Graz, 1982), 21. Also see Grove, *Dictionary of Music* (1980), XII, 316ff.

A l'Etendart, to the colors. In the battle it is a signal for the scattered troops to reassemble.

Alarme

Apell blasen, to signal the retreat.

Ban, for announcements and proclamations

Charge, the signal to attack.

Fanfare, for days of celebration and gala occasions. It is of two kinds, first, one of an Intrada nature, a short prelude or introduction to a musical piece; this is usually improvised. Second, the *Tusch*, also improvised, as a short fantasy consisting of nothing but arpeggios and runs, played when noblemen drink a toast. Altenburg further observes, "it makes noise enough, but contains neither art nor order."

Guet, for changing the guard. Altenburg says the Prussian army trumpeters here played a *"Bicinium* in the clarin register."

Altenburg says the Germans were superior in playing these field signals because they employed certain embellishments, or "tricks of the trade"; especially the lowest part, or Principal, was very much ornamented or improved. The secret was a system of tonguing based on syllables, following the Renaissance tradition. Altenburg reveals only one, for single-tonguing, "ritiriton," or "kitikiton," together with the observation that either could be turned into double-tonguing by the addition of another "ti" in front.

The military timpani, which were so closely identified with the trumpeters, actually borrowed technical terms from the trumpets to name some of their drum strokes, as for example *Einfache Zungen* and *Doppel Zungen*.[5] Zedler, in his *Universallexikon* (1735), describes the timpanist as one "who knows how to strike the drum elegantly." Altenburg mentions their improvisation, called *Praambulieren* or *Fantasieren*, and their playing, "now loud, now soft, now fast, now slow."[6]

There is one German military signal which had its origin for drums which is particularly interesting, the "Zapfenstreich." This term which continues well into the nineteenth

[5] Richard Leppert, "Musical Instruments and Performing Ensembles in Flemish Paintings of the Seventeenth Century" (Unpublished dissertation, Indiana University, 1973), 206. Curt Sachs, in *The History of Musical Instruments* (New York, 1940), 330, in discussing the flamboyant style of sticking by the military timpanists, adds this anecdote,

> When, about the middle of the 16th century, a German, Baron von Dohna, came to France, his ostentatious entrance annoyed the French so much that the Duke of Guise ordered his timpani to be dashed to pieces "to his great abashment."

[6] Quoted in Wilhelm Ehmann, *Tibilustrium* (Kassel, 1950), 14.

century appears as the title of a well-known band composition by Beethoven. It takes its name from the spigot of the wine cask and apparently dates from some remote time when the signal announced the hour for the soldiers to depart from the tavern.[7] The earliest form of the signal was "Zapfenschlag" (to hit or close the spigot) and is mentioned in an edict from 1636, which we paraphrase,

[7] Panoff, *Militarmusik* (Berlin, 1944), 89ff.

> Moreover We command that as soon as the drum plays, at nine o'clock from our Church of the Holy Trinity, no tavern, private or public should pour more wine or beer, but [rather] point out that it is time to go home.[8]

[8] *Zur Herstellung der guten Ordnung*, Colln an der Spree, August 29, 1636.

A similar order of 1672 refers specifically to soldiers,

> ... no soldier should go to a tavern after the "Zapffen Schlag," or be found in the alley; in addition the Innkeeper should not serve beer after the Zapffen Schlag and if he [does not adhere to this], he will be punished and made an example of.[9]

[9] War Article (1672) from Berlin, quoted in Panoff, *Militarmusik*, 90.

An edict from the same period is more firm, indicating that any soldier not in his quarters after the Zapffen-Schlage will be punished by running the gauntlet.[10] A similar ordinance is found from the period of Fredrich Wilhelm I (1713–1740) in Berlin.

[10] Ibid.

> In the evening after the sun has set, the artillery will fire a shot and at the same time all the drummers of the army will beat a Zapfenstreich. After this there should be no running around and in case a soldier does, he will be required to run the gauntlet 30 times.[11]

[11] Ibid., 91.

The military trumpeter, following an ancient tradition, also served as the ambassador, carrying messages to the enemy commander and back. Altenburg provides an interesting review of the facets of this responsibility. First, he says, one must take care to put the message in a safe place, where it will not get dirty. One must not show the message, or disclose his purpose, to anyone—not even the officers of his own regiment. One must be careful to get a receipt from the enemy commander to prove the message was delivered.

One must be careful not to say anything that might reveal your own army's poor circumstances, but must discreetly look around for anything that might be welcome information to one's own commander. In summary, one must "conduct oneself soberly, moderately, and carefully, since one can otherwise easily run the risk of being shot dead!"[12]

A final piece of diplomatic tradition is mentioned by Altenburg. After military funerals the trumpeter usually was allowed to receive the dead man's boots and dagger, but only after an established ritual. The trumpeter removed the boots and dagger from the top of the coffin, where they were placed during the ceremony, and gave them to the captain in charge, offering the captain at the same time a "tip" appropriate to the rank of the deceased, whereupon the captain was supposed to offer the boots and dagger back to the trumpeter.[13]

Before the advent of standing armies, the free German cities maintained their own militia. When the civic militia appeared in ceremonies, it was the civic wind band which joined them in temporary military duty. The basic wind band of shawms, with a few drums, can be seen in the "Schalmeier, Pfeifer and Trommler," of 1625 Hamburg, and in the three musicians of the "guardia" in 1603 Augsburg.[14] A particularly valuable reference to one of these civic bands participating with the civic militia is found in an account of the celebration of the birthday of the Archduke of Austria in Frankfurt in 1716, in which an eye-witness speaks of the six-member Hautboisten band performing a march by Telemann.[15]

[12] Altenburg, *Versuch einer Anleitung zur heroischmusikalischen Trompeter- und Pauker-Kunst ...*, 42ff.

[13] Ibid., 53.

[14] H. Engel, *Musik und Gesellschaft, Beitrage zu einer Musiksoziologie* (Berlin-Halensee, 1960), 212, 225.

[15] C. Valentin, *Geschichte der Musik in Frankfurt a. M.* (Frankfurt, 1906), 240.

Military Shawm Bands of the Seventeenth Century

THE FIRST TRUE INDEPENDENT military band tradition in Germany coincides with the seventeenth century decision to create standing armies. One might point to the date of 1646, when the elector Friedrich Wilhelm (1640–1688), "the Great Elector," founded his *Charbrandenburgische Liebguardie*, which consisted of two hundred troops and a band of four *Schalmeyer* (two discant and an alto shawm, with a dulcian) with drums which concertized [*konzertierte*] for the troops.[16] Degele also indicates the typical German infantry *Regimentskapellen* by 1670 was still three shawms and a dulcian, called *Feldpfeifer*, but he adds that the sound of these ancient shawms was so offensive that the military band was made to march twenty-five to thirty paces in front of the troops.[17]

These Renaissance shawms provided the basic German military music until 1681 when one begins to find the introduction of the modern oboe. At this time the elector in Berlin had twelve instruments, divided between "teutschen Schalmeyern" and "franzsischen hoboisten." A chronicle of 1690 speaks of the "French shawm, called Hautbois," and also informs us that these musicians followed the troops into actual battle.[18]

It was this period that the African blacks began to appear in European military bands. The first colony of these persons were acquired from the West African coast in 1683 and appear as military timpanists in the Berlin court by 1685.[19] This became a tradition in Berlin and Friedrich Wilhelm I (1713–1740) had an entire band in his personal regiment composed of fifteen black musicians.[20] A contemporary account relates hearing, as the king sat down to his midday meal in the great hall in Potsdam, a procession of twenty-six blacks, playing in the "Moorish and Turkish" style with cymbals, timpani and wind instruments. By the beginning of the eighteenth century these musicians were found in many European regimental bands. Even in Poland, under August der Starke, one finds twenty-nine "Mohren" employed in 1730.[21]

Friedrich I (1688–1713)

DURING THE REIGN of the Elector Frederick III (1688–1713) the Hohenzollern family finally succeeded in having their electorate become a kingdom and so, in 1701, Frederick

---

[16] Johannes Reschke, "Zur Geschichte der Deutschen Militarmusik des 17. und 18. Jahrhunderts," in *Deutsche Musik-Kultur* (1937), II, 11.

[17] Ludwig Degele, *Die Militarmusik* (Wolfenbüttel, 1937), 113.

[18] W. C. Printz, *Historische Beschreibung der Edelen Sing- und Klingkunst* (Dresden, 1690) and H. Riedel, *Musik und Musikerlebnis in der erzahlenden deutschen Dichtung* (Bonn, 1959), 520.

[19] Panoff, *Militarmusik*, 96.

[20] Ibid., 97.

[21] Johannes Reschke, *Studie zur Geschichte der brandenburgisch-preussischen Heeresmusik* (Berlin, 1935), 16.

became Frederick I of Prussia. It was during his reign that the new Hautboisten band begins to replace the older shawm band. He maintained a standing army of some 31,000 men with each battalion consisting of a grenadier company with two "pfeifer" and three drums and five musket companies with only three drums in each. His headquarters troops, the *Leibgarde zu Fuss*, had a regimental drummer and six pfeifer.[22] This last band was probably oboes, and not shawms [*pfeifer*] as a court record mentions that in 1706 he transferred this military "Hautboisten" band to the palace musical establishment.[23] As a testimony of his interest we note that Friedrich I arranged for his Hautboisten to study composition for two years under Johann Theile (1646–1724)[24]

Also in Austria these new Hautboisten bands began to appear. Suppan even lists a typical infantry band in 1706 as having two oboes, two clarinets (!), two bassoons, trumpet and trombone.[25] An engraving by J. A. Pfeffel pictures a military Hautboisten band of three oboes and bassoon performing in Vienna in 1712.[26]

But it would probably be a mistake to assume that these first *military* Hautboisten bands were as musically capable as the *court* Hautboisten bands discussed in a previous chapter. For one thing, during the first generation of military Hautboisten the military shawm players were no doubt struggling with the new French oboes. Indeed in the town of Stade a document by the local civic band complains that the nearby army Hautboisten "have not correctly learned nor do they understand their music."[27]

It was also during this period that the first examples of Turkish Music began to appear in this part of Europe.[28] One early exponent was the King of Poland, August der Starke, who by 1699 had an entire *Janitscharen-Bataillon*, including a *Janitscharen-Musikkorps* of twenty-seven: nine shawms, four timpani, four cymbals and ten drummers, all German players. For his coronation in the same year he assembled 170 *Janitscharenleibgarde* members, again with Turkish music, as is clear from an eyewitness:

[22] Panoff, *Militarmusik*, 77.

[23] Curt Sachs, *Musik und Oper*, 66.

[24] *Die Musik in Geschichte und Gegenwart* (Kassel, 1949-1968), XIII, 278.

[25] Wolfgang Suppan, *Lexikon des Blasmusikwesens* (Freiburg, 1973), 40. While this seems early for clarinets to appear, Kappey in *A Short History of Military Music* (1894) mentions a march for a band with clarinets dating from c. 1720.

[26] Reproduced in Brixel, *Das ist Osterreichs Militarmusik*, 24–25.

[27] O. Spreckelsen, "*Der Stader Ratsmusikanten*," in *Stader Archiv* (Stade, 1924), 32.

[28] Reschke, *Studie zur Geschichte der brandenburgisch-preussichen Heeresmusik*, 12, where he dates the arrival from c. 1697.

They played with Turkish army music, small oboes, cymbals played by twelve year old boys, large drums and a pair of small copper timpani.[29]

[29] Arnold Schering, *Musikgeschichte Leipzigs* (Leipzig, 1926), II, 297ff.

Frederick William I (1713–1740)

FREDERICK WILLIAM I was an extraordinary man who worked hard to develop his nation and his court into a strong entity with an emphasis on German, rather than French, qualities. Whereas his father had had a standing army of 31,000, Frederick William, known as the "Soldier-King," increased it to 80,000 and left it as a highly disciplined bequest to his more famous son, Frederick the Great. A contemporary account describes him as,

> both the master and the servant of the state. He cut in half the number of pompous commissioners whose conflicting authority had obstructed the business of government. He sold the jewels, horses,[30] and fine furniture bequeathed to him, reduced the royal household to the simplicity of a burgher's home, gathered taxes wherever they could be made to grow ...[31]

[30] Voltaire offered the advice that he should instead get rid of the asses at court.

[31] Quoted in Will and Ariel Durant, *The Age of Voltaire* (New York, 1965), 437.

In building his army he conscripted the tallest and strongest men he could find, even in one case snatching a man away while he was praying in church.[32] In each infantry regiment, Frederick William had two battalions and ten companies, totaling forty officers, 110 under-officers, 130 grenediers and 1,080 muskets. The military music consisted of only three drums in each company, except for the command regiment which had a Hautboisten band of two soprano oboes, two tenor oboes and two bassoons[33] and six fifes.[34] Frederick seems to have taken a keen interest in this Hautboisten band and even used it to replace the usual court "art" music.[35]

[32] *Cambridge Modern History* (New York, 1907), VI, 214.

[33] Panoff, *Militarmusik*, 87.

[34] Reschke, *Studie zur Geschichte der brandenburgisch-preussischen Heeresmusik*, 31.

[35] Panoff, *Militarmusik*, 86.

Eventually Frederick added the trumpet to the Hautboisten band and one source says this trumpeter marched in front of the Hautboisten, alternating his fanfares with their music.[36] Brixel, quotes an unnamed 1737 source who

[36] G. Thouret, *Frederick der Grosse als Musikfreund und Musiker* (Leipzig, 1898).

believes the Hautboisten, in turn, took their cue from the drums, beginning to play when they heard the drums begin behind them.[37] The often reproduced engraving by Ch. Weigel (c. 1720) pictures just such an Hautboisten band of oboes, horns and bassoon and the trumpeter marching in front. Frederick must have also added timpani, the constant companion of the aristocratic trumpeter, for it is known that he had built a special "timpani wagon." One observer of a parade in Prague saw an entire "turkische musik," consisting of nine blacks, riding and performing on this wagon.[38]

Frederick William I also founded the first military music school in 1724.[39] The school was housed in the Military Orphans Home in Potsdam and its original purpose seems to have been to create Hautboisten musicians from the orphans. The first director of the school was Gottfried Pepush and he appears to have been in charge of about twenty students by 1750. The king seems to have taken a personal interest in the school and in an extant note calls Pepusch's attention to a young boy whom he wanted placed in the school.[40]

The most interesting first-hand account of German military music during the Baroque Period is found in a publication (1726) on the subject by Hans von Fleming.[41] He includes a long discussion of the method of performing the standard drum signals[42] and mentions a player called the "Quer-Pfeiffer." This player, the "good companion of the drummer," plays a morning song during Reveille and also plays during marching. He carries both a large and small instrument in a wooden case and, according to Fleming, when he played these instruments his performance varied considerably with the printed page.[43] Fleming relates seeing these instruments in a procession in Dresden for the changing of the guard.

> In Dresden I have observed that 12 Querpfieffer and 24 drums, 6 in rank and 6 in front of the Head Guard, in the New Market Place. As soon as the clock struck 12, the eldest regimental drummer gave an orderly cadence to the drummers, which was a signal for them to remove their instruments from their shoulder harnesses before preparing to play. Then he com-

[37] Brixel, *Das ist Osterreichs Militarmusik*, 28.

[38] Panoff, *Militarmusik*, 98.

[39] The first music school in France was also a military music school and it evolved into the present Paris Conservatoire.

[40] Panoff, *Militarmusik*, 108. This book also includes a drawing of the building.

[41] Hans von Fleming, *Der vollkommene deutsche Soldat* (Leipzig, 1726).

[42] Quoted in Panoff, *Militarmusik*, 79.

[43] Ibid. *Die Methode zu pfeifen und die Stuckgen zu componiren ist different.*

manded them to play the "Changing of the Guard," which occurred to their slow beating.[44]

His description of the new oboe, as compared to the old shawm is particularly interesting.

> During the time of the shawm there were 4 players: 2 discant, an alto and a Dulcian. After the oboe took their place, one finds 6 oboes as the oboes were not so strong but had a softer sound. The harmonie was now completed with 2 discant, 2 taille and 2 bassoons.[45]

This Hautboisten band, he says, marched in front of the troops and generally was attached to the headuarters command; the players carried the rank of corporal.[46]

The most frequently quoted passage from Fleming's work is a passage in which he describes performances by one of the Hautboisten bands which were more in the nature of concert music.

> In the morning, in front of the commander's quarters, the Hautboisten play a Morning Song, a newly composed march, an Intrada, and a pair of minuets, which the commander likes; these are often repeated in the evening [or one might also hear at that time] string instruments, or recorders and other instruments.[47]

Today we know a large number of multi-movement concert works for Hautboisten from the Baroque Period, but very few which were of military origin. A rare extant example is the *lustige Feld-Music* (1704) by Johann Philipp Kreiger (1649–1725), consisting of six *Suites* [*Ouverture*] scored for Oboe I [three players], Oboe II [two players], Taille[48] [one player] and Bassoon [three players]. The composer states that these works may be played either at court or in the field and, in the latter case, he hopes when his music is heard in the field it will be heard "like a ray of sun on a stormy day." In the case of the military Hautboisten "who march before the company or perform for the officers," he notes that almost all the *Entrees* among these *Partien* can also serve as marches.[49]

Another example of such repertoire might have been the *Parade Sinfonien* for two oboes, taille and bassoon by Gallo,

[44] Ibid., 80.

[45] Ibid., 81.

[46] Werner Braun, "Entwurf fur eine Typlogie der Hautboisten," in *Der Sozialstatus des Befursmusikers vom 17. bis 19. Jahrhundert* (Kassel, 1971), 53.

[47] Ibid., 52.

[48] There is substantial evidence, including iconography, which identifies the taille as a tenor oboe (English horn).

[49] Quoted in *Denkmaler Deutscher Tonkunst*, LIII–LIV, lxxiv.

which was advertised in the 1762 catalog of Breifkopf & Härtel.

Even though these German military bands were very small, one member appears to have served as a conductor. Several icons from this period picture an oboist–conductor and, as mentioned above, Pepusch served in this role in Berlin.[50] A contemporary account (1740) speaks of the Waldeck Kapellmesiter not only conducting his twelve member Hautboisten, but composing for them as well.[51] Johann Graf, who had served courts at Mainz and Bamberg, used the title, "Hoboistenmeister," in referring to a period during which he served in this capacity for six years in Hungary.[52]

Horns begin to appear in the military records during the 1720s. Fleming speaks of the addition of the horns to the Saxony-Polish army in 1723 as resulting in a "pleasant harmony."[53] One finds two horns, together with two oboes and two bassoons, in the oldest extant music of this army, a set of marches dated 1729.[54] Horns appear in the military in 1722 in Bavaria[55] and in 1730 in Austria.[56] The period of Frederick the Great in Prussia belongs properly to the Classical Period, but we might mention that he had a military band of sixteen players already in 1741.[57]

Finally, the oldest composition we know which carries the name "marsch," is dated 1711 by Johann Storl, for two oboes, two horns and bassoon, although Kreiger mentions the name in 1704, as mentioned above. There are also known Baroque examples by Grafe, Graun, Heinrich and Hertel, but we imagine the form must have come to life near the time of the reinstitution of co-ordinated marching.

When the composer Franz Benda made a gift of some marches to a dragoon regiment, he specified that his name not be used. The generals perhaps had a greater appreciation for the new form, for Kastner quotes an unnamed Prussian general as boasting,

> With a good march and my Hautboisten, it is a true pleasure to speak to Europe with the punctuation of the cannon.[58]

[50] Panoff, *Militarmusik*, Plate 41, reproduces an engraving from this period picturing a five-member band with a conductor.
[51] D. Rouvel, "Zur Geschichte der Musik am Fürstl. Waldeckschen Hof zu Arolsen," in *Kölner Beitrage zur Musikforschung* (Regensburg, 1962), XXII, 102ff.
[52] P. Gluke, *Musik und Musiker in Rudolstadt* (Rudolstadt, 1963), 14ff.

[53] Braun, "Entwurf fur eine Typologie der Hautboisten," 52.
[54] *Die Infanterie Marsche der vormaligen Churfürstl. Sachsischen Armee 1729*. DDR-Dla [Aktenband Loc. 10945].
[55] Reschke, "Zur Geschichte," gives six oboes and two horns for the Kurprinz regiment of 1728.
[56] Brixel, in correspondence with us, gives a typical Austrian military band for 1730 as two oboes, two clarinets, two bassoons, two horns, trumpet and bass drum.
[57] Reschke, *Studie zur Geschichte der brandenburgisch-preussichen Heeresmusik*, 14.

[58] Georges Kastner, *Manuel General de Musique Militaire* (Paris, 1848), 124.

16
On the Influence of Turkish Music

THE REPEATED BATTLES between the West and the Ottoman Empire from 1526 to 1699 made the Turkish nation for a time the primary fear of Western civilization. This empire was a particular source of anxiety for the Viennese for their city lay on the border between East and West and more than once the Turkish armies were at the very gates of the city. There followed, of course, a great curiosity about these "heathen" neighbors and consequently the museums in Vienna today are filled with objects collected from the fields outside the city walls after the Turkish troops had withdrawn. Every visitor to Vienna today is told of the discovery, in this manner, of a bag of coffee beans which was the beginning of the craze for drinking coffee in Vienna.

This curiosity was shared by musicians and a rare account exists of a musical "duel" held during a lull in a battle fought in 1683 between the military musicians of East and West. The Turkish musicians were heard playing "*Cymbeln, Glocklein and Schalmeyen,*" and the Viennese answered with trumpets and timpani.[1] This musical fascination continued in the West, and in Vienna in particular, for a long time. Mozart's first real success in Vienna was, of course, his *The Abduction from the Seraglio* of the 1782 season. Similar examples of music "alla Turca" followed in the works of Gluck, Haydn and the *Ninth Symphony* of Beethoven.

---

[1] Eugen Brixel, *Das ist Oesterreichs Militarmusik* (Graz, 1982), 21. It was from this same battle that the folksong, "Prinz-Eugen, das edle ritter," used in Hindemith's *Konzertmusik*, Op. 42, had its origin.

The Turkish influence on Western military music was much more fundamental, as it helped solve the basic problem of mass movement among the new standing armies. This influence was so generally recognized throughout the Classical and Romantic Periods that Western military bands were often called simply, "Turkische musik." Ironically, the Sultan Mahmut II ended the indigenous Turkish military band tradition in 1826, when he decided to model his bands after the West and decided to hire the most famous composer known to him, Donizetti, to move to Istanbul to guide this reorganization. On someone's error he instead hired Donizetti's *brother*, who in fact moved to Turkey to work for the Sultan.

The Turkish Mehter Band

THE TURKISH wind and percussion band tradition is very old. Their early history is best known in the West today through the chronicles of the Crusades of the late Middle Ages, but the tradition is much older. A Chinese chronicle tells of a Chinese general who visited the Turkish city of Balasagun in the year 200 BC and was so impressed that he brought an entire band back with him to China.[2]

The basic Turkish military band unit was a five-member ensemble called the *Mehter* band, which was doubled and redoubled according to the rank of the person by whom they were employed. The Sultan's band, called *Mehterhane*, was usually the largest and consisted of a nine-fold version of the same basic instruments. For great battles even larger proportions were assembled. The Sultan Selim (1512–1520) took more than two hundred players to the battle of Mercidabik, as did Suleiman the Great (1520–1566) to Vienna. Salim III (1789–1807) also maintained a two hundred piece band.[3]

The instruments included a conical and wild-sounding medieval shawm. Made of plum or apricot wood, it was decorated with precious stones and silver bracelets and called by the Turks, the *zurna*. There was a primitive trumpet, which seems to have been used more as a rhythmic than a melodic

[2] Much of our information is taken from a publication (no date) under the direction of Sabahattin Doras, curator of the Military Museum in Istanbul, *Mehterhane (Turkiye Turing Ve Otomobil Kurumu)*, to whom we are all indebted.

[3] Ibid., 32.

instrument, called the *boruzen*. The percussion instruments were the most influential in the West. There were cymbals, *Zil,* the player being called *Zilzen,* very much like the modern ones. There were prototype small timpani, called *Nekkare,* with leather stretched over twin copper bowls, played in a sitting position on the ground. The final member of the normal *Mehter* band was a large bass drum, played with a large stick in the right hand and a smaller one, sometimes a branch of a tree, with the left hand.

In larger bands the *Cevgen* was added, played by a musician who also sang. In English we call this instrument the "Jingling Jonnie," or "Turkish crescent," and in German, *Schellenbaum*. It was a high pole surmounted by one or more metal crescents (*Mehter,* itself, being derived from the Persian *Mahi-ter,* for "moon"), from which hung many small bells and on each end, horsehair plumes. The contemporary Western bell-lyre is nothing but a surrogate for this instrument.

In one of the multiple *Mehter* bands there would be a leader for each instrument, called *Aga,* and the players of each instrument would be grouped together by the instrument. The smaller groups would then be configured into a large half-circle ("moon" again),[4] or in the case of the nine-fold band, a full circle. The over-all conductor was called *Mehterbasi Aga*.

The royal *Mehter* band, a nine-fold band attached to the Topkapi Palace, was composed not of Turkish players, oddly enough, but rather of Armenians and Greeks who had been converted to Islam. The *viziers,* or governors, and commanders of the army troops had seven-fold bands. Civilian organizations, such as trade guilds, were allowed to form *Mehter* bands for special occasions, processions, etc., but were not allowed to maintain them independently.

The bands dressed in striking uniforms, typically gowns with wide sleeves, turbans wrapped with gauze, leggings, and short, slip-on boots. The conductor, of course, was dressed in colors apart from the musicians.

These bands played at regular times during the day, beginning early in the morning. A Prussian soldier, sent to

---

[4] Arif Pascha, *Les anciens costumes de l'Empire Ottoman* (Paris, 1863) suggests that the reason for the half-circle formation was that it helped in immediately identifying any player of wrong notes.

Istanbul early in the eighteenth century, recalled that the band which marched before his quarters every morning, "split the ears with its incredible charivari."[5] On fortresses, these bands also performed a watch duty.

[5] Quoted in *Musikalische Nachrichten und Anmerkungen auf das Jahr 1770* (Leipzig, 1770), III.

It was in battle that the *Mehter* band was considered most valuable. Their playing thrilled and excited the soldiers, lifting their morale and driving them into action. Many accounts also remark on the effect of this thundering noise in diminishing the morale and dissipating the enemy. One of the band leaders during the Kara Mustafa Pasha's attack on Vienna, remembered,

> Toward the middle of the afternoon the grand Viszier's mehter band started to play first. Then the bands of the governors of provinces and the bands on the right started to play all together. Thus, after the evening prayer and at dawn, the sound of drums, oboes, kettle-drums, and cymbals joined from every corner the rumble of cannon and gunfire, and the whole countryside echoed with these sounds.[6]

[6] Doras, *Mehterhane*, 27.

The sultan's band performed concerts each afternoon in the palace during peace time as well as during coronations and other ceremonies. During battle, concerts were performed in front of the royal tent. One such concert performed before a guest, Osman Gazi, began a tradition somewhat similar to the curious tradition in the West of audiences standing during the famous chorus in the Messiah by Handel. Gazi, out of respect for the Selijuk Sultan, stood during the concert by the *Mehter* band and for the following two hundred years, until Mohammed II (1451–1481), sultans stood when these bands performed concerts.[7]

[7] Ibid., 32.

There are some interesting eyewitness accounts from the West dating from the seventeenth century, the period in which these Turkish bands began to influence Western military bands. The percussion instruments, while not unknown in the West, caught the attention of Western ears for their use in large numbers combined with fewer melodic instruments. For many this was a shock on first hearing, as in the case of one listener early in the seventeenth century.

In Turkey there are also many kinds of instruments which they usually play in a confused manner and without the use of consonances, unless these happen to arrive by accident; and the Turks only take satisfaction in hearing loud and confused noise.[8]

[8] Salomon De Caus, *Institution Harmonique* (Frankfurt, 1615), fol. 22v.

Another early writer who gave special attention to the description of the percussion instruments, as heard later during the seventeenth century, was Count Luigi Ferdinando Marsigli. Based on a journey to Istanbul, his account divides the instruments into those which produce shock (the various drums) and those which make musical sounds (shawms and perhaps trumpets). The bass drum he describes as being played on one side with a large wooden mallet (*Gross Baguette de buis*) and on the other with a *Petite Baguette*. This instrument was thus played on both sides alternatively, "with such artistry and solemnity, in a most agreeable manner." These bass drums, he adds, were played,

> when the Army is approaching that of its enemies ... and they are beaten around the soldiers guarding the Camp, in order to keep them awake. Meanwhile the drummers cry out "Jegder-Alla," that is to say, "the Lord is good!"[9]

[9] *Il Sato Militare dell' Imperio Ottomano, Incremento e Decremento Del Medesimo Dell Signore Conte di Marsigli ...* (Hague, 1732), 54ff.

He heard this instrument as having the effect of somehow pulling together the sounds of all the other percussion instruments into a more homogeneous effect.

> The different sounds of all these instruments would be harsh to the ear, if they were not corrected by that of the *Grand Caisse*; but when they are reunited the concert that they produce is agreeable enough.

The smaller timpani-type instruments he heard as being played in the Western tradition, with a pair of hard sticks.

> They are reserved for the honor of the Family of the *Bacha*, and serve to signal the march; they enter the concert of Music extremely well, and they are called the *Sadar Nagara*. The *Bachas* march in three lines and have two *Timbalists*, and the *Timbales* are at each side of the procession, and they are beaten in the same way we do in our own army.

Another seventeenth century observer, Evilya Efendi, in a manuscript account of travels throughout Turkey, says that the musicians of the Ottoman Empire were organized into more than forty different guilds of builders, players and singers.[10] The *Mehter* band he heard had nine players, including the conductor who was the shawmist. The large bass drum, he wrote, was "as big as the dome of a Turkish bath. They are played day and night. Their sound is like thunder."

This same writer gives us an eyewitness account of the daily routine of the royal band.

[10] *Narrative of Travels in Europe, Asia, and Africa in the Seventeenth Century*, trans. Joseph von Hammer (London, 1834), 225ff.

> The mehters' lodging quarters is an old building at the Demirkapi site of the Palace gates. It has a tall four cornered tower in the middle. Every night after the evening prayer they play three tunes (*Fasil*) ending in a martial tune and pray for the Sultan. At dawn three hours before morning, they play three very pleasant tunes to invite the members of the court to the assembly, and wake everybody for the morning prayer. If a member of the palace was promoted, the Mehters used to go to his place in order to congratulate him and play for him three tunes. If he were not at home, they played one tune to the people at home. At the palace, the grand council of state which gathered in the council room used to begin their discussions after the mehter band performed.

This account hints at the variety of music, as well as the variety of functions, in the repertoire of these Turkish bands during the seventeenth century. More valuable information regarding the nature of the music itself is given by the same eyewitness, contained in an interesting description of an argument between the conductor of the royal *Mehter* band and the chief architect of the palace. They had come into conflict over the issue of who should take precedence in a procession during the reign of Murat IV and had taken the issue to the Sultan himself for resolution. The architect spoke first,

> Your Majesty, we are the dancers of Habib Neccar, the mehters are a crowd with no patron-saint, who seem to have embraced the Art of Jamshid. We build palaces, mosques, and mausoleums for our Sultan. We repair fortresses when they are

> captured, and we build bridges. We are indispensable for the Islamic Army, and we serve it well. There is no doubt that we should march in front of the mehters.

The conductor of the *Mehter* band answered,

> Your Majesty, wherever you go, you should walk with the sound of drums and trumpet for the sake of your magnificence, grandeur, and fame toward friend and foe. At the battlefields we are the ones who beat the gigantic drums in order to incite the soldiers to combat. We are the ones who excite the soldiers to a fighting condition. When our Sultan is upset about something, we entertain him by performing 12 kinds of mood [*Makam*], 24 kinds of fundamental cadence [*Usul*], and 48 kinds of music [*Terkibi musiki*]. Old wise men have said that music, poetry and song give joy to the hearts of men. We are the trades people who feed the spirit. The workers of the chief architect are Greeks, Armenians and gypsies. They are cement workers, conduit repairers, plumbers and even latrine cleaners. We will not allow these trades people to march in front of us. Wherever the flag of the Prophet is seen the drums of the Ottoman Dynasty have to be present.

How could any sultan refuse an argument like that?

Another seventeenth century reference to the music performed by these bands mentions that out of a group of twenty-four tunes heard, six were of a melancholy nature, six were allegro and light-spirited, six furious and six mellifluous or even amorous.[11] He too was impressed by the percussion, for he noted,

[11] Giovanni Battista Donado, *Della Letteratura de' Turchi* (Venice, 1688), 130ff.

> Now, to speak the truth, their universal and ordinary music feels the effect of tumult, since the Turkish Nation is fraught with war.

When one considers how different all this was from the music and practices of the Western military traditions, one can certainly appreciate the curiosity in the exotic and the sense of surprise found in almost all these early encounters.

The Influence of Turkish Music on the Western Armies

BECAUSE THE REPEATED CONFLICTS between the West and the Ottoman Empire offered numerous points of contact, it is impossible to pinpoint a precise date for the introduction of this "Turkische musik," the percussion instruments in particular, in Western military bands. Most sources give the approximate date as the end of the seventeenth century, but we suspect it may have been somewhat earlier. Certainly, for example, it was the new Turkish percussion instruments which Samuel Pepys heard in London in 1661.

> So to White Hall; where I staid to hear the trumpets and kettle-drums, and then the other drums, which are much cried up, though I think it dull, vulgar musique.[12]

The adoption of these instruments became wide spread near the beginning of the eighteenth century, following a visit to the King of Prussia in Berlin by the Turkish Ambassador, Achmet Effendi. Prussia had apparently been experimenting with these new instruments and in honor of the ambassador's visit the king arranged a performance with them. The ambassador reacted by exclaiming, "This isn't Turkish at all!" meaning, we suspect, that even if the instruments were familiar, the nature of playing them was not. His reaction seems to have embarrassed the king, who then arranged through the ambassador to import actual Turkish musicians to train his own.[13]

The fact that the King of Prussia had actual Turkish musicians in residence seems to have made such players an instant "status symbol" among Europe's leading aristocracy. Almost immediately, Augustus II of Poland (d. 1735) acquired a complete Turkish band as a gift from the sultan, the emperor of Austria obtained one and Anne of Russia sent to Istanbul for a band that included not only the percussion instruments, but shawms in both treble and tenor sizes.[14]

The vital contribution these new percussion instruments made to Western armies must be understood in context

[12] *The Diary of Samuel Pepys* (London, 1924), III, 315, entry for January 31–February 3, 1661.

[13] Georges Kastner, *Manuel general de Musique Militaire* (Paris, 1848), 131.

[14] Ibid., and Grove, *Dictionary* (1980), IX, 497.

with a fundamental change in the nature of these armies during the seventeenth century. It was at this time that the concept of a standing army began to be employed in Western Europe, whereas for centuries earlier when battles were necessary they were conducted by troops hired for that purpose, mercenaries. With a standing army, which could practice marching, the generals could at last successfully introduce coordinated marching. This was a concept which had long been appreciated in theory in the West, but was not practical with short-term mercenaries. Neither the drums, which were still needed for signals, nor the ancient fifes, nor the new oboes and bassoons were sufficient to convey the beat necessary for successful coordinated marching by massed troops. It was the addition of all the extra Turkish percussion which had the potential for making the beat audible to the common soldier. Even then, the whole idea of coordinated marching to a beat seemed so new and tenuous that even a single beat's rest represented a threat to the order of the feet. The famous German critic, Schubart, wrote that it was here especially that a great clash of percussion helped prevent anyone from getting out of step.[15]

This important association between the new musical instruments and the new concept of the standing army can also be seen in the fact that for a time these newly equipped bands were called *Janissaries*, after the Turkish, *Yeni cherik*, for "new troops."

[15] Gottfried Veit, *Die Blasmusik* (Innsbruck, 1972), 32.

Bibliography

Chapter 1 Thoughts on the Musical Scene in Baroque Germany

David, Hans T. and Arthur Mendel. *The Bach Reader.* New York: Norton, 1966.

Donnington, Robert. *The Interpretation of Early Music.* New York, 1964.

Fend, Barthold. *Gedanken von der Opera* (1708). Quoted in Lorenzo Biaconi, *Music in the Seventeenth Century.* Cambridge: Cambridge University Press, 1989.

Fuhrmann, Martin. *Satans-Capelle.* Köln, 1729.

Grimmelshausen, Hans Jacob Christoffel von. *The Adventurous Simplicissimus.* Translated by A. T. Goodrick. Lincoln: University of Nebraska, 1962

———. *The Singular Life Story of Heedless Hopalong.* Detroit: Wayne State University Press, 1981.

Grossmann, Burckhart. *116th Psalm* (Jena, 1623). Quoted in Hans Moser, *Heinrich Schütz.* St. Louis: Concordia, 1936.

Moser, Hans. *Heinrich Schütz.* St. Louis: Concordia, 1936.

Norman, Gertrude and Miriam Shrifte. *Letters of Composers.* New York, Knopf, 1946.

Morgenstern, Sam. *Composers on Music.* New York: Pantheon, 1956.

Muffat, Georg. *Florilegia.*

———. *Florilegium Secundum* (1698).

Niedt, Friedrich Erhard. *Musicalische Handleitung.* Hamburg, 1700.

Scheibe, Johann. *Critischer musicus* (1737). Translated by Claude Palisca, *Baroque Music*. Englewood Cliffs: Prentice Hall, 1981.

Schütz, Henrich. *Geistliche Chormusik* (1648).

———. *Kleine geistliche Concerte.*

———. *Symphoniae sacrae I.*

———. *Symphoniae sacrae II. (1647).*

Strunk, Oliver. *Source Readings in Music History.* New York: Norton, 1950.

Chapter 2 Leibniz on Music

Leibniz, Gottfried Wilhelm. "Mars Christianissimus" (1683), in *The Political Writings of Leibniz.* Translated by Patrick Riley. Cambridge: Cambridge University Press, 1972.

———. *New Essays Concerning Human Understanding* (1704). Translated by Alfred Langley. La Salle: The Open Court Publishing Company, 1949.

———. *Leibniz Selections.* Edited by Philip Wiener. New York: Scribner's, 1951.

———. *Philosophical Essays.* Translated by Roger Ariew and Daniel Garber. Indianapolis: Hackett, 1989.

Loemker, Leroy. *Philosophical Papers and Letters* [of Leibniz]. Dordrecht: Reidel, 1956.

Chapter 3 Mattheson on the Nature of Music

Cannon, Beekman. *Johann Mattheson, Spectator in Music.* Archon Books, 1968.

Mattheson, Johann. *Behauptung der Himmlischen Musik ...* (1739).

———. *Das Beschutzte Orchestre.*

———. *Das Forschende Orchestre* (1721).

———. *Das Neu-Eröffnete Orchestre* (Hamburg, 1713).

———. *Der vollkommene Capellmeister* (1739). Translated by Ernest Harriss. Ann Arbor: UMI Research Press, 1981.

Weiss, Piero. *Letters of Composers Through Six Centuries.* Philadelphia: Chilton, 1967.

Chapter 4 On Emotion in Music in the German Baroque

Bernard, Chr. *Tractatus compositionis augmentatus* (c. 1650).
Bukofzer, Manfred. *Music in the Baroque Era.* New York: Norton, 1947.
———. "Allegory in Baroque Music," in *Journal of the Warburg and Courtauld Institutes, 1939-1940.* Vaduz: Kraus Reprint, 1965
Caldenbach, Chr. *Dissertatio musica* (1664).
Calvisius, S. *Exercitationes duae* (1600).
Cruger, J. *Synopsis musica* (1624)
David, Hans T. and Arthur Mendel. *The Bach Reader.* (New York: Norton, 1966.
Decorus, Volupius. *Architectonice musices universalis* (1631).
Donnington, Robert. *The Interpretation of Early Music.* New York, 1964.
Harris, Ellen. "Voices," in *Performance Practice: Music after 1600.* New York: Norton, 1989.
Heinichen, Johann. *Anweisung zum Generalbass* (1711).
Kuhnau, Johann. *Der musicalische Quack-Salber.* Dresden, 1700.
Lang, Paul Henry. "Musical Thought of the Baroque: The Doctrine of Temperaments and Affections," in *Twentieth-Century Views of Music History.* Edited by William Hays. New York: Scribner's, 1972.
Marpurg, F. W. *Der critische Musicus an der Spree* (Berlin), September 2, 1749.
Mattheson, Johann. *Der vollkommene Capellmeister* (1739). Translated by Ernest Harriss. Ann Arbor: UMI Research Press, 1981.
———. *Critica Musica* (1725).
Nucius, J. *Musices poeticae* (1613).
Palisca, Claude. *Baroque Music.* Englewood Cliffs: Prentice Hall, 1981.
Praetorius, Michael. *Syntagma musicum* (1619).
Printz, J. C. *Phrynidis Mytilinaei* (1696).
Scheibe, J. *Critischer Musicus.* (1743).

Schoolfield, George. *The German Lyric of the Baroque.* New York: AMS Press, 1966.

Speer, Daniel. *Grundrichtiger . . . musikaliches Kleeblatt* (1697).

Strunk, Oliver. *Source Readings in Music History.* New York: Norton, 1950.

———. "Francois Raguenet, Comparison between the French and Italian Music (1702)," *The Musical Quarterly* 32, no. 3 (1946): 411–436.

Vogt, M. *Conclave thesauris magnae artis musicae* (1719).

Chapter 5 Mattheson on Emotion in Music

La Mothe le Vayer, François. *Oeuvres de François de la Mothe le Vayer.* Paris (1656).

Leipziger Zeitungen von gelehrten Sachen (1733).

Mattheson, Johann. *Der vollkommene Capellmeister* (1739). Translated by Ernest Harriss. Ann Arbor: UMI Research Press, 1981.

———. *Das Neu-Eröffnete Orchestre* (Hamburg, 1713).

Observations de Medecine sur la maladie, appellée convulsions par un Medecine de la Faculte de Paris. Paris, 1732.

Rousseau, Jean. *Methode claire, certaine et facile pour apprendre a chanter la musique.* Paris, 1678.

Chapter 6 On German Baroque Performance Practice

Buelow, George. *Thorough-Bass Accompaniment according to Johann David Heinichen.* Ann Arbor: UMI Research Press, 1986.

Bukofzer, Manfred. *Music in the Baroque Era.* New York: Norton, 1947.

David, Hans T. and Arthur Mendel. *The Bach Reader.* New York: Norton, 1966.

Donnington, Robert. *The Interpretation of Early Music.* New York, 1964.

Marpurg. *Legende einiger Musikheiligen.* Köln (1786).

Mattheson, Johann. *Der vollkommene Capellmeister* (1739). Translated by Ernest Harriss. Ann Arbor: UMI Research Press, 1981.

Moser, Hans. *Heinrich Schütz*. St. Louis: Concordia, 1936.
Muffat, Georg. *Auserlesene Instrumental-Music* [1701].
Norman, Gertrude and Miriam Shrifte. *Letters of Composers*. New York: Knopf, 1946.
Praetorius. *Syntagma Musicum,* Book III (1619).
Schütz, Heinrich. *Resurrection History* [1623].
———. *Cantiones sacrae,* Op. 4 [1625].
———. *Geistliche Chormusik* [1648].
Strunk, Oliver.   New York: Norton, 1950.

Chapter 7 Praetorius on Performance Practice

Praetorius, Michael. *Syntagma Musicum*. Kassel: Bärenreiter, 1958.

Chapter 8 Mattheson on Performance Practice

Mattheson, Johann. *Das Neu-Eröffnete Orchestre.* Hamburg (1713).
———. *Der vollkommene Capellmeister* [1739]. Translated by Ernest Harriss. Ann Arbor: UMI Research Press, 1981.
———. *Der musicalische Patriot.* Hamburg (1744).
———. *Die neueste Untersuchung der Singspiele.* Hamburg (1744).

Chapter 9 Mattheson on the Composition of Good Melody

Beekman, Cannon. *Johann Mattheson, Spectator in Music.* Archon Books, 1968.
Gresset, Jean Baptiste. *Discours sur l'harmonie*. Paris, 1737.
Mattheson, Johann. *Der vollkommene Capellmeister* [1739]. Translated by Ernest Harriss. Ann Arbor: UMI Research Press, 1981.

Chapter 10 On Court Music in the German Baroque

The Autobiography of Karl von Dittersdorf. Translated by A. D. Coleride. London, 1896.

Baselt, Bernd. "Brandenburg-Prussia and the Central German Courts," in *The Late Baroque Era*. Englewood Cliffs: Prentice Hall, 1994.

Beer, Johann. *Musicalische Diskurse*. Nürnberg (1710).

Buelow, George. "Dresden in the Age of Absolutism," in *The Late Baroque Era*. Englewood Cliffs: Prentice Hall, 1994.

Burney, Charles. *Memoirs of the Life and Writings of the Abate Metastasio*. New York: Da Capo Press, 1971.

Castiglione, Baldassare. *Il Cortigiano*.

David, Hans T. and Arthur Mendel. *The Bach Reader*. New York: Norton, 1966.

Doering, O. *Des Augsburger Patriciers Philipp Hainhofer Reisen nach Innsbruck und Dresden*. Vienna, 1901.

Griesheim. *Die Stadt Hamburg* (1760).

Mattheson, Johann. *Das neu-eröffnete Orchestre*. Hamburg, 1713.

Moser, Hans. *Heinrich Schütz*. St. Louis: Concordia, 1936.

Pietzsch, G. *Sachsen als Musikland*. Dresden, 1938.

Seraunky, W. *Musikgeschichte der Stadt Halle*. Halle-Berlin, 1939.

Spagnoli, Gina. "Dresden at the Time of Heinrich Schutz," in *The Early Baroque Era*. Englewood Cliffs: Prentice Hall, 1994.

Werner, A. *Stadtische und fürstliche Musikpflege in Weissenfels*. Leipzig, 1911.

Wilson, John. *Roger North on Music*. London: Novello, 1959.

Chapter 11 On the Hautboisten

Braun, Werner. "Entwurf für ein Typologie der 'Hautboisten'," in *Der Sozialstatus des Berufsmusikers vom 17. bis 10. Jahrhundert*. Kassel, 1971.

Bottrigari. *Il desiderio ovvero De' concerti de varii stromenti musicali* (1594).

Frederick II von Brandenburg. *Memoires pour servir a l'histoire de Brandenbourg*. (1750).

Grove. *Dictionary of Music* 1980.

Hirsching. *Historische-Litterarisches Handbuch Beruhmter und Denkwurdiger Personen.* Leipzig (1792).

Hutchings, Arthur. *The Baroque Concerto.* New York: Scribner's Sons.

Mattheson, Johann. *Das neu-eröffnete Orchestre.* Hamburg, 1713.

———. *Ehren-Pforte* (Hamburg (1740).

Mersenne, Marin. *Harmonie Universelle* (1635). Translated by Roger Chapman. The Hague, 1957.

Morley-Pegge, R. *The French Horn.* London: Ernest Benn.

Muffat, Georg. *Ausserlesene Instrumental-Music* of 1701, quoted in Oliver Strunk, *Source Readings in Music History.* New York, 1950.

Panoff, Peter. *Militarmusik.* Berlin, 1944.

Reschke, Johannes. "Zur Geschichte der Deutschen Militarmusik des 17. und 18. Jahrhunderts," in *Deutsche Musik-Kultur* (1937).

Sachs, Curt. *Musik und Oper am kurbrandenburgischen Hof.* Berlin, 1910.

Schmidt, G. *Die Musik am Hofe der Markgrafen von Brandenburg-Ansbach.* Kassel, 1956.

Serauky, W. *Musikgeschichte der Stadt Halle.* Halle-Berlin, 1939.

Sittard, J. *Zur Geschichte der Musik und des Theaters am Württembergischen Hofe.* Stuttgart, 1891.

Smithers, Don. *The Music and History of the Baroque Trumpet.* London: Dent.

Werner, A. *Stadtische und fürstliche Musikpflege in Weissenfels.* Leipzig, 1911.

Chapter 12 On the Golden Age of the Trumpet in Germany

Altenburg, Detlef. *Untersuchungen zur Geschichte der Trompete im Zeitalter der Clarinblaskunst.* Regensburg, 1973.

Altenburg, Ernst. *Versuch einer Anleitung zur heroischmusikalischen Trompeter- und Pauker-Kunst ...* Halle (1795).

The Diary of John Evelyn [1673–1689]. Oxford, 1955.

Ehmann, Wilhelm. *Tibilustrium.* Kassel, 1950.

Fabrum, Antonium. *Europaischer Staats-Kantzley.* Leipzig (1700).

Menke, Werner. *History of the Trumpet of Bach and Handel.* London, 1934.

Nichols, John. *The Progresses of King James the First.* London, 1828.

Reschke, Johannes. *Studie zur Geschichte der brandenburgisch-preussischen Heeresmusik.* Berlin, 1936.

Schering, Arnold. *Musikgeschichte Leipzigs von 1650–1723.* Leipzig, 1926.

Viet, Gottfried. *Die Blasmusik.* Innsbruck, 1972.

Werner, A. *Stadtische und furstliche Musikpflege in Zeitz.* Buckeburg & Leipzig, 1922.

Chapter 13 On Civic Music of the German Baroque

Bernhard, M. B. "Notice sur la Confrerie des Joueurs d'Instruments d'Alsace," in *La Revue historique de la Noblesse.* Paris, 1844.

Brixel, Eugen and Wolfgang Suppan. *Das Grosse Steirische Blasmusikbuch.* Vienna, 1981.

Cannon, Beekman. *Johann Mattheson, Spectator in Music.* Archon Books, 1968.

David, Hans T. and Arthur Mendel. *The Bach Reader.* New York: Norton, 1966.

Ehmann, Wilhelm. *Tibilustrium.* Kassel, 1950.

Grosse, H. and H. R. Jung, ed. *Georg Philipp Telemann Briefwechsel.* Leipzig, 1972.

Grove, George, ed. *Dictionary of Music.* 1980.

Kruckeberg, Elisabeth. "Ein historisches Konzert zu Nürnberg im Jahre 1643," in *Archiv für Musikwissenschaft* (1918–1919).

Kruger, Liselotte. *Die Hamburgische Musikorganisation in XVII Jahrhundert.* Leipzig, 1933.

Kuhnau. *Musicus vexatus* (1690).

Mattheson, Johann. *Matthesons bewahrte Panacea* (1750).

Morgenstern, Sam. *Composers on Music.* New York: Pantheon, 1956.

Muller von Asow, E. H. *Johann Sebastian Bach Briefe.* Regensburg, 1950.

Pezel, Johann. *Bicinia variorum instrumentorum, ut a Violinis, Cornettis, Flautis, Clarinis et Fagottis com apprendice a 2 Bombardinis vulgo Schalmeyen.* Leipzig, 1675).

Rasmussen, Mary. "Gottfried Reiche..." *Brass Quarterly* (1960).

Schering, Arnold. *Musikgeschichte Leipzigs.* Leipzig, 1941.

———. "The Leipziger Ratsmusik von 1650 bis 1775," in *Archiv für Musikwissenschaft* (1921).

Sirman, Mitchel. *The Wind Sonatas in Daniel Speer's Musicalisch-Türkischer Eulen-Spiegel* (Unpublished dissertation, University of Wisconsin, 1972).

Sittard, J. *Geschichte des Musik- und Concertwesens in Hamburg.* Altona and Leipzig, 1890.

Smithers, Don. *The Music and History of the Baroque Trumpet.* London: Dent.

Werner, Arno. *Stadtische und fürstliche Musikpflege in Zeitz.* Buckenburg, 1922.

Wustmann, G. *Quellen zur Geschichte Leipzig.* Leipzig.

Chapter 14 On Church Music in Baroque Germany

Baselt, Bernd. "Brandenburg-Prussia and the Central German Courts," in *The Late Baroque Era.* Englewood Cliffs: Prentice Hall, 1994.

Buelow, George. "Dresden in the Age of Absolutism," in *The Late Baroque Era.* Englewood Cliffs: Prentice Hall, 1994.

———. "Hamburg and Lübeck," in *The Late Baroque Era.* Englewood Cliffs: Prentice Hall, 1994.

———. *Thorough-Bass Accompaniment according to Johann David Heinichen* Ann Arbor: UMI Research Press, 1986.

David, Hans T. and Arthur Mendel. *The Bach Reader.* New York: Norton, 1966.

Ehmann, Wilhelm. *Tibilustrium.* Kassel, 1950.

Fitzpatrick, Horace. "Jacob Denner's Woodwinds for Göttweig Abbey," *The Galpin Society Journal* (1968).

Freeman, Robert. *The Practice of Music at Melk Monastery in the Eighteenth Century.* Los Angeles (Dissertation, UCLA, 1971).

Gottron, Adam. *Mainzer Musikgeschichte.* Mainz, 1959.

Grove, George, ed. *Dictionary of Music.* 1980.

Hoenegg, Mathias Hoe von. "Parasceve ad solemnitatem evangelicam" [1617], quoted in Carol MacClintock. *Readings in the History of Music in Performance.* Bloomington: Indiana University Press, 1979.

Kruger, Liselotte. *Die Hamburgische Musikorganisation im XVII Jahrhundert.* Leipzig, 1933.

Mattheson, Johann. *Ehrenpforte* (1740).

———. *Der musicalische Patriot.*

Morgenstern, Sam. *Composers on Music.* New York: Pantheon, 1956.

Moser, Hans. *Heinrich Schütz.* St. Louis: Concordia, 1936.

Norman, Gertrude and Miriam Shrifte. *Letters of Composers.* New York, Knopf, 1946.

Praetorius, Michael. *Syntagma Musicum* (1619).

Sachs, Curt. *Musik und Oper am Kurbrandenburgischen Hof.* Berlin, 1910.

Schering, Arnold. "Einleitung," *Denkmaler Deutscher Tonkunst.* Wiesbaden, 1958. (XXIX-XXX).

———. *Musikgeschichte Leipzigs.* Leipzig, 1941.

Sittard, Josef. *Zur Geschichte der Musik... am Württembergischen hofe.* Stuttgart, 1890.

Weiss, Piero. *Letters of Composers Through Six Centuries.* Philadelphia: Chilton, 1967.

Werner, Arno. "Die alte Musikbibliothek und die Instrumentsammlung an St. Wenzel in Naumberg a. d. S.," in *Archiv fur Musikwissenschaft* (1926).

———. *Vier Jahrhunderte im Dienste der Kirchenmusik.* Leipzig: Merseburger.

———. *Stadtische und fürstliche Musikpflege in Weissenfels.* Leipzig, 1911.

———. *Stadtische und fürstliche Musikpflege in Zeitz.* Buckeburg, 1922.

Chapter 15 On Military Music in Baroque Germany

Altenburg, Ernst. *Versuch einer Anleitung zur heroischmusikalischen Trompeter- und Pauker-Kunst . . .* Translated by Edward Tarr. Halle, 1795.

Braun, Werner. "Entwurf fur eine Typlogie der Hautboisten," in *Der Sozialstatus des Befursmusikers vom 17. bis 19. Jahrhundert.* Kassel, 1971.

Brixel, Eugen. *Das ist Osterreichs Militarmusik.* Graz, 1982.

Cambridge Modern History. New York, 1907.

Durant, Will and Ariel. *The Age of Voltaire.* New York, 1965.

Ehmann, Wilhelm. *Tibilustrium.* Kassel, 1950).

Engel, H. *Musik und Gesellschaft, Beitrage zu einer Musiksoziologie.* Berlin-Halensee, 1960.

Farmer, Henry. *Military Music.* London, 1912.

Fleming, Hans von. *Der vollkommene deutsche Soldat.* Leipzig (1726).

Gluke, P. *Musik und Musiker in Rudolstadt.* Rudolstadt, 1963.

Grove, George, ed. *Dictionary of Music.* 1980.

Die Infanterie Marsche der vormaligen Churfürstl. Sachsischen Armee 1729. DDR-Dla [Aktenband Loc. 10945].

Kastner, Georges. *Manuel General de Musique Militaire.* Paris, 1848.

Leppert, Richard. "Musical Instruments and Performing Ensembles in Flemish Paintings of the Seventeenth Century." Unpublished dissertation, Indiana University, 1973.

Die Musik in Geschichte und Gegenwart. Kassel, 1949–1968.

Panoff, Peter. *Militarmusik.* Berlin, 1944.

Printz, W. C. *Historische Beschreibung der Edelen Sing- und Klingkunst.* Dresden (1690).

Reschke, Johannes. "Zur Geschichte der Deutschen Militarmusik des 17. und 18. Jahrhunderts," in *Deutsche Musik-Kultur* (1937).

———. *Studie zur Geschichte der brandenburgisch-preussichen Heeresmusik.* Berlin, 1935.

Riedel, H. *Musik und Musikerlebnis in der erzahlenden deutschen Dichtung.* Bonn, 1959.

Rouvel, D. "Zur Geschichte der Musik am Fürstl. Waldeckschen Hof zu Arolsen," in *Kölner Beitrage zur Musikforschung*. Regensburg, 1962.
Sachs, Curt. *The History of Musical Instruments*. New York, 1940.
Schering, Arnold. *Musikgeschichte Leipzigs*. Leipzig, 1926.
Spreckelsen, O. "Der Stader Ratsmusikanten," in Stader Archiv. Stade, 1924.
Suppan, Wolfgang. *Lexikon des Blasmusikwesens*. Freiburg, 1973.
Thouret, G. *Frederick der Grosse als Musikfreund und Musiker*. Leipzig, 1898.
Valentin, C. *Geschichte der Musik in Frankfurt a. M*. Frankfurt, 1906.

Chapter 16 On the Influence of Turkish Music

Brixel, Eugen. *Das ist Oesterreichs Militarmusik*. Graz, 1982.
De Caus, Salomon. *Institution Harmonique*. Frankfurt (1615).
The Diary of Samuel Pepys (entry for January 31–February 3, 1661).
Donado, Giovanni Battista. *Della Letteratura de' Turchi*. Venice (1688).
Doras, Sabahattin. *Mehterhane*. Military Museum in Istanbul.
Grove, George, ed. *Dictionary of Music*. 1980.
Kastner, Georges. *Manuel General de Musique Militaire*. Paris, 1848.
Musikalische Nachrichten und Anmerkungen auf das Jahr 1770. Leipzig.
Narrative of Travels in Europe, Asia, and Africa in the Seventeenth Century. Translated by Joseph von Hammer. London, 1834.
Pascha, Arif. *Les anciens costumes de l'Empire Ottoman*. Paris, 1863.
Il Sato Militare dell' Imperio Ottomano, Incremento e Decremento Del Medesimo Dell Signore Conte di Marsigli ... Hague (1732).
Veit, Gottfried. *Die Blasmusik*. Innsbruck, 1972.

About the Author

Dr. David Whitwell is a graduate ("with distinction") of the University of Michigan and the Catholic University of America, Washington DC (PhD, Musicology, Distinguished Alumni Award, 2000) and has studied conducting with Eugene Ormandy and at the Akademie für Musik, Vienna. Prior to coming to Northridge, Dr. Whitwell participated in concerts throughout the United States and Asia as Associate First Horn in the USAF Band and Orchestra in Washington DC, and in recitals throughout South America in cooperation with the United States State Department.

At the California State University, Northridge, which is in Los Angeles, Dr. Whitwell developed the CSUN Wind Ensemble into an ensemble of international reputation, with international tours to Europe in 1981 and 1989 and to Japan in 1984. The CSUN Wind Ensemble has made professional studio recordings for BBC (London), the Köln Westdeutscher Rundfunk (Germany), NOS National Radio (The Netherlands), Zürich Radio (Switzerland), the Television Broadcasting System (Japan) as well as for the United States State Department for broadcast on its "Voice of America" program. The CSUN Wind Ensemble's recording with the Mirecourt Trio in 1982 was named the "Record of the Year" by *The Village Voice*. Composers who have guest conducted Whitwell's ensembles include Aaron Copland, Ernest Krenek, Alan Hovhaness, Morton Gould, Karel Husa, Frank Erickson and Vaclav Nelhybel.

Dr. Whitwell has been a guest professor in 100 different universities and conservatories throughout the United States and in 23 foreign countries (most recently in China, in an elite school housed in the Forbidden City). Guest conducting experiences have included the Philadelphia Orchestra, Seattle Symphony Orchestra, the Czech Radio Orchestras of Brno and Bratislava, The National Youth Orchestra of Israel, as well as resident wind ensembles in Russia, Israel, Austria, Switzerland, Germany, England, Wales, The Netherlands, Portugal, Peru, Korea, Japan, Taiwan, Canada and the United States.

He is a past president of the College Band Directors National Association, a member of the Prasidium of the International Society for the Promotion of Band Music, and was a member of the founding board of directors of the World Association for Symphonic Bands and Ensembles (WASBE). In 1964 he was made an honorary life member of Kappa Kappa Psi, a national professional music fraternity. In September, 2001, he was a delegate to the UNESCO Conference on Global Music in Tokyo. He has been knighted by sovereign organizations in France, Portugal and Scotland and has been awarded the gold medal of Kerkrade, The Netherlands, and the silver medal of Wangen, Germany, the highest honor given wind conductors in the United States, the medal of the Academy of Wind and Percussion Arts (National Band Association) and the highest honor given wind conductors in Austria, the gold medal of the Austrian Band Association. He is a member of the Hall of Fame of the California Music Educators Association.

Dr. Whitwell's publications include more than 127 articles on wind literature including publications in *Music and Letters* (London), the *London Musical Times*, the *Mozart-Jahrbuch* (Salzburg), and 50 books, among which is his 13-volume *History and Literature of the Wind Band and Wind Ensemble* and an 8-volume series on *Aesthetics in Music.* In addition to numerous modern editions of early wind band music his original compositions include five symphonies.

David Whitwell was named as one of six men who have determined the course of American bands during the second half of the twentieth century, in the definitive history, *The Twentieth Century American Wind Band* (Meredith Music). A doctoral dissertation by German Gonzales (2007, Arizona State University) is dedicated to the life and conducting career of David Whitwell through the year 1977. David Whitwell is one of nine men described by Paula A. Crider in *The Conductor's Legacy* (Chicago: GIA, 2010) as "the legendary conductors" of the twentieth century.

> "I can't imagine the 2nd half of the 20th century—without David Whitwell and what he has given to all of the rest of us."
> Frederick Fennell (1993)

About the Editor

CRAIG DABELSTEIN began studying the piano at age seven and took up the saxophone at age twelve. Mr Dabelstein has Bachelor of Arts (Music) and Bachelor of Music degrees from the Queensland Conservatorium of Music and a Graduate Diploma of Learning and Teaching and a Graduate Certificate in Editing and Publishing from the University of Southern Queensland. He has held the principal saxophone chairs in the Australian Wind Orchestra and has been an augmenting member of the Queensland Philharmonic and Symphony Orchestras. He was a member of the Queensland Saxophone Quartet and has previously been a saxophone teacher at the Queensland Conservatorium of Music. He is a regular conductor of the Queensland Wind Orchestra and has been a research associate for the *Teaching Music Through Performance in Band* series of books. He is the editor of more than forty books by Dr. David Whitwell including *A Concise History of the Wind Band, Foundations of Music Education, Music Education of the Future, The Sousa Oral History Project, Wagner on Bands, Berlioz on Bands, The Art of Musical Conducting, Aesthetics of Music* (8 volumes) and *The History and Literature of the Wind Band and Wind Ensemble* (13 volumes). He currently teaches saxophone and clarinet, and conducts bands at St Joseph's College, Gregory Terrace.

Books by David Whitwell

- The Sousa Oral History Project
- The Art of Musical Conducting
- The Longy Club: 1900–1917
- La Téléphonie and the Universal Musical Language
- Extraordinary Women
- A Concise History of the Wind Band
- Essays on the Modern Wind Band
- Essays on Performance Practice
- A New History of Wind Music
- The College and University Band
- The Early Symphonies of Mozart
- Band Music of the French Revolution
- A Conductor's Diary
- Essays on Music of the German Baroque: Philosophy and Performance Practice
- Essays on Music of the French Baroque: Philosophy and Performance Practice
- Essays on Italian and Spanish Music of the Baroque: Philosophy and Performance Practice
- Philosophy and Performance Practice of Music during Jacobean England

On Composers

- Wagner on Bands
- Berlioz on Bands
- Chopin: A Self-Portrait
- Liszt: A Self-Portrait
- Schumann: A Self-Portrait in His Own Words
- Mendelssohn: A Self-Portrait in His Own Words

On Education

- Philosophic Foundations of Education
- Foundations of Music Education
- Music Education of the Future

Aesthetics of Music

- Aesthetics of Music in Ancient Civilizations
- Aesthetics of Music in the Middle Ages
- Aesthetics of Music in the Early Renaissance
- Aesthetics of Music in Sixteenth-Century Italy, France and Spain
- Aesthetics of Music in Sixteenth-Century Germany, the Low Countries and England
- Aesthetics of Baroque Music in Italy, Spain, the German-Speaking Countries and the Low Countries
- Aesthetics of Baroque Music in France
- Aesthetics of Baroque Music in England

The History and Literature of the Wind Band and Wind Ensemble Series

- Volume 1 The Wind Band and Wind Ensemble Before 1500
- Volume 2 The Renaissance Wind Band and Wind Ensemble
- Volume 3 The Baroque Wind Band and Wind Ensemble
- Volume 4 The Wind Band and Wind Ensemble of the Classical Period (1750–1800)
- Volume 5 The Nineteenth-Century Wind Band and Wind Ensemble
- Volume 6 A Catalog of Multi-Part Repertoire for Wind Instruments or for Undesignated Instrumentation before 1600
- Volume 7 Baroque Wind Band and Wind Ensemble Repertoire
- Volume 8 Classical Period Wind Band and Wind Ensemble Repertoire
- Volume 9 Nineteenth-Century Wind Band and Wind Ensemble Repertoire
- Volume 10 A Supplementary Catalog of Wind Band and Wind Ensemble Repertoire
- Volume 11 A Catalog of Wind Repertoire before the Twentieth Century for One to Five Players
- Volume 12 A Second Supplementary Catalog of Early Wind Band and Wind Ensemble Repertoire
- Volume 13 Name Index, Volumes 1–12, The History and Literature of the Wind Band and Wind Ensemble

Ancient Voices

- Ancient Views on Music and Religion
- Ancient Views on the Natural World
- Ancient Views on What Is Music
- Contemporary Descriptions of Early Musicians
- Early Views of Music and Ethics
- Early Thoughts on Performance Practice
- Music Performance in Ancient Societies

Renaissance Voices

- Essays on Renaissance Philosophies of Music
- Renaissance Men on Music

www.whitwellbooks.com

www.ingramcontent.com/pod-product-compliance
Lightning Source LLC
Chambersburg PA
CBHW081350230426
43667CB00017B/2777